Rick Steves'

Best of
GERMANY, AUSTRIA, AND SWITZERLAND

*Make the Most of Every Day
and Every Dollar*

**John Muir Publications
Santa Fe, New Mexico**

Thanks to my hardworking team at Europe Through the Back Door; Steve Smith for research assistance; the many readers who shared tips and experiences from their travels; my wife, Anne; and the many Europeans who make travel such good living.

Other JMP travel guidebooks by Rick Steves:
  Asia Through the Back Door (with Bob Effertz)
  Europe 101: History and Art for Travelers (with Gene Openshaw)
  Kidding Around Seattle
  Mona Winks: Self-Guided Tours of Europe's Top Museums
    (with Gene Openshaw)
  Rick Steves' Best of the Baltics and Russia (with Ian Watson)
  Rick Steves' Best of Europe
  Rick Steves' Best of France, Belgium, and the Netherlands
    (with Steve Smith)
  Rick Steves' Best of Great Britain
  Rick Steves' Best of Italy
  Rick Steves' Best of Scandinavia
  Rick Steves' Best of Spain and Portugal
  Rick Steves' Europe Through the Back Door
  Rick Steves' Phrase Books: German, French, Italian, and Spanish
    and Portuguese

John Muir Publications, P.O. Box 613, Santa Fe, NM 87504
© 1995 by Rick Steves
Cover © 1995 by John Muir Publications
All rights reserved.
Printed in the United States of America
First Printing January 1995

ISBN 1-56261-199-2
ISSN 1078-8050

Distributed to the book trade by
Publishers Group West
Emeryville, California

Editor Risa Laib
Production Kathryn Lloyd-Strongin, Sarah Johansson
Editorial Support Elizabeth Wolf, Nancy Gillan, Dianna Delling
Maps Dave Hoerlein
Cover Design Tony D'Agostino
Design Linda Braun
Typesetting Marcie Pottern
Printer Quebecor/Kingsport
Cover Photo Leo de Wys Inc./Masa Uemura

Although the author and publisher have made every effort to provide accurate, up-to-date information, they accept no responsibility for loss, injury, loose stools, or inconvenience sustained by any person using this book or eating strudel recommended herein.

The 12 Best Destinations in Germany, Austria, and Switzerland

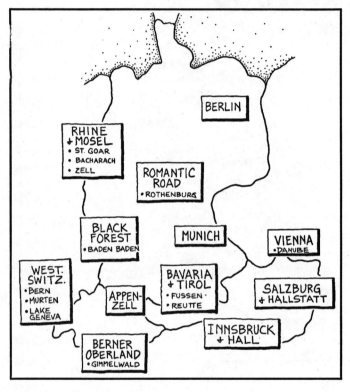

CONTENTS

HOW TO USE THIS BOOK

This book breaks Germany, Austria, and Switzerland into its top 12 big-city, small-town, and rural destinations. It then gives you all the information and opinions necessary to wring the maximum value out of your limited time and money in each of these destinations.

If you plan a month or less in the German-speaking part of Europe, and have a normal appetite for information, this lean and mean little book is all you need. If you're a travel info fiend (like me), this book sorts through all the superlatives and provides a handy rack upon which to hang your supplemental information.

Experiencing this region's culture, people, and natural wonders economically and hassle-free has been my goal for twenty years of traveling, tour guiding, and travel writing. With this book, I pass on to you the lessons I've learned, updated for 1995.

Rick Steves' Best of Germany, Austria, and Switzerland is your friendly Franconian, your German in a jam, a tour guide in your pocket. Places covered are balanced to include big cities and tiny villages, mountaintop hikes and forgotten Roman ruins, sleepy river cruises, and sky-high gondola rides. It covers the predictable biggies and mixes in a healthy dose of Back Door intimacy. Along with Rhine castles, Mozart's house, and the Vienna Opera, you'll ride on a thrilling Austrian mountain luge, soak in a Black Forest mineral spa, share a beer with Bavarian monks, and ramble through traffic-free Swiss alpine towns. I've been very selective, including only the most exciting sights. For example, you won't visit both the Matterhorn and the Jungfrau. I take you up and around just the best of the two.

I don't recommend anything just to fill a hole. If you find no tips on eating in a town, I've yet to find a restaurant worth recommending above the others. In the interest of smart use of your time, I favor hotels and restaurants handy to your sightseeing activities. Rather than list hotels scattered throughout a city, I describe my favorite two or three neighborhoods, and recommend the best accommodations values in each, from $10 bunks to $120 doubles.

The best is, of course, only my opinion. But after two busy decades of travel writing, lecturing, and tour guiding,

I've developed a sixth sense of what strokes the traveler's wanderlust. Just thinking about the places featured in this book makes me want to slap dance and yodel.

This Information Is Accurate and Up-to-date

This book is updated every year. Most publishers of guide-books that cover a country from top to bottom can afford an update only every two or three years (and even then, it's often by letter). Since this book is selective, covering only the places I think make the top month or so in Germany, Austria, and Switzerland, I am able to personally update it each year. Even with an annual update, things change. But if you're traveling with the current edition of this book, I guarantee you're using the most up-to-date information available. If you're packing an old book, you'll understand the gravity of your mistake by Day Two. (You're trip costs about $10 per waking hour. Your time is valuable. This guidebook saves lots of time.)

2 to 22 Days Out . . . Modularity In!
Top 12 Destinations in Germany, Austria, and Switzerland

This book used to be called *2 to 22 Days in Germany, Austria, and Switzerland*, and was organized as a proposed 22-day route. It's now restructured into a more flexible modular system. Each recommended module, or "destination," is covered as a mini-vacation on its own, filled with memorable experiences; exciting sights; homey, affordable places to stay; and hard opinions on how to best use your limited time. As before, my assumption is that you have limited time and money. My goal remains to help you get the most travel experience out of each day and each dollar. Each destination is divided into these sections:

Planning Your Time, a suggested schedule with thoughts on how to best use your time.

Orientation, including transportation within a destination, tourist information, and a DCH map designed to make the text clear and your entry smooth.

Sights with ratings: ▲▲▲—Worth getting up early and skipping breakfast for; ▲▲—Worth getting up early for; ▲—Worth seeing if it's convenient; No rating—Worth knowing about.

Sleeping and **Eating**, with addresses and phone numbers of my favorite budget hotels and restaurants.

Transportation Connections to nearby destinations by train and **Route Tips for Drivers** with ideas on roadside attractions along the way.

The Appendix is a traveler's toolkit with information on climate, telephone numbers, and public transportation.

With this book you can browse through then choose your favorite destinations, link them up, and have a great trip. You'll travel like a temporary local, getting the absolute most out of every mile, minute, and dollar. You won't waste time on mediocre sights because, unlike other guidebooks, I cover only my favorites. Since a major financial pitfall is lousy, expensive hotels, I've worked hard to assemble the best accommodations values for each stop. And, as you travel the route I know and love best, I'm happy you'll be meeting some of my favorite Europeans.

Costs

Five components make up your trip cost: airfare, surface transportation, room and board, sightseeing, and shopping/entertainment/miscellany.

Airfare: Don't try to sort through the mess. Don't go direct. Get and use a good travel agent. A basic round-trip U.S.A.-to-Frankfurt flight should cost $600 to $1,000, depending on where you fly from and when. Consider "open-jaws."

Surface Transportation: For a three-week whirlwind trip of all my recommended destinations, allow $650 per person for public transportation (train pass and buses), or $600 per person (based on two people sharing car and gas) for a three-week car rental, parking, gas, and insurance. Car rental is cheapest from the U.S.A. Train passes are normally only available outside of Europe. You may save money by simply buying tickets as you go (see below).

Room and Board: You can thrive in this region on $80 a day plus transportation costs in 1995. Students and tightwads will do it on $40. A $80-a-day budget allows $60 for a double with breakfast, $5 for lunch, and $15 for dinner. That's doable. But budget sleeping and eating requires the skills and information covered below.

Sightseeing: In big cities, figure $5 to $10 per major sight,

$2 for minor ones, $25 for splurge experiences (e.g., tours, Alpine lifts, conducting the beer-hall band). An overall average of $15 a day works for most. Don't skimp here. After all, this category directly powers most of the experiences all the other expenses are designed to make possible.

Shopping/Entertainment/Miscellany: This can vary from nearly nothing to a small fortune. Figure $2 per coffee, beer, and ice-cream cone, $1 per postcard, $10 to $20 for evening entertainment. Good budget travelers find that this category has little to do with assembling a trip full of lifelong and wonderful memories.

Prices and Discounts

I've priced things in local currencies. Prices, hours and telephone numbers are accurate as of late 1995. Things are always changing, and I know you'll understand that this, like any other guidebook, starts to yellow even before it's printed. While discounts are not listed in this book, seniors (60 and over), students (only with International Student Identity Cards), and youths (under 18) often get discounts—but only by asking.

Whirlwind Three-Week Tour

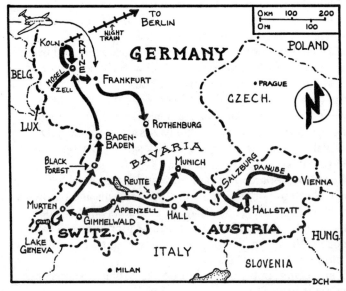

Sample Itineraries
Priority of Sightseeing Stops in Germany, Austria, and Switzerland

3 days:	Munich, Bavaria, Salzburg
5 days, add:	Romantic Road, Rhine castles
7 days, add:	Rothenburg, slow down
10 days, add:	Berner Oberland (Swiss Alps)
14 days, add:	Vienna, Hallstatt
17 days, add:	Bern, Danube Valley, Tirol (Reutte)
21 days, add:	West Switzerland, Baden-Baden, Mosel Valley, Köln
24 days, add:	Berlin, Appenzell
30 days, add:	Black Forest, slow down

(The map on page 4 and suggested 22-day itinerary below include everything in the top 24 days except Berlin.)

Germany, Austria, and Switzerland
Best 22-Day Trip

Day	Plan	Sleep in
1	Arrive in Frankfurt	Rothenburg
2	Rothenburg	Rothenburg
3	Romantic Road to the Tirol	Reutte
4	Bavaria and Castle Day	Reutte
5	Reutte to Munich	Munich
6	Munich	Munich
7	Salzburg	Salzburg
8	Salzkammergut Lakes District	Hallstatt
9	Mauthausen, Danube to Vienna	Vienna
10	Vienna	Vienna
11	Vienna to the Tirol	Hall
12	Tirol to Swiss Appenzell	Ebenalp
13	Appenzell to Berner Oberland	Gimmelwald
14	Free Day in the Alps, Hike	Gimmelwald
15	Bern, west to French Switzerland	Murten
16	French Switzerland	Murten
17	Murten to Black Forest	Staufen
18	Black Forest	Baden-Baden
19	Baden-Baden, relax, soak	Baden-Baden
20	Drive to the Rhine, castles	Bacharach
21	The Mosel Valley, Berg Eltz	Bacharach/Zell
22	Koln and Bonn, night train to Berlin, or fly home	

While this 22-day itinerary is designed to be done by car, with slight modifications it works by train. For the best three weeks by train I'd modify it to sleep in Füssen rather than Reutte, sleep on the train from Vienna to the Swiss Alps (skipping Hall and Appenzell), skip French Switzerland, skip the Black Forest, and add two days in Berlin, connecting it by night trains.

When to Go

Summer is peak season—best weather, snow-free Alpine trails, and the busiest schedule of tourist fun, but crowded and most expensive. The only serious peak-season problem is finding a room. Call ahead (nearly every place will hold a room until late afternoon if you call that morning) or arrive early.

"Shoulder season" travel (May, June, September, and early October) is ideal. Shoulder-season travelers enjoy minimal crowds, decent weather, and the ability to just grab a room almost whenever and wherever they like.

Winter travelers find absolutely no crowds, but many sights and accommodations are closed or run on a limited schedule. The weather can be cold and dreary, and nighttime will draw the shades on your sightseeing before dinnertime. The weather is predictably unpredictable, but you may find the climate chart in the back of this book helpful.

Scheduling

Your overall itinerary is a fun challenge. To maximize rootedness, minimize one-night stands. Alternate intense and relaxed periods. Every trip (and every traveler) needs at least a few slack days.

Read through this book and note special days (festivals, colorful market days, and days when sights are closed). Sundays have pros and cons, as they do for travelers in the U.S.A. (special events, limited hours, shops and banks closed, limited public transportation, no rush hours). Saturdays are virtually weekdays. Popular places are even more popular on weekends. Most sights are closed during one weekday (often Monday).

Travel Smart

When you arrive in a town, arrange for your departure. Use the telephone for reservations and confirmations, reread this book as you travel, and visit local tourist information offices (abbreviated "TI" and listed with phone numbers for every town in this book). Enjoy the hospitality of the Germanic people. Ask questions. Most locals are eager to point you in their idea of the right direction. Carry a phone card, wear a money belt, organize your thoughts and keep your mind clear with a pocket notepad, and practice the virtue of simplicity. If you insist on being confused, your trip will be a mess. Those who expect to travel smart, do.

Tourist Information

Any town with much tourism has a tourist office (I refer to them as "TIs" for "Tourist Information"), usually well-organized and English-speaking. The TI should be your first stop in a new city. Try to arrive, or at least telephone, before they close.

As national budgets tighten, many TIs have been privatized. This means they become sales agents for big tours and hotels and their "information" becomes unavoidably colored. While the TI has listings of all the rooms and is eager to book you one, use their room-finding service only as a last resort. Across Europe, room-finding services are charging commissions from hotels, taking fees from travelers, blacklisting establishments that buck their materialistic rules, and are unable to give hard opinions on the relative value of one place over another. The accommodations stakes are too high to go potluck through the TI. And with the listings in this book, there's generally no need to.

Each country's national tourist office in the U.S.A. is a wealth of information. Before your trip, get their free general information packet and request any specific information you may want (such as city maps and schedules of upcoming festivals).

Austrian National Tourist Office: P.O. Box 491938, Los Angeles, CA 90049, 310/477-3332, fax 310/477-5141; Box 1142 Times Square, New York, NY 10108-1142, 212/944-6880, fax 212/730-4568. Ask for their "Vacation Kit" map.

German National Tourist Office: 122 E. 42nd St., 52nd Floor, New York, NY 10168, 212/661-7200, fax 212/661-7174; 11766 Wilshire Blvd., Suite 750, Los Angeles,

CA 90025, 310/575-9799, fax 310/575-1565. Germany map, Romantic Road map, city maps, Rhine schedules, events, very helpful.

Swiss National Tourist Office: 608 Fifth Ave., New York, NY 10020, 212/757-5944, fax 212/262-6116; 150 North Michigan Ave. #2930, Chicago IL 60601, tel. 312/630-5840, fax 312/630-5848; 222 North Sepulveda Blvd #1570, El Segundo, CA 90245, tel. 310/335-5980, fax 310/335-5982. Great maps and service.

Recommended Guidebooks

Especially if you'll be traveling beyond the recommended destinations, you may want some supplemental information. When you consider the improvements they'll make in your $3,000 vacation, $25 or $35 for extra maps and books is money well spent. Especially for several people traveling by car, the weight and expense are negligible.

The Lonely Planet Guides to Germany, Austria, and Switzerland are thorough, well researched, and packed with sidebar-type information. The hip Rough Guides (British researchers, more insightful) and *Let's Go: Germany/ Switzerland* and *Let's Go: Austria* (by Harvard students, better hotel listings) are great for students and vagabonds. If you're a trainpass-carrying backpacker interested in the youth and night scene, get *Let's Go. Let's Go: Europe* is the best-seller, but it's pretty skimpy on the coverage and everyone has it. The popular, skinny, green Michelin Guides to Germany, Austria, and Switzerland are excellent, especially if you're driving. They're known for their city and sightseeing maps, dry but concise and helpful information on all major sights, and good cultural and historical background. English editions are sold locally at gas stations and tourist shops.

Rick Steves' Books

Rick Steves' Europe Through the Back Door (Santa Fe, NM: John Muir Publications, 1995) gives you budget-travel skills on things such as minimizing jet lag, packing light, driving or train travel, finding budget beds without reservations, changing money, theft, terrorism, hurdling the language barrier, health, travel photography, things to do in your bidet, ugly-Americanism, laundry, itinerary strategies, and more.

The book also includes chapters on more than 35 of my favorite "Back Doors."

Rick Steves' Country Guides are a series of eight guidebooks covering Europe, Britain, France, Italy, Spain and Portugal, Scandinavia, and the Baltics and Russia, just as this one covers Germany, Austria, and Switzerland.

Europe 101: History and Art for the Traveler (co-written with Gene Openshaw, John Muir Publications, 1990) gives you the story of Europe's people, history, and art. A little *101* background knowledge really helps the sights come alive.

Mona Winks (also co-written with Gene Openshaw, John Muir Publications, 1993) gives you fun, easy-to-follow self-guided tours of Europe's top twenty museums. (It's most appropriate for a trip to Italy, Paris, or London).

My *Rick Steves' German Phrase Book* (John Muir Publications, 1995) is a fun and practical tool for independent budget travelers. With everything from beer-hall vocabulary to sample telephone hotel reservation conversations to German tongue twisters, you'll be glad to have this handy book in your pocket.

Maps

The maps in this book are concise and simple, designed and drawn by Dave Hoerlein (who travels in Germany, Austria, and Switzerland each year as a tour guide). His maps are designed to help you follow the text, orient you, and direct you until you pick up a more in-depth map (usually free) at the local tourist information office.

Many European bookstores, especially in tourist areas, have good selections of maps. For drivers, I'd recommend the *Deutschland Auto Atlas* (30 DM, by RV Verlag, 1:200,000 scale) for Germany and the *Österreich Euro-Reiseatlas* (also by RV Verlag, 18 DM, 1:300,000 scale) for Austria. Each of these atlases has good coverage of the entire country with an extensive index and handy maps of all major cities. For Switzerland, use Michelin maps 216 and 217 (or *Die General Karte* maps 1 and 2) with 1:200,000 scale. Train travelers can usually manage fine with the freebies they get with their train pass and at the local tourist offices.

Transportation in Germany, Austria, and Switzerland

Car or Train?

The train is best for single travelers, those who'll be spending more time in big cities, and those who don't want to drive in Europe. While a car gives you the ultimate in mobility and freedom, enables you to search for hotels more easily, and carries your bags for you, the train zips you effortlessly from city to city, normally dropping you in the center and near the tourist office. Cars are great in the countryside but a worthless headache in places like Munich, Bern, and Vienna.

By Train

The trains are punctual and cover all the cities very well, but frustrating schedules make a few out-of-the-way recommendations (such as the concentration camp at Mauthausen) not worth the time and trouble for the less determined.

If you're doing a whirlwind trip of all of my recommended destinations, a three-week first-class Eurailpass is worthwhile—especially for a single traveler (about $650, available from your travel agent or by mail from *Europe Through the Back Door*—see Catalog). You can save about $100 by managing with the "any ten days out of two months" Eurail Flexipass. But this small saving requires some serious streamlining. Each individual country has its own train passes. Patchworking several second-class country passes together may be cheaper than a single first-class Eurailpass for the total traveling time. For example, a $286 ten-days-in-a-month second-class German Railpass, $103 four-days-in-ten Austrian Rabbit pass, and a $186 eight-day Swiss Pass give you 22 days of second-class rail travel for about $575. But the $75 savings entails a lot of complexity and you'll be going second class rather than first class.

Eurailers should know what extras are included on their pass—such as any German buses marked "Bahn" (run by the train company); city S-bahn systems; boats on the Rhine, Mosel, and Danube rivers and the Swiss lakes; and the Romantic Road bus tour.

If you decide to buy tickets as you go, look into local specials. Seniors (women over 60, men over 65) and youths (under 26) can enjoy substantial discounts with the appropriate ID cards. While Eurailers (over 26) automatically travel first class, those buying individual tickets should remember that second-class tickets provide the same transportation for 33 percent less.

Hundreds of local train stations rent bikes for about $5 a day (discounted for train-pass holders, ask for a Fahrrad am Bahnhof brochure at any station).

Railpass Analysis

Germany: Before buying a German railpass consider the first-class-only **Central Europe Pass**, which gives you any eight days in a month traveling in Germany, as well as in the Czech Republic, Slovakia, and Poland, for $346. That's $43 a day, about the same price per day as the five- or ten-days-in-a-month German Railpasses. In fact, even if you're traveling only in Germany, if you need eight days, the Central Europe Pass is your best bet for a first-class pass.

Austria: When considering the Austrian Rabbit flexipass, remember there is a first-class **European East Pass**, which gives you any five days in 15 for $185, or any ten days in a month for $299—and it covers Austria, Czech Republic, Slovakia, Hungary, and Poland to boot. If you're going to Prague or Budapest, this may actually beat the Rabbit. Austria sells a one-month **Bundesnetzkarte** (Network Pass, first class is 5,400 AS or about $500, second class is 3,600 AS or about $350) at Austrian train stations. It offers unlimited travel on Austrian railways. Groups of up to six travelers can buy and share a discount mileage pass called a **Kilometerbank**, which gives 2,000 km of rail travel for 2,100 AS or about $165 (children go for half the rate, sold only in Austria). A couple traveling the 320 km from Salzburg to Vienna and back on regular tickets would pay $160 ($40 per second-class ticket each way). For about the same money, they could buy the Kilometer ticket, use up about 1,280 km for the trip, and still have 620 km to play with.

Switzerland: Those traveling in the Alps (where many scenic rides are not covered by rail passes) should give the various Alps passes (sold at Swiss train stations) a look. The Swiss Family Card (free with Swiss train passes if you ask) allows children under 16 to travel free with their parents.

Note: See the Appendix for railpass costs in Germany, Austria, and Switzerland.

Driving

Every long drive between my recommended destinations is autobahn (super-freeway), and nearly every scenic back-country drive is paved and comfortable.

Drivers over 21 need only their U.S. license and the insurance that comes automatically with the rental car. Besides the rare insurance card check, there are no border formalities to worry about.

Learn the universal road signs (charts explain them in most road atlases and at service stations). Seat belts are required, and two beers under those belts is enough to land you in jail.

Use good local maps and study them before each drive. Familiarize yourself with which exits you need to look out for, which major cities you'll travel in the direction of, where the ruined castles lurk, and so on. For parking, pick up the "cardboard clock" (*Parkscheibe*, available free at gas stations, police stations, and Tabak shops) and display your arrival time on the dashboard so parking attendants can see you've been there less than the posted maximum stay (blue lines indicate 90-minute zones on Austrian streets).

To understand the complex but super-efficient auto-bahn (no speed limit, toll-free) pick up the "Autobahn Service" booklet at any autobahn rest stop (free, lists all intersection signs, stops, services, road symbols, and more). Study the intersection signs: *Dreieck* means three corners, a "Y" in the road; *Autobahnkreuz* is a "cross" or intersection. Gas stations are spaced about every 30 miles, normally with a restaurant, a "mini-market," and sometimes a tourist infor-mation desk. Unleaded (*Bleifrei*) gas is everywhere. Exits are often 20 miles apart. Know what you're looking for—*nord, süd, ost, west,* or *mittel*—miss it and you're long autobahn-gone. Don't cruise in the passing lane. When driving slower than 120 kph, stay on the right hand curb. Remember, in Europe the shortest distance between any two points is the autobahn. Signs directing you to the autobahn are green in Austria and Switzerland, blue in Germany.

Get used to metric. A liter is about a quart, four to a gallon; a kilometer is six-tenths of a mile. I figure kilometers to miles by cutting them in half and adding back 10 percent of the original (120 km is 60 + 12 miles, 300 km is 150 + 30 miles).

I keep a box in the trunk for things I don't need to cart in and out of hotels. My pantry box sits on the back seat, and I equip it for easy and enjoyable, time- and money-saving car picnics (either at the very pleasant autobahn picnic areas or as I drive—if my navigator agrees to cook). I stock up with plenty of orange juice in liter boxes, paper towels, plastic cups, and so on. Copy the car key as soon as possible for safety and so two people have access to the car.

Car Rental

It's cheapest to rent a car through your travel agent well before departure (not in Germany). You'll want a weekly rate with unlimited mileage. For three weeks or longer, leasing is cheaper (a scheme that saves you money on taxes and insurance).

Comparison shop through your agent. DER (tel. 800/782-2424), a German company, often has the best rates. Expect to pay $500 to $600 for a small car for three weeks with unlimited mileage, plus around $70 a week for the collision-damage waiver full-insurance option. If you drop your car off early or keep it longer, you'll be credited or charged at a fair, prorated price.

I normally rent a small inexpensive model (e.g., Ford Fiesta). For a bigger, roomier, and more powerful inexpensive car, move up to the Ford 1.3-liter Escort or VW Polo category. For peace of mind, I splurge for the CDW (collision-damage waiver insurance supplement, ridiculously expensive because the base rental price doesn't really allow a reasonable profit), which gives a zero deductible rather than the standard deductible—which can be as high as the value of the car. With the luxury of CDW you can enjoy the autobahns knowing you can bring back the car in an unrecognizable shambles and just say, "S-s-s-sorry."

Sleeping in Germany, Austria, and Switzerland

While accommodations in these three countries are fairly expensive, they are normally very comfortable and come with breakfast. Plan on spending $70 per hotel double in big cities, $50 in towns and in private homes.

A triple is much cheaper than a double and a single. While hotel singles are most expensive, private accommodations (*Zimmer*) have a flat per-person rate. Hostels and dorms always charge per person. Especially in private homes, where the boss changes the sheets, people staying several nights are most desirable. One-night stays are sometimes charged extra.

In recommending a hotel, I favor places that are in convenient, central, quiet, and safe locations; small, family-run places with local character; simple facilities not catering to American "needs"; inexpensive, friendly, English-speaking, clean, and not listed in other guidebooks. Obviously a friendly, clean, quiet, central, cheap room that no other guidebook knows about is rare, and all of my recommendations fall short of perfection—sometimes miserably. But I've listed the best values for each price category, given the above criteria. The best values are family-run and centrally located, with showers down the hall and no elevator.

Unless I note a difference, the cost of a room includes a continental breakfast, taxes, service, and showers and toilet either in the room or down the hall. This price is usually posted in the room. Before accepting, confirm your understanding of the complete price. The only tip the hotels I've listed would like is a friendly, easy-going guest. The accommodations prices listed in this book should be good through 1995. I appreciate feedback on your hotel experiences.

The Accommodations Description Code
To save space while giving more specific information for people with special concerns, I've described my recommended hotels with a standard code. When there is a range of prices in one category, the price will fluctuate with the season, size of room, or length of stay.

S—single room or price for one person using a double.

D—double or twin room. Double beds are usually big enough for non-romantic couples.

T—three-person room (often a double bed with a single bed moved in).

Q—four-adult room (an extra child's bed is usually cheaper).

B—private shower (most likely) or bath in the room. Most B rooms have a WC (toilet). All rooms have a sink. B rooms are often bigger and renovated while the cheaper rooms without B often will be on the top floor or yet to be refurbished. Any room without B has access to a B on the corridor (free unless otherwise noted). Rooms with baths often cost more than rooms with showers.

WC—I include this only to differentiate between rooms that have only a B and those with BWC. With no WC mentioned, B rooms generally have a WC.

CC—accepts credit cards: **V**=Visa, **M**=Mastercard, **A**=American Express. Many also accept Diners (which I ignored). If CC is not mentioned, assume they accept only cash.

SE—the likelihood that an English-speaking staff person is available is graded A through F.

Finding a Room

While you could do this entire trip without reservations, if you want to stay in my best listings, make calling a day or three ahead your standard operating procedure. You might make a habit of calling between 9:00 and 10:00 on the day you plan to arrive, when the hotel knows who's checking out and just which rooms will be available. I've taken great pains to list telephone numbers with long distance instructions (see Appendix). Use the telephone and the convenient telephone cards. A hotel receptionist will trust you and hold a room until 17:00. Reconfirm by telephone for safety. Don't let these people down—I promised you'd call and cancel if for some reason you won't show up. Don't needlessly confirm rooms through the tourist office; they'll take a commission.

Room lists are always available at local tourist offices, and remaining vacancies are often posted there after hours.

Camping and Hosteling

While campers can manage with the *Let's Go* listings and help from the local TI, you're more in control with a serious camping guide. Your hometown travel bookstore has guidebooks for camping Europe. You'll find campgrounds just about wherever you need them. Look for *Campingplatz* signs. Camping is a popular middle-class family way to go among

Germans. You'll find that campgrounds are cheap ($4-$5 per person), friendly, safe, more convenient than rustic, and very rarely full.

Youth hostelers can take advantage of the wonderful network of hostels. Follow the signs marked *Jugendherberge*. Triangles and the "tree next to a house" are also youth hostel symbols. Generally, you must have your membership card ($25 per year, sold in most U.S. cities), though non-members are often admitted for an extra charge.

Hostels are open to members of all ages (except in Bavaria where a maximum age of 26 is strictly enforced). They usually cost $8-$15 per night (cheaper for those under 27, plus $4 sheet rental if you don't have your own) and serve good, cheap meals and/or provide kitchen facilities. While many have couples' or family rooms available upon request for a little extra money, plan on beds in segregated dorms—four to twenty per room. Hostels can be idyllic and peaceful, or school groups can raise the rafters. School groups are most common on summer weekends and on school-year weekdays. I like small hostels best. While many hostels may say they're full over the telephone, most hold a few beds for people who drop in, or they can direct you to budget accommodations nearby.

Eating in Germany, Austria, and Switzerland

The local cuisine is heavy and hearty. While it's tasty, it can get monotonous if you fall into the schnitzel-or-wurst-and-potatoes rut. To eat well, use a phrase book or menu translator and be adventurous. The *Marling German Menu Master* is the best phrase book for galloping gluttons. Each region has its local specialties which, while not the cheapest, are often the best values on the menu.

There are many kinds of restaurants. Hotels often serve fine food. A *Gaststatte* is a simple, less-expensive restaurant. The various regions' many ethnic restaurants provide a welcome break from the basic Germanic fare. Foreign food is either from the remnants of a crumbled empire (Hungarian and Bohemian—where Austria gets its goulash and dumplings) or a new arrival to feed the many hungry-but-poor guest workers. Italian, Turkish, and Greek food is commonplace and a good value. The cheapest meals are found in department-store cafeterias, *Schnell-Imbiss* (fast-food) stand-up joints, university cafeterias (*mensas*), and youth hostels. For a quick, cheap bite, have a deli or butcher make you a *Wurstsemmel*, a hearty meat sandwich.

Most restaurants tack a menu onto their door for browsers and will usually have an English menu inside. Only a rude waiter will rush you. Good service is relaxed (slow to an American). When you want the bill, ask, *"Die Rechnung, bitte."* Service is included although it's customary to round the bill up after a good meal. Wish others happy eating with a cheery *"Guten Appetit."*

A basic Continental-style breakfast of coffee and rolls almost always comes with your hotel or *Zimmer* (room in a private home). A breakfast roll and a tiny tub of cheese zip-locked away before you leave your hotel makes a handy snack or light lunch later.

For most visitors, the rich pastries, the wine, and the beer provide the fondest memories of Germany's cuisine. The wine (85% white) is particularly good from the Mosel, Rhine, Danube, eastern Austria, and southwestern Switzer-land areas. Order wine by the *Viertel* (quarter-liter) or *Achtel* (eighth-liter). You can say, *"Ein Viertel suss* (sweet), *halbe trocken* (medium) or *trocken* (dry), *weiss* (white) or *rot* (red) *Wein* (wine), *bitte* (please)." *Sekt* is German champagne. Mosel and Saar wines come in a slender green bottle, Rhine wines in a tall brown one, and Franconian in a jug-shaped bottle.

The Germans enjoy a tremendous variety of great beer. The average German, who drinks forty gallons of beer a year, knows that *dunkles* is dark, *helles* is light, *Flaschenbier* is bottled, and *vom fass* is on tap. *Pils* is barley-based, *Weize* is wheat-based, and *Malzbier* is the malt beer that children learn on. *Radler* is half beer and half lemonade. When you order beer, ask for *ein Halb* for a half-liter or *ein Mass* for a whole liter. Some beer halls only serve it by the liter (about a quart). Menus list drink size by the tenth of a liter (e.g., .2l is a small juice, .5l is a big beer).

Red Tape, Business Hours, and Money
You currently need a passport but no visa and no shots to travel in Europe. Even as borders fade, when you change

countries you still change money, telephone cards, postage stamps, and *unterhosen*.

In Europe—and in this book—you'll be using the 24-hour clock. After 12:00 noon, keep going-13:00, 14:00, etc. For anything over 12, subtract 12 and add p.m. (For example, 14:00 is 2:00 p.m.).

This book lists in-season hours for sightseeing attractions. Off-season, roughly October through April, expect generally shorter hours, longer lunchtime breaks, and fewer activities.

Enjoy the differences. While we think shower curtains are logical, many countries just cover the toilet paper and let the rest of the room shower with you. In Europe, what we call the second floor is the "first" and Christmas is 25-12-95. Europeans give their 1s an upswing and cross their 7s. If you don't adapt, your 7 will be mistaken for a sloppy 1 and you'll miss your train.

I've priced things in local currencies. Figure about 1.6 deutsche marks (DM) per dollar, 11 Austrian schillings (AS) per dollar, and 1.5 Swiss francs (SF) per dollar. Roughly: 1 DM = $.60, 1 AS = $.10, and 1 SF = $.70.

To convert to dollars, subtract a third off prices in DM and SF (e.g., 60 DM or 60 SF = $40) and divide prices in AS by 10 (e.g., 450 AS = about $45). So that 30-DM cuckoo clock is about $20, the 15-SF lunch is about $10, and the 800-AS taxi ride through Vienna is . . . uh-oh.

Stranger in a Strange Land

We travel all the way to the Rhine or the Alps to enjoy differences—to become temporary locals. You'll experience frustrations. Certain truths that we find "God-given" or "self-evident"—like cold beer; ice; a bottomless cup of coffee; long, hot showers; body odor smelling bad; and bigger being better—are suddenly not so true. One of the benefits of travel is the eye-opening realization that there are logical, civil, and even better, alternatives. Travel tends to pry open one's hometown blinders. If the beds are too short, the real problem is that you are too long. Don't look for things American on the other side of the Atlantic and you're sure to enjoy a good dose of Germanic hospitality.

Back Door Manners

While updating this book, I heard over and over that my readers are considerate and fun to have as guests. Thank you for traveling as temporary locals who are sensitive to the culture. It's fun to follow you in my travels.

Send Me a Postcard, Drop Me a Line

While I do what I can to keep this book accurate and up-to-date, things are always changing. If you enjoy a successful trip with the help of this book and would like to share your discoveries, please send any tips, recommendations, criticisms, or corrections to me at Europe Through the Back Door, Box 2009, Edmonds, WA 98020. To update the book before your trip or share tips, tap into our free computer bulletin board travel information service (206/771-1902:1200 or 2400/8/N/1). All correspondents will receive a two-year subscription to our "Back Door Travel" quarterly newsletter (it's free anyway).

Judging from the positive feedback and happy postcards I receive from travelers using this book, it's safe to assume you're on your way to a great vacation—independent, inexpensive, and with the finesse of an experienced traveler. Thanks, and *Gute Reise!*

BACK DOOR TRAVEL PHILOSOPHY
As Taught in *Rick Steves' Europe Through the Back Door*

Travel is intensified living—maximum thrills per minute and one of the last great sources of legal adventure. Travel is freedom. It's recess, and we need it.

Experiencing the real Europe requires catching it by surprise, going casual . . . "Through the Back Door."

Affording travel is a matter of priorities. (Make do with the old car.) You can travel—simple, safe, and comfortable—anywhere in Europe for $50 a day plus transportation costs. In many ways, spending more money only builds a thicker wall between you and what you came to see. Europe is a cultural carnival, and time after time, you'll find that its best acts are free and the best seats are the cheap ones.

A tight budget forces you to travel close to the ground, meeting and communicating with the people, not relying on service with a purchased smile. Never sacrifice sleep, nutrition, safety, or cleanliness in the name of budget. Simply enjoy the local-style alternatives to expensive hotels and restaurants.

Extroverts have more fun. If your trip is low on magic moments, kick yourself and make things happen. If you don't enjoy a place, maybe you don't know enough about it. Seek the truth. Recognize tourist traps. Give a culture the benefit of your open mind. See things as different but not better or worse. Any culture has much to share.

Of course, travel, like the world, is a series of hills and valleys. Be fanatically positive and militantly optimistic. If something's not to your liking, change your liking. Travel is addicting. It can make you a happier American, as well as a citizen of the world. Our Earth is home to nearly six billion equally important people. It's humbling to travel and find that people don't envy Americans. They like us but, with all due respect, they wouldn't trade passports.

Globe-trotting destroys ethnocentricity. It helps you understand and appreciate different cultures. Travel changes people. It broadens perspectives and teaches new ways to measure quality of life. Many travelers toss aside their hometown blinders. Their prized souvenirs are the strands of different cultures they decide to knit into their own character. The world is a cultural yarn shop. And Back Door Travelers are weaving the ultimate tapestry. Come on, join in!

GERMANY (DEUTSCHLAND)

- United Germany is 136,000 square miles (the size of Montana).
- Population is 77 million (about 650 per square mile, declining slowly).
- The West was 95,000 square miles (like Wyoming) with 61 million people.
- The East was 41,000 square miles (like Virginia) with 16 million people.
- 1 deutsche mark (DM) is about 60 cents; $1 is about 1.6 DM.

Deutschland is energetic, efficient, and organized, and Europe's muscleman—economically and wherever people are lining up. Its cities hold 85 percent of its people; and average earnings are among the highest on earth. Ninety-seven percent of the workers get a one-month paid vacation, and during the other eleven months they create a gross national product that's about one-third of the United States' and growing. Germany has risen from the ashes of World War II to become the world's fifth-biggest industrial power, ranking fourth in steel output and nuclear power and third in automobile production. Its bustling new cities are designed to make people feel like they belong. It shines culturally, beating out all but two countries in production of books, Nobel laureates, and professors.

While its East-West division lasted about forty years, historically Germany has been and continues to be divided north and south. While northern Germany was barbarian, is Protestant, and assaults life aggressively, southern Germany was Roman, is Catholic, and enjoys a more relaxed tempo of life. The southern German, or Bavarian, dialect is to High (northern) German what the dialect of Alabama or Georgia is to the speech of the northern United States. The American image of Germany is Bavaria (probably because that was "our" sector immediately after the war) where the countryside is most traditional. This historic north-south division is less pronounced these days as Germany becomes a more mobile society. Of course, the big chore facing Germany today is integrating the rotten and wilted economy of what was East Germany into the powerhouse economy of

Germany

the West. This monumental task has given the West higher taxes (and second thoughts).

Germany's most interesting tourist route today—Rhine, Romantic Road, Bavaria—was yesterday's most important trade route, along which its most prosperous and important medieval cities were located. Germany as a nation is just 120 years old. In 1850, there were 35 independent countries in what is now Germany. In medieval times, there were over 300, each with its own weights, measures, coinage, king, and lotto. Many were surrounded by what we would call iron curtains. This helps explain Germany's many diverse customs.

Germans eat lunch from 11:30 to 14:30 and dinner between 18:00 and 21:00. Each region has its own gastronomic twist, so order local house specials whenever possible. Pork, fish, and venison are good, and don't miss the bratwurst and sauerkraut. Potatoes are the standard vegetable. Great beers and white wines abound. Try the small local brands—go with whatever beer is on tap. "Gummi Bears" are a local gumdrop candy with a cult following (beware of imitations—you must see the word "Gummi"), and Nutella is a chocolate-nut spread specialty that may change your life. Service and tips are included in your restaurant bills.

Banks are generally open from 8:00 to 12:00 and 14:00 to 16:00, other offices from 8:00 to 16:00. Beware: some banks charge per traveler's check.

August is a holiday month for workers, but that doesn't really affect us tourists (unless you're on the road on the 15th, when half of Germany is going over the Alps one way and half returning the other).

MUNICH (MÜNCHEN)

Munich, Germany's most livable city, is also one of its most historic, artistic, and entertaining. It's big and growing, with a population of over 1,500,000. Just a little more than a century ago, it was the capital of an independent Bavaria. Its imperial palaces, jewels, and grand boulevards constantly remind visitors that this was once a political as well as a cultural powerhouse. Its recently-bombed-out feeling reminds us that 50 years ago it lost a war.

Orient yourself in Munich's old center with its colorful pedestrian mall. Immerse yourself in Munich's art and history—crown jewels, baroque theater, Wittelsbach palaces, great art, and beautiful parks. Munich evenings are best spent in frothy beer halls—oompah bunny-hopping and belching Bavarian atmosphere. Pry big pretzels from no-nonsense, buxom beer maids.

Planning Your Time
Munich is worth two days, including a half-day side trip to Dachau. If necessary, its essence can be nicely captured in a day (walk the center, tour a palace and a museum, and enjoy a beer-filled evening). Those without a car and in a hurry can do the castles of Ludwig as a daytrip from Munich by tour. Even Salzburg can be done as a daytrip from Munich.

Orientation (tel. code: 089)
The tourist's Munich is circled by a ring road (which was the town wall) marked by four old gates: Karlstor (near the train station), Sendlinger Tor, Isartor (near the river), and Odeonsplatz (near the palace). Marienplatz is the city center. A great pedestrian-only street cuts this circle in half, running nearly from Karlstor and the train station through Marienplatz to Isartor. Orient yourself along this east-west axis. Most sights are within a few blocks of this people-filled walk. Nearly all the sights and hotels I recommend are within about a 20-minute walk of Marienplatz and each other. Most Munich sights are closed on Monday.

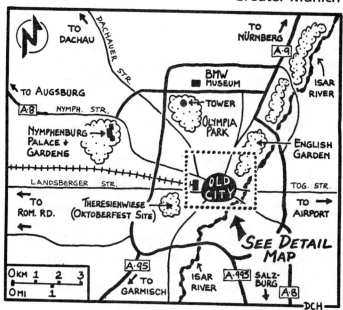

Tourist Information

Take advantage of the TI in the train station (Monday-Saturday 8:00-22:00, Sundays 11:00-19:00, tel. 089/2391-256 or 257, near street exit at track 11). Have a list of questions ready, confirm your sightseeing plans, and pick up brochures, the free and excellent city map, and subway map. Consider buying the 2.50-DM "Monatsprogram" for a German-language list of sights and calendar of events or the "Young People's Guide" (1 DM, in English, good regardless of your age). They have a room-finding service (5 DM, you'll save money by contacting my recommended hotels directly.). If the line is worse than your questions are important, skip your questions and go directly to the cash window to pick up the map and other brochures (or go to EurAide, described below).

Trains

Munich's station is a sight in itself, one of those places that stoke anyone's wanderlust. For a quick orientation in the station, use the big wall maps of the train station, Munich, and

Bavaria (through the center doorway as you leave the tracks on the left). For a quick rest stop, the Burger King upstairs has toilets as pleasant and accessible as its hamburgers. Sussmann's Internationale Presse (across from track 24) is great for English-language books, papers, and magazines including *Munich Found* (the informative English-speaking residents' monthly).

The industrious, eager-to-help **EurAide** office (halfway to the Bahnhof Mission, down track 11, daily May-early October, 7:30-11:30, 13:00-18:00, closes at 16:30 in May, tel. 089/593889, fax 550-3965) is an American whirlpool of travel information ideal for Eurailers and budget travelers. Alan Wissenberg and his staff know your train travel and accommodations questions and have answers in clear American English. The German rail company pays them to help you design your best train travels. They also have Dachau and Neuschwanstein tours (frustrating without a car), advice on cheap money-changing, transit tickets, a "Czech Prague Out" train pass (convenient for Prague-bound Eurailers), and a free newsletter; they can also find you a room, for a fee.

At the other end of the station, near track 30, **Radius Touristik** (daily, 10:00-18:00, May through mid-October, tel. 596113, run by Englishman Patrick Holder) rents three-speed bikes (5 DM/hour, 20 DM/day, 25 DM/24 hours, 40 DM/48 hours) and organizes city bike tours. Patrick dispenses all the necessary tourist information (city map, bike routes).

Getting Around Munich

The great Munich tram, bus, and subway system is a sight in itself. Subways are called U- or S-bahns. Subway lines are numbered (e.g., S3 or U5). Eurail passes are good on the S-bahn (actually an underground-while-in-the-city commuter railway). Regular tickets cost 3.50 DM and are good for 2 hours of changes in one direction. For the shortest rides (one or two stops) get the smallest 2-DM ticket. The 10-DM all-day pass is a great deal. One pass is good for up to two adults and three kids. If more than one adult is using it on a weekday, it's good only after 9:00. Get a pass, validate it in a machine, and you have Munich-by-rail for a day (purchase at tourist offices, subway booths, and in machines at

Munich Center

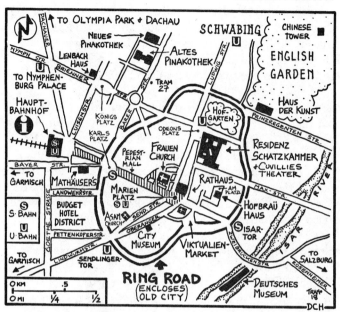

TO OLYMPIA PARK & DACHAU
SCHWABING
CHINESE TOWER
NEUES PINAKOTHEK
ALTES PINAKOTHEK
ENGLISH GARDEN
LENBACH HAUS
TO NYMPHEN-BURG PALACE
TRAM 27
HAUPT-BAHNHOF
HAUS DER KUNST
KONIGS PLATZ
HOF-GARTEN
KARLS PLATZ
ODEONS PLATZ
RESIDENZ SCHATZKAMMER + CUVILLIES THEATER
FRAUEN CHURCH
PEDESTRIAN MALL
TO GARMISCH
MATHÄUSER'S
RATHAUS
AM PLATZL
S-BAHN
U-BAHN
BUDGET HOTEL DISTRICT
MARIEN PLATZ
HOFBRAÜ HAUS
ASAM CHURCH
ISAR-TOR
TO GARMISCH
CITY MUSEUM
VIKTUALIEN-MARKET
TO SALZBURG
SENDLINGER-TOR
RING ROAD (ENCLOSES OLD CITY)
DEUTSCHES MUSEUM
0 KM .5
0 MI ¼ ½

most stops). The entire system (bus/tram/subway) works on the same tickets. You must punch your own ticket before boarding. (Plainclothes ticket-checkers enforce this "honor system," rewarding freeloaders with stiff fines.) I see the town by bike, rentable quick and easy at the train station (see above). Munich—level and compact, with plenty of bike paths—feels good on two wheels. Taxis are expensive and needless.

Sights—Munich

▲▲**Marienplatz and the Pedestrian Zone**—The glory of Munich will slap you in the smile as you ride the escalator out of the subway and into the sunlit Marienplatz (Mary's Place): great buildings bombed flat and rebuilt, the ornate facades of the new and old City Halls (the Neues Rathaus, built in neo-Gothic style from 1867 to 1910, and the Altes Rathaus), outdoor cafés, and people bustling and lingering like the birds and breeze they share this square with. From here the pedestrian mall (Kaufingerstrasse and

Neuhauserstrasse) leads you through a great shopping area past carnivals of street entertainers, the twin-towering Frauenkirche (built in 1470, rebuilt after World War II), and several fountains, to Karlstor and the train station. The not-very-old Glockenspiel "jousts" on Marienplatz daily through the tourist season at 11:00, 12:00, 17:00, and a shorty at 21:00.

▲▲**City Views**—The highest viewpoint is from a 350-foot-high perch on top of the **Frauenkirche** (elevator, 4 DM, 10:00-17:00, closed Sunday). **Neues Rathaus** (2 DM, elevator from under the Marienplatz Glockenspiel, 9:00-19:00, closed Sunday). For a totally unobstructed view, but with no elevator, climb the **St. Peter's Church** tower just a block away. It's a long climb, much of it with two-way traffic on a one-way staircase, but the view is dynamite (2.50 DM, 9:00-18:00, Sunday 10:00-18:00). Try to be two flights from the top when the bells ring at the top of the hour (and when your friends ask you about your trip, you'll say, "What?"). The church, built upon the hill where the first monks founded the city in the 12th century, has a fine interior with photos of the WWII bomb damage on a column near the entrance.

▲▲**Residenz**—For a long hike through rebuilt corridors of gilded imperial Bavarian grandeur, tour the family palace of the Wittelsbachs, who ruled Bavaria for more than 700 years (4 DM, 10:00-16:30, closed Monday, enter on Max-Joseph Platz, 3 blocks from Marienplatz). The **Schatzkammer** (treasury) shows off a thousand years of Wittelsbach crowns and knickknacks (same hours, another 4 DM from the same window). Vienna's palace and jewels are better, but this is Bavaria's best.

▲**The Cuvillies Theater**—Attached to the Residenz, this National Theater, designed by Cuvillies, is dazzling enough to send you back to the days of divine monarchs (3 DM, Monday-Saturday 14:00-17:00, Sunday 10:00-17:00).

▲▲**Münchner Stadtmuseum**—The underrated Munich city museum is a pleasant surprise. Exhibits include: life in Munich through the centuries (including WWII and Hitler's planned urban fantasy) illustrated in paintings, photos, and models, historic puppets and carnival gadgets; a huge collection of musical instruments from around the world; old photography; and a first-class medieval armory. No crowds, bored and playful guards (5 DM, 7.50 DM for families, Tuesday-Sunday 10:00-17:00, Wednesday until 20:30, closec Monday; 3 blocks off Marienplatz at St. Jakob's Platz 1, a fine children's playground faces the entry).

▲▲**Alte Pinakothek**—Bavaria's best collection of art is closed for renovation at least through 1996. Thankfully, most of its top masterpieces will be displayed in the normally-much-less-interesting neighboring Neue Pinakothek (6 DM, Tuesday-Sunday 10:00-17:00, Tuesday and Thursday 10:00-20:00, closed Monday, tel. 238-05195). The collection's forte is Italian and North European artists, such as Rubens and Dürer. (U-2 to Königsplatz or tram #27).

▲**Haus der Kunst**—Built by Hitler as a temple of Nazi art, this bold and fascist building now houses modern art, much of which the Führer censored. It's a fun collection—Kandinsky, Picasso, Dali, and much more from this century (3.50 DM, 9:00-16:30, Thursday evening 19:00-21:00, closed Monday).

Bayerisches Nationalmuseum—An interesting collection of Riemenschneider carvings, manger scenes, traditional living rooms, and old Bavarian houses (5 DM, free on Sunday, 9:30-17:00, closed Monday; tram #20 or bus 53 or 55 to Prinzregentenstrasse 3).

▲▲**Deutsches Museum**—Germany's answer to our Smithsonian Institution has everything of scientific and technical interest from astronomy to zymurgy but can be disappointing because of its overwhelming size and lack of English descriptions (there is an English guidebook). With 10 miles of exhibits, even those on roller skates will need to be selective. Technical types enjoy lots of hands-on gadgetry, a state-of-the-art planetarium and an IMAX theater (8 DM, self-serve cafeteria, museum open daily 9:00-17:00; S-Bahn to Isartorplatz).

Schwabing—Munich's artsy, bohemian university district or "Greenwich Village" has been called "not a place but a state of mind." All I experienced was a mental lapse. The bohemians run the boutiques. I think the most colorful thing about Schwabing is the road leading back downtown. U3 or U6 will take you to the Münchener-Freiheit Center if you want to wander. Most of the jazz and disco joints are near

Occamstrasse. The Haidhausen neighborhood (U-bahn: Max Weber Platz) is becoming the "new Schwabing."

▲**Englischer Garten**—One of Europe's great parks, Munich's "Central Park" is the Continent's largest, laid out in 1789 by an American. There's a huge beer garden near the Chinese Pagoda. Caution: while a local law requires sun-worshippers to wear clothes on the tram, this park is sprinkled with nude sunbathers. A rewarding respite from the city, it's especially fun on a bike under the summer sun (rental shop where Veterinar Strasse hits the park).

Asam Church—Near the Stadtmuseum, this private church of the Asam brothers is a gooey, drippy masterpiece by Bavaria's top two rococonuts, showing off their very popular baroque-concentrate style.

The Centre of Unusual Museums is a collection of mediocre but occasionally interesting one-room museums featuring goofy topics such as padlocks, Easter bunnies, chamber pots, and so on (not worth 8 DM, daily 10:00-18:00; near Marienplatz and Isartor at Westenriederstr. 26).

▲**Olympic Grounds**—Munich's great 1972 Olympic stadium and sports complex is now a lush park offering a tower (5 DM, commanding but so high it's a boring view from 820 feet, 8:00-24:00), an excellent swimming pool (5 DM 7:00-22:30, Monday from 10:00, Thursday closed at 18:00,), a good look at its striking "cobweb" style of architecture, and plenty of sun, grass, and picnic potential. Take U3 to Olympiazentrum direct from Marienplatz.

BMW Museum—The BMW headquarters, located in a striking building across the street from the Olympic Grounds, offers free factory tours (normally one a day in English) and a 5-DM museum (daily 9:00-17:00, last ticket sold at 16:00, tel. 389-53307, closed much of August). The museum is popular with car buffs.

Bus Tours of the City and Nearby Countryside— Panorama Tours (at the train station, tel. 591504) offers all-day tours of Neuschwanstein and Linderhof (75 DM) and 1-hour city orientation bus tours (at 10:00, 11:30, and 14:30, 15 DM). EurAide does a train/bus Neuschwanstein-Linderhof-Wies Church day tour twice a week in June and July (transportation only, 70 DM, 55 DM with a train pass).

Renate Suerbaum (tel. 283374, 130-DM tours) is a good local guide.

▲▲**Nymphenburg Palace**—This royal summer palace is impressive, but if you've already seen the Residenz, it's only mediocre. If you do tour it, don't miss King Ludwig's "Gallery of Beauties"—a room stacked with portraits of Bavaria's loveliest women—according to Ludwig (who had a thing about big noses). The palace park, good for a royal stroll, contains the tiny, more-impressive-than-the-palace Amalienburg hunting lodge, a rococo jewel by Cuvillies. The sleigh and coach collection (Marstallmuseum) is especially interesting for "Mad" Ludwig fans (9:00-12:30 and 13:30-17:00, closed Monday, shorter hours October-March, admission to all 6 DM, less for individual parts, use the little English guidebook, tel. 179080, reasonable cafeteria; U1 to Rotkreuzplatz than tram or bus #12).

Oktoberfest

When King Ludwig the First had a marriage party in 1810 it was such a success that they made it an annual bash. These days the Oktoberfest lasts 16 days, ending with the first full weekend in October. It starts (usually on the third Saturday in September) with an opening parade of more than 6,000 participants and fills eight huge beer tents with about 6,000 people each. A million gallons of beer later, they roast the last ox.

It's crowded, but if you arrive in the morning (except Friday or Saturday), and haven't called ahead for a room, the TI can normally find you a place. The fairground, known as the Wies'n (a few blocks from the train station), erupts in a frenzy of rides, dancing, and strangers strolling arm-in-arm down rows of picnic tables, while the beer god stirs tons of beer, pretzels, and wurst in a bubbling caldron of fun. The "three-loops" roller coaster must be the wildest on earth (best before the beer drinking). During the fair, the city functions even better than normal, and it's a good time to sightsee even if beer-hall rowdiness isn't your cup of tea. The Fasching carnival time (early January to mid-February) is nearly as crazy. And the Oktoberfest grounds are set up for a mini-Oktoberfest to celebrate spring for the two weeks around May Day.

Sights—Near Munich

▲▲**Andechs**—A fine baroque church in a Bavarian setting at a monastery that serves hearty food and the best beer in Germany in a carnival atmosphere full of partying locals? That's the Andechs Monastery, crouching quietly with a big smile between two lakes just south of Munich. Come ready to eat chunks of tender pork chain-sawed especially for you, huge and soft pretzels (best I've had), spiraled white radishes, savory sauerkraut, and Andecher monk-made beer that would almost make celibacy tolerable. Everything is served in medieval proportions; two people can split a meal. Great picnic center, too. Open daily 9:00-21:00, first-class view, second-class prices (TI tel. 08152/5227). To reach Andechs from Munich without a car, take the S5 train to Herrsching and catch a "Rauner" shuttle bus (hourly) or walk 2 miles from there. Don't miss a stroll up to the church where you can sit peacefully and ponder the striking contrasts a trip through Germany offers.

▲▲**Dachau**—Dachau was the first Nazi concentration camp (1933). Today it's the most accessible camp to travelers and a very effective voice from our recent but grisly past, warning and pleading "Never Again," the memorial's theme. This is a valuable experience and, when approached thoughtfully, well worth the trouble. In fact, it may change your life. See it. Feel it. Read and think about it. After this most powerful sightseeing experience, many people gain more respect for history and the dangers of not keeping tabs on their government.

Upon arrival, pick up the mini-guide and note when the next documentary film in English will be shown (25 minutes, normally at 11:30 and 15:30). The museum and the movie are exceptional. Notice the Expressionist fascist-inspired art near the theater, where you'll also find English books, slides, and a WC. Outside, be sure to see the reconstructed barracks and the memorial shrines at the far end (9:00-17:00, closed Monday; 45 minutes from downtown taking S2, direction: Petershausen, to Dachau, then bus 722, Dachau-Ost, from the station to "Gedenkstätte"; the two-zone 6-DM ticket covers the entire trip; with a train pass, just pay for the last leg) If you're driving, follow Dachauerstrasse from downtown Munich. If lost, signs to Augsburg will lead to signs to Dachau. Then follow the KZ-Gedenkstätte signs.

The town of Dachau (TI tel. 08131/84566) is more pleasant than its unfortunate image.

Sleeping in Munich
(1.6 DM = about $1, tel. code: 089)
There are no cheap beds in Munich. Youth hostels strictly enforce their 25-year-old age limit, and side-tripping in is a bad value. But there are plenty of decent, moderately priced rooms, most located within a few blocks of the Haupt-bahnhof (central train station). August, September, and early October are most crowded, but conventions can clog the city on any day. Call ahead and reserve one of my recommenda-tions. Assuming these hotels honor their 1995 prices, you won't get a better value through a TI room service.

Sleep code: **S**=Single, **D**=Double/Twin, **T**=Triple, **Q**=Quad, **B**=Bath/Shower, **WC**=Toilet (if not listed, a WC is normally included with B), **CC**=Credit Card (**V**isa, **M**astercard, **A**mex). English is spoken at nearly all places; prices include breakfast and increase with conventions and festivals. The cheapest rooms with no showers usually charge a few marks for one down the hall.

Hotels
Budget hotels (90-DM doubles, no elevator, shower down the hall) cluster in the area immediately south of the station. It's seedy after dark (erotic cinemas, barnacles with lingerie tongues, men with moustaches in the shadows) but danger-ous only to those in search of trouble. Still, I've listed places in more polite neighborhoods, generally a 5- or 10-minute walk from the station and handy to the center. Those far-thest from the station are most pleasant. The last four list-ings are in the nearly traffic-free old town center. Places are listed in order of closeness to the station.

Jugendhotel Marienherberge (S-35 DM, 30 DM per bed in D and T, 25 DM 4- to 7-bed rooms, open 8:00-24:00; 1 block from the station at Goethestrasse 9, tel. 555805) is a pleasant, friendly convent accepting young women only (loosely enforced 25-year age limit). These are the best cheap beds in town.

Hotel Gebhardt (D-95 DM, DB-120 DM, T-120 DM, TB-160 DM, Q-150 DM, QB-170 DM, CC:VMA;

Goethestrasse 38, Munich, 4 blocks from the station, tel. 539446, fax 53982663) offers a combination of decent neighborhood, comfort, and price surrounded by cold institutional hotel plastic and plaster.

YMCA (CVJM), open to people of all ages and sexes (D-80 DM, T-108 DM, a bed in a shared triple-36 DM; Landwehrstrasse 13, 80336 Munich, elevator, tel. 5521410, fax 5504282), has modern, simple rooms and serves cheap dinners (18:00-21:00, Tuesday-Friday).

Hotel Pension Luna (D-95 DM, DB-110 DM, T-125 DM, TB-135 DM, CC:VMA, lots of stairs; 5 Landwehrstrasse, tel. 597833, fax 550-3761) employs a loving touch to give a dumpy building quiet, bright, and cheery rooms. **Hotel Pension Erika** (D-85 DM, DB-95 DM, DBWC-115 DM, TB-120 DM, showers 3 DM, CC:VMA; Landwehrstrasse 8, tel. 554327), bright as dingy yellow can be, is sleepable.

Hotel Pension Zöllner (small twin-85 DM, big double-95 DM, DB-129 DM; near Karlstor at Sonnenstrasse 10, tel. 554035, fax 550-3714, elevator) is plain, clean, and concrete on the big ring road between the station and the old center.

Hotel Pension Utzelmann (S-50 DM, D-90 DM, DB-110 DM, T-125 DM, TB-150 DM; showers loosely 5 DM each, Pettenkoferstrasse 6, tel. 594889) has huge rooms, especially the curiously cheap Room 6. Each lacy room is richly furnished. It's in an extremely decent neighborhood a 10-minute walk from the station, a block off Sendlinger Tor.

Hotel Uhland (DB-140, TB-180 DM, all with WC, elevator, reserve with CC number, huge breakfast; 1 Uhlandstrasse, 80336 Munich, near the Theresienwiese Oktoberfest grounds, 10-minute walk from the station, tel. 539277, fax 531114), a mansion with sliding glass doors and a garden, is a worthwhile splurge. Easy parking.

Pension Westfalia overlooks the Oktoberfest grounds from the top floor of a quiet and elegant old building. Well-run by Peter Deiritz, this is a great value if you prefer sanity and personal touches to centrality (S-60 DM, SB-80 DM, D-85 DM, DB-110 DM, extra bed 25 DM, showers 3 DM, includes buffet breakfast; Mozartstr 23, 80336 Munich, easy parking, U3 or U6 to Goetheplatz, tel. 53037778, fax 5439120).

Pension Mariandl (D-95 DM, CC:VMA, 41 DM per person in larger rooms, CC:VA; Goethestrasse 51, tel. 534108, fax 543 8471, will hold rooms until 18:00) is an uppity place in an old, formerly elegant mansion with peeling vinyl floors, weak lights, and yellow corridors. The rooms are basic but fine, the neighborhood is peaceful and residential, and the classy dining hall plays free classical music Monday through Friday with dinner.

Hotel Westend, a big group-friendly place on the fifth floor of a nondescript office building on the big road parallel to the tracks a 10-minute walk away from the center from the station, offers affordable comfort rather than character (D-95 DM, DB-130 DM with this book, higher on Fair days, CC:VMA; Landsbergerstr 20, 80339 Munich, S-bahn: Hackerbrucke, tel. 504004, fax 5025896).

Pension Diana (D-98 DM, T-132 DM, Q-172, CC: VA; Altheimer Eck 15, U- or S-bahn to Karlsplatz, tel. 2603107, fax 263934; run by Mr. Geza Szabo, who is from Hungary, and Atilla the son), 70 steps up and no elevator, 17 bright and airy doubles, narrow halls, and two power showers, is my home in Munich. It's in the old center, a block off the pedestrian mall (through the green "Arcade"). 16-DM/day parking garage across the street.

Pension Linder (S-55 DM, D-95 DM, DB-120 DM, DBWC-135 DM; Dultstrasse 1, just off Sendlinger Strasse, 80331 Munich, tel. 263413, Marion Sinzinger) is clean, quiet, and modern, with pastel-bouquet rooms hiding behind a concrete stairway. Along with the Diana, this is the most central of my listings, a few blocks from Marienplatz.

Hotel Herzog Wilhelm is hotelesque with a few simple rooms (S-69 DM, D-99 DM, T-125 DM, DB-150 DM, CC:VMA, elevator; Herzog-Wilhelm Str 23, 80331 Munich, tel. 230360, fax 23036701). Around the corner, the forgettable **Hotel Atlanta** is cheap, beautifully located, and more comfortable than a youth hostel (DB-90 DM, Sendlinger Str 58, tel. 263605).

Hostels and Cheap Beds

Munich's youth hostels charge 25 to 32 DM with sheets and breakfast and strictly limit admission to YH members who are under 26. The **Burg Schwaneck hostel** (30 minutes from the center, S7 to Pullach, then walk 10 minutes to Burgweg 4, tel. 7930643) is a renovated castle. Other hostels are at Miesingstrassse 4 (U-bahn: Thalkirchen, tel. 7236560) and Wendl-Dietrichstrasse 20 (U-bahn to Rothreuzplatz, tel. 131156).

"The Tent," Munich's **International Youth Camp Kapuzinerhölzl**, offers 400 places on the wooden floor of a huge circus tent with a mattress, blankets, good showers, and free tea in the morning for 6 DM to anyone under 25 (flexible). It's a fun experience—kind of a cross between a slumber party and Woodstock (if anyone under 25 knows what that was). Call 1414300 (recorded message before 17:00) before heading out. No curfew. Cool ping-pong-and-frisbee atmosphere throughout the day. Take U1 to Rotkreuzplatz, then tram #12 to Botanischer Garten (direction Amalienburgstrasse), and follow the youthful crowd down Franz-Schrank-strasse to the big tent. This is near the Nymphenburg Palace. Open late June through August. There is a theft problem, so sleep on your bag or leave it at the station.

Eating in Munich

Munich's most memorable budget food is in the beer halls. You have two basic choices: famous touristy places with music or mellower beer gardens with Germans.

The touristy ones have great beer, reasonable food, and live music, and are right downtown. These days Germans go there for the entertainment—to sing "Country Roads," see how Texas girls party, and watch salarymen from Tokyo chug beer. The music-every-night atmosphere is thick; the fat and shiny-leather band has even church mice standing up and conducting three-quarter time with a breadstick. Meals are inexpensive (for a light 10-DM meal, I like the local favorite, *Schweinswurst mit Kraut*); huge, liter beers called *ein Mass* (or "ein pitcher" in English) are 9 DM; white radishes are salted and cut in delicate spirals; and surly beermaids pull mustard packets from their cleavages. You can order your beer *"Helles"* (light, what you'll get if you say "ein beer"), *"Dunkle"* (dark), or *"Radler"* (half lemonade, half light beer). Notice the vomitoriums in the WC.

The most famous beer hall, the **Hofbräuhaus** (Platzl 9, near Marienplatz, tel. 221676, music for lunch and dinner), is most touristy. But check it out; it's fun to see 200 Japanese people drinking beer in a German beer hall. (They have a gimmicky folk evening upstairs in the "Festsaal" nightly at 19:00, 8 DM, tel. 290136-10, food and drinks are sold from the same menu.) My long-time favorite, **Mathäser Bierstadt** (dinner #94 is light, good, typical, and cheap; tel. 592896, Bayerstrasse 5, halfway between the train station and Karlstor, music after 17:00) has joined the Hofbräuhaus as the tour-group beer hall. For typical Bavarian fast food, try the self-serve at Mathäser's entry.

The **Weisses Bräuhaus** (Tal 10, between Marienplatz and Isartor) is more local and features the local fizzy "wheat beer." Hitler met with fellow fascists here in 1920 when his Nazi party had yet to ferment. The **Augustiner Beer Garden** (across from the train tracks, 3 blocks from the station away from the center on Arnulfstrasse) is a sprawling haven for local beer-lovers on a balmy evening. Upstairs in the tiny **Jodlerwirt** (4 Altenhofstrasse, between the Hofbräuhaus and Marienplatz, after 19:00, closed Sunday) is a woodsy, smart-aleck, yodeling kind of pub. For a classier evening stewed in antlers and fiercely Bavarian, eat under a tree or inside at the **Nürnberger Bratwurst Glöckl am Dom** (Frauenplatz 9, under the twin-domed cathedral, tel. 220385, closed Sunday).

For outdoor atmosphere and a cheap meal, spend an evening at the **Englischer Garten's Chinese Pagoda** (*Chinesischer Turm*) **Biergarten.** You're welcome to BYO food and grab a table or buy from the picnic stall (*Brotzeit*) right there. Don't bother to phone ahead: there are six thousand seats! For similar BYOF atmosphere right behind Mairienplatz, eat at Viktualien market's beer garden. Lunch or dinner here taps you into about the best budget eating in town. Countless stalls surround the beer garden selling wurst, sandwiches, produce, and so on. This BYOF tradition goes back to the days when monks were allowed to sell beer but not food. (A tablecloth indicates picnics are *verboten*.)

The crown in its emblem indicates that the royal family assembled its picnics in the historic, elegant, and expensive **Alois Dallmayr** delicatessen at 14 Dienerstrasse just behind the Rathaus (9:00-18:30, Saturday 9:00-14:00, closed Sunday). Wander through this dieter's purgatory, put together a royal picnic, and eat it in the nearby, adequately royal Hofgarten. To save money, browse at Dallmayr's, but buy in the basement of the Kaufhof across Marienplatz.

Transportation Connections
Munich is a super transportation hub (one reason it was the focus of so many WWII bombs). Direct trains connect **Munich to: Berlin** (6/day, in 8 hrs), **Frankfurt** (14/day, 3½ hrs), **Salzburg** (12/day, 2 hrs), **Vienna** (4/day, 5 hrs), **Venice** (2/day, 9 hrs), **Paris** (3/day, 9 hrs), **Prague** (2/day, 7-10 hrs), **Füssen** (10/day, in 2 hrs, the 8:50 departure is good for a castles day trip), and just about every other point in western Europe. By train, Munich is 3 hours from **Reutte** (hrly departures to Garmish where you connect to Reutte). Munich's airport is an easy 40-minute ride on the S-bahn (10 DM or free with train pass).

BAVARIA AND TIROL

Straddling the border, 2 hours south of Munich between Germany's Bavaria and Austria's Tirol, is a timeless land of fairy-tale castles, painted buildings shared by cows and farmers, and locals who still yodel when they're happy.

In Germany's Bavaria, tour "Mad" King Ludwig's ornate Neuschwanstein Castle, Europe's most spectacular. Stop by the Wies Church, a textbook example of Bavarian rococo bursting with curly curlicues, and browse through Oberammergau, Germany's wood-carving capital and home of the famous Passion Play. In Austria's Tirol, hike to the Ehrenberg ruined castle, scream down a nearby ski slope on an oversized skateboard, then catch your breath for an evening of yodeling and slap-dancing.

In this chapter, I'll cover Bavaria first, then Tirol. My favorite home base for exploring Bavaria's castles is actually in Austria, in the town of Reutte. Füssen, in Germany, is a handier home base for train travelers.

Planning Your Time

While locals come here for a week or two, the typical speedy American traveler will find two days worth of sightseeing. With a car and some more time you could enjoy the more remote corners but the basic visit ranges anywhere from a long day-trip from Munich to a three-night, two-day visit. If the weather's good and you're not going to Switzerland, be sure to ride a lift to an Alpine peak.

Getting Around Bavaria and Tirol

This region is ideal by car. All the sights are within an easy 60-mile loop. It's frustrating by train. Local bus service in the region is spotty for sightseeing. Without wheels, Reutte, the luge ride, and the Wies church are probably not worth the trouble. Füssen (with a direct 2-hour train ride to and from Munich every 2 hours) is 3 miles from Neuschwanstein castle with easy bus and bike connections. Oberammergau (hourly 2-hour trains from Munich with one change) has decent bus connections to nearby Linderhof castle. Oberammergau to

Bavaria and Tirol Castle Loop

Füssen is a pain. If you're interested only in Bavarian castles, consider an all-day organized bus tour of the Bavarian biggies as a side trip from Munich (see Munich chapter).

This is great biking country. Most train stations (including Reutte and Füssen) and many hotels rent bikes for 9 DM a day (tandems for 20 DM). Hitchhiking is a slow-but-possible way to connect the public transportation gaps.

Füssen, Germany

Füssen has long been a strategic place. Its main street sits on the Via Claudia Augusta, which crossed the Alps (over Brenner Pass) in Roman times. And the town was the southern terminus of a medieval trade route which happens to be today's Romantic Road. Dramatically situated under a renovated castle on the lively Lech River, that liveliness will spread through the town in 1995 as Füssen celebrates its 700th birthday.

Unfortunately, in the summer it's entirely overrun by tourists. Traffic can be exasperating, but by bike or on foot, it's not bad. Off-season, the town is a jester's delight.

Apart from Füssen's cobbled and arcaded town center, there's little real sightseeing. The striking-from-a-distance castle houses a boring picture gallery. The city museum in the monastery below the castle exhibits lifestyles of 200 years ago, the story of the monastery, and displays on the development of the violin for which Füssen was famous (explanations in German only, 11:00-16:00, closed Monday). Halfway between Füssen and the border (as you drive, or a woodsy walk from the town) is the Lechfall, a thunderous waterfall with a handy potty stop.

The train station is a few minutes' walk from the TI, the town center (a cobbled shopping mall), the youth hostel, and good rooms (listed at the end of this chapter).

Orientation

Tourist Information
The TI, 2 blocks past the train station, has a free room-finding service (look for *Kurverwaltung*, 8:00-12:00, 14:00-18:00, Saturday 10:00-12:00, Sunday 10:00-12:00, closed off-season Sundays, tel. 08362/7077 or 7078, fax 39181).

Trains
Füssen is well connected only to Munich (2-hour trip, almost hourly). The station rents bikes. Buses go twice an hour to Neuschwanstein and four times a day to Reutte. The Romantic Road bus tour leaves at 8:00 and arrives at 20:05 (bus stop: Hotel Hirsch, just past the TI at the Green and Yellow sign). Taxis from Füssen station to Reutte cost 35 DM. Füssen's laundromat, "Self serve Wäsche service," is next to the TI (Sebastianstrasse 3, tel. 4529).

Sights—Bavaria
(These are listed in driving order from Füssen.)
▲▲▲**Neuschwanstein and Hohenschwangau Castles (Königsschlösser)**—The fairy-tale castle, Neuschwanstein,

looks medieval, but it's only about as old as the Eiffel Tower.
It was built to suit the whims of Bavaria's King Ludwig II
and is a textbook example of the romanticism that was popular in 19th-century Europe.

Beat the crowds. See Neuschwanstein, Germany's most
popular castle, early in the morning. The castle is open every
morning at 8:30; by 11:00, it's packed. Rushed 25-minute
English-language tours are less rushed early. They leave regularly, telling the sad story of Bavaria's "mad" king.

After the tour, climb up to Mary's Bridge to marvel at
Ludwig's castle, just as Ludwig did. This bridge was quite an
engineering accomplishment a hundred years ago. From the
bridge, the frisky can hike even higher to the "Beware—
Danger of Death" signs and an even more glorious castle view.
For the most interesting (but 15-minute longer and extremely
slippery when wet) descent, follow signs to the Pöllat Gorge.

The big yellow Hohenschwangau Castle nearby was
Ludwig's boyhood home. It's more lived-in and historic and
actually gives a better glimpse of Ludwig's life. (Each castle

Neuschwanstein

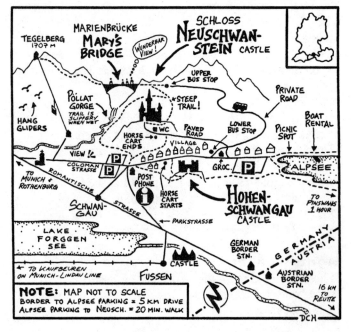

costs 9 DM and is open daily 8:30-17:30, October-March
10:00-16:00, tel. 08362/81035. If not enough English-
speakers gather, you may have to do Hohenschwangau with
a German group. TI tel. 08362/8198-40)

The "village" at the foot of the castles was created
for and lives off the hungry, shopping tourists who come
in droves to Europe's "Disney" castle. The big yellow
Bräustüberl restaurant by the lakeside parking lot is cheapest,
with food that tastes that way. Next door is a little family-
run, open-daily souvenir/grocery store with the makings for
a skimpy picnic and a microwave fast-food machine. Picnic
in the lakeside park or in one of the old-fashioned rent-
by-the-hour rowboats. The bus stop, the post/telephone
office, and a helpful TI cluster around the main intersection.

It's a steep hike to the castle. (The best and closest
parking lot is the lakeside Schloss Parkplatz am Alpsee—all
lots cost 6 DM.) To reach the castle, you can take a 20-
minute uphill hike or take advantage of the buses (3.50 DM
up, 5 DM round-trip, dropping you at Mary's Bridge, a steep
10 minutes above the castle) or horse carriages (slower than
walking, stops 5 minutes short of the castle, 7 DM up, 3.50
DM down) that go constantly (watch your step). Your work
continues inside the castle as your tour takes you up and
down more than 300 stairs. Signposts and books often refer
to these castles in the German, "*Königsschlösser.*"

To give your castle experience a romantic twist, hike or
bike over from Austria (trailhead is at Hotel Schluxenhof in
Pinswang). When the dirt road forks at the top of the hill, go
right (downhill), cross the Austrian/German border (marked
by a sign and deserted hut), and follow the paved road to the
castles. It's an hour's hike with bus connections back to
Füssen and Reutte or a great circular bike trip.

From Reutte, you can bus directly to the castle at
Neuschwanstein (11:25-12:00) and return (15:45-16:10).
Buses from the Füssen station to Neuschwanstein run hourly
(4.40 DM round-trip).

▲**Tegelberg Gondola**—Just north of Neuschwanstein,
you'll see hang gliders hovering like vultures. They jumped
from the top of the Tegelberg gondola. For 23 DM, you can
ride high above the castle to the 5,500-foot summit and back
down (last lift at 17:00, tel. 08362/81018). On a clear day,

you get great views of the Alps and Bavaria and the vicarious thrill of watching hang gliders and parasailers leap into airborne ecstasy. From there, it's a pleasant 2-hour hike down to Ludwig's castle.

▲▲**Wies Church**—Germany's greatest Rococo-style church, *Wieskirche* (the church in the meadow), is newly restored and looking as brilliant as the day it floated down from heaven. With flames of decoration, overripe but bright and bursting with beauty, this church is a divine droplet, a curly curlicue, the final flowering of the Baroque movement. The ceiling depicts the Last Judgment.

This is a pilgrimage church. In the early 1700s, a carving of Christ, too graphic to be accepted by that generation's church, was the focus of worship in a peasant's private chapel. Miraculously, it wept. And pilgrims came from all around. Bavaria's top Rococo architects, the Zimmerman brothers, were then commissioned to build this church, which features the amazing carving above its altar and still attracts countless pilgrims. Take a commune-with-nature-and-smell-the-farm detour back through the meadow to the car park.

Wieskirche (daily 8:00-20:00, admission for a donation) is 30 minutes north of Neuschwanstein. The northbound Romantic Road bus tour stops here for 15 minutes. Füssen-to-Wieskirche buses go twice a day. By car, head north, turn right at Steingaden, and follow the signs. If you can't visit Wies, other churches that came out of the same heavenly spray can are Oberammergau's church, Munich's Asam church, the Würzburg Residenz chapel, or the splendid Ettal Monastery (free and near Oberammergau).

If you're driving from Wies church to Oberammergau you'll cross the Echelsbacher Bridge, arching 250 feet over the Pöllat Gorge. Drivers should let their passengers walk across and meet them at the other side. Any kayakers? Notice the painting of the traditional village woodcarver (who used to walk from town to town with his art on his back) on the first big house on the Oberammergau side, a shop called Almdorf Ammertal. It has a huge selection of overpriced carvings and commission-hungry tour guides.

▲**Oberammergau**—The Shirley Temple of Bavarian villages and exploited to the hilt by the tourist trade, Oberammergau wears way too much makeup. It's worth a wander, only if you're passing through anyway. Browse through the woodcarvers' shops—small art galleries filled with very expensive whittled works—or the local Heimat (folk art) Museum. (TI tel. 08822/1021; off-season, closed Saturday afternoon and Sunday.)

Visit the church, a poor cousin of the one at Wies. This church looks richer than it is. Put your hand on the "marble" columns. If they warm up they're painted fakes. Wander through the graveyard. Ponder the deaths that two wars dealt Germany. Behind the church are the photos of three Schneller brothers, all killed within two years in World War II.

Still making good on a deal the townspeople made with God if they were spared devastation by the Black Plague 350 years ago, once each decade Oberammergau performs the Passion Play. The next show is in the year 2000 when 5,000 people a day for 100 summer days will attend Oberammergau's all-day dramatic story of Christ's crucifixion. For the rest of this millenium, you'll have to settle for browsing through the theater's exhibition hall (4 DM, 9:30-12:00 and 13:30-16:00, tel. 32278), seeing Nicodemus tooling around town in his VW, or reading the Book.

Gasthaus zum Stern (SB-45 DM, DB-90 DM; Dorfstrasse 33, 8103 Oberammergau, tel. 08822/867) is friendly, serves good food, and for this tourist town, is a fine value (closed Tuesday and November). Oberammergau's modern **youth hostel** (18 DM beds, open all year, tel. 08822/4114) is on the river a short walk from the center.

Driving into town from the north, cross the bridge, take the second right, follow "Polizei" signs, and park by the huge gray Passionsspielhaus. Leaving town, head out past the church and turn toward Ettal on road 23. You're 20 miles from Reutte via the scenic Plansee.

▲▲**Linderhof Castle**—This was Mad Ludwig's "home," his most intimate castle. It's small and comfortably exquisite, good enough for a minor god. Set in the woods, 15 minutes by car or regular bus from Oberammergau, surrounded by fountains and sculpted, Italian-style gardens, it's the only palace I've toured that actually had me feeling envious. Don't miss the grotto (8 DM, April-September 9:00-17:30, off-season 10:00-16:00, fountains often erupt on the hour,

English tours constantly, tel. 08822/3512). Plan for lots of crowds, lots of walking, and a 2-hour stop.

▲▲**Zugspitze**—The tallest point in Germany is a border crossing. Lifts from Austria and Germany go to the 10,000-foot summit of the Zugspitze. Straddle two great nations while enjoying an incredible view. There are restaurants, shops, and telescopes at the summit. The hour-long trip from Garmisch on the German side costs 60 DM (by direct lift or a combo cogwheel train/cable car ride, tel. 08821/7970). On the Austrian side, from the less crowded Talstation Obermoos, above the village of Erwald, the tram zips you to the top in ten minutes (385 AS round-trip, 8:40 to 16:40, tel. 05673/2309). The German ascent is easier for those without a car. But buses do connect the Erwald train station and the Austrian lift nearly twice an hour.

Reutte, Austria

Reutte (pronounced "ROY-teh," rolled "r"), population 5,000, is a relaxed town, far from the international tourist crowd but popular with Germans and Austrians for its climate. Doctors recommend its "grade 1" air.

You won't find Reutte in any American guidebook. Its charms are subtle. It never was rich or important. Its castle is ruined, its buildings have paint-on "carvings," its churches are full, its men yodel for each other on birthdays, and lately its energy is spent soaking its Austrian and German guests in *gemütlichkeit*. Because most guests stay for a week, the town's attractions are more time-consuming than thrilling. If the weather's good, hike to the mysterious Ehrenberg ruins or ride the luge. For a slap-dancing bang, enjoy a Tirolean folk evening.

Orientation

Tourist Information

The helpful Reutte TI is a block in front of the train station (weekdays 8:30-12:00 and 13:00-17:00 or 18:00, Saturday 8:00-12:00, and mid-July to mid-August on Saturday and Sunday afternoons from 16:00-18:00; tel. 05672/2336, or direct from Germany, 0043-5672/2336). Go over your sightseeing plans, ask about a folk evening, pick up a city map, ask

Reutte in Tirol

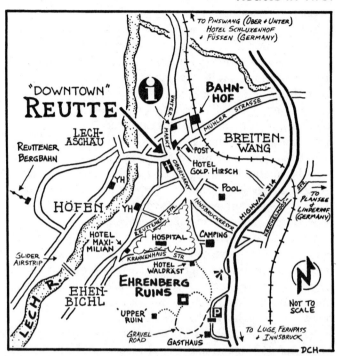

TO PINSWANG (OBER + UNTER)
HOTEL SCHLUXENHOF
+ FÜSSEN (GERMANY)

"DOWNTOWN"
REUTTE

BAHN-HOF

LECH-ASCHAU

MÜHLER STRASSE

BREITEN-WANG

REUTTENER
BERGBAHN

POST

HOTEL
GOLD. HIRSCH

OBERMARKT

UNTER MARKT

YH

HÖFEN

YH

POOL

INNSBRUCKER STR.

HIGHWAY 314

KREGELBERG

TO
PLANSEE
+
LINDERHOF
(GERMANY)

HOTEL
MAXI-MILIAN

REUTTENER STR.

HOSPITAL

CAMPING

GLIDER
AIRSTRIP

KRANKENHAUS STR.

HOTEL
WALDRAST

EHEN-BICHL

EHRENBERG
RUINS

LECH R.

UPPER
RUIN

P

N

NOT TO
SCALE

GRAVEL
ROAD

GASTHAUS

TO LUGE, FERNPASS
+ INNSBRUCK

DCH

about discounts with the hotel guest cards. Don't ask about a laundromat. Unless you can infiltrate the local campground, the town has none. (Accommodations are listed at the end of this chapter.)

Getting Around
While Reutte is a short bus ride from Füssen (departures at 8:35, 12:10, 13:50, 16:45; returning from Füssen to Reutte at 9:30, 12:50, 15:20 and 17:10), its train line goes to Garmisch (2/hr, 60 min ride). The station rents bikes cheaply. From Reutte, you can bus directly to the castle at Neuschwanstein (11:25-12:00) and return (15:45-16:10).

Sights—Reutte
▲▲**Ehrenberg Ruins**—The brooding ruins of Ehrenberg (two castle ruins atop two neighboring hills) are a mile outside of Reutte on the road to Lermoos and Innsbruck. These

13th-century rock piles, a great contrast to King Ludwig's "modern" castles, are a great opportunity to let your imagination off its leash. Hike up from the parking lot at the base of the hill; it's a 15-minute walk to the small (*kleine*) castle for a great view from your own private ruins. (Facing the hill from the parking lot, the steeper but more scenic trail is to the right, the easy gravelly road is to the left.) Imagine how proud Count Meinrad II of Tirol (who built the castle in 1290) would be to know that his castle repelled 16,000 Swedish soldiers in the defense of Catholicism in 1632.

You'll find more medieval mystique atop the taller neighboring hill in the big (*gross*) ruins. You can't see anything from below and almost nothing when you get there, but these bigger, more desolate and overgrown ruins are a little more romantic (and a lot harder to get to).

The easiest way down is via the small road from the gully between the two castles. The car park, with a café/guest house (offering a German language flyer about the castle), is just off the Lermoos/Reutte road. Reutte is a pleasant 60-minute walk away. The town museum and many Reutte hotels have sketches of the intact castle.

Folk Museum—Reutte's *Heimatmuseum* (10:00-12:00, 14:00-17:00, closed Monday; in the Green House on Untermarkt, around the corner from Hotel Goldener Hirsch) offers a quick look at the local folk culture and the story of the castle, but so do the walls and mantels of most of the hotels.

▲▲Tiroler Folk Evening—Ask in your hotel if there's a Tirolean folk evening scheduled. About two evenings a week in the summer, Reutte or a nearby town puts on an evening of yodeling, slap-dancing, and Tirolean frolic—usually worth the 70 AS and short drive. Off-season, you'll have to do your own yodeling.

Swimming—Plunge into Reutte's Olympic-sized swimming pool to cool off after your castle hikes (58 AS, 10:00-21:00, off-season 14:00-21:00, closed Monday).

The Reuttener Bergbahn (mountain lift) swoops you high above the tree line to a starting point for several hikes and an Alpine flower park with special paths leading you past countless local varieties.

Flying and Gliding—For a major thrill on a sunny day, drop by the tiny airport in Hofen across the river and fly. A small single-prop plane (three people for 30 minutes, 1,200 AS; 60 minutes for 1,900 AS) can buzz the Zugspitze and Ludwig's castles and give you a bird's-eye peek at Reutte's Ehrenberg ruins (that's about the cost of three lift tickets up the Zugspitze, and a lot easier). Or for something more angelic, how about *Segelfliegen*? For 280 AS, you get 30 minutes in a glider for two (you and the pilot). Just watching the tow rope launch the graceful glider like a giant slow motion rubber-band gun is thrilling (late May-October, 11:00-19:00, in good weather, tel. 05672/3207).

Sights—In Tirol, Near Reutte

▲▲*Sommerrodelbahn*, the Luge—Near Lermoos, on the Innsbruck-Lermoos-Reutte road, you'll find two rare and exciting luge courses. In the summer, these ski slopes are used as luge courses, or *Sommerrodelbahn*. To try one of Europe's great $5 thrills, take the lift up, grab a sled-like go-cart, and luge down. The concrete bobsled course banks on the corners, and even a novice can go very, very fast. Most are cautious on their first run and speed demons on their second. (Recently, a woman showed me her journal illustrated with her husband's dried 5-inch-long luge scab. He disobeyed the only essential rule of luging: keep both hands on your stick.) No one emerges from the course without a windblown hairdo and a smile-creased face. Both places charge a steep 70 AS per run, with five-trip or ten-trip discount cards; both are open weekends from late May and daily from about mid-June through September and into October if weather permits, from 9:00 or 10:00 until about 17:00. They're closed in wet weather, so call before going out. Unfortunately, you'll need a car to get to the luge.

The small and steep luge: The first course (100-meter drop over 800-meter course) is 6 kilometers beyond Reutte's castle ruins. Look for a chairlift on the right and exit on the tiny road at the yellow Riesenrutschbahn sign (call ahead, tel. 05674/5350, the local TI at 05674/5354 speaks more English).

The longest luge: The Biberwier Sommerrodelbahn, 15 minutes closer to Innsbruck, just past Lermoos in Biberwier (the first exit after a long tunnel), is a better luge, the longest in Austria—1,300 meters—but has a shorter

season. (9:00-16:30, tel. 05673/2111, local TI tel. 05673/
2922.) A block or two down hill from this luge, behind
the Sport und Trachtenstüberl shop, is a wooden church
dome with a striking Zugspitze backdrop. If you have sun
shine and a camera, don't miss it.

▲**Fallershein**—A special treat for those who may have been
Kit Carson in a previous life, this extremely remote log-
cabin village is a 4,000-foot-high, flower-speckled world of
serene slopes and cowbells. Thunderstorms roll down the
valley like it's God's bowling alley, but the pint-sized church
on the high ground, blissfully simple in a land of baroque,
seems to promise that this huddle of houses will survive and
the river and breeze will just keep flowing. The couples
sitting on benches are mostly Austrian vacationers who've
rented cabins here. Many of them, appreciating the remote-
ness of Fallershein, are having affairs.

For a rugged chunk of local Alpine peace, spend a night
in the local **Matratzenlager Almwirtschaft Fallershein,**
run by friendly Kerle Erwin (80 AS per person with breakfast; open, weather permitting, May-November; 27 very
cheap beds in a very simple loft dorm, meager plumbing,
good inexpensive meals; 6671 Weissenbach 119a, b/Reutte,
tel. 05678/5142, rarely answered, and then not in English).
It's crowded only on weekends. Fallershein is at the end of a
miserable 2-kilometer fit-for-jeep-or-rental-car-only gravel
road that looks more closed than it is, near Namlos on the
Berwang road southwest of Reutte. To avoid cow damage, park
300 meters below the village at the tiny lot before the bridge.

Sleeping in Bavaria and Tirol

Austria's Tirol is easier and cheaper than touristy Bavaria.
The town of Reutte, just inside the Austrian border, is my
home base for the area. But if you're relying on public transportation, Füssen, with its quicker, easier connections, is
handier.

Sleep code: **S**=Single, **D**=Double/Twin, **T**=Triple,
Q=Quad, **B**=Bath/Shower, **WC**=Toilet, **CC**=Credit Card
(Visa, Mastercard, Amex). Breakfast is included, showers
down the hall are free, nearly all speak at least a little
English. Prices listed are for one-night stays. Some places
give a discount for longer stays. Always ask.

[Handwritten annotations:] ? Hotel Schluxen(Hof) ? It's a farmhouse w/ balcony overlooking Alps... Can walk to Neuschwanstein... all I know... just heard it was great! see pg 52 53

Sleeping in Füssen, Germany

(1.6 DM = about $1, zip code: 87629, tel. code: 08362)

Füssen, 2 miles from Ludwig's castles, is a cobbled, cren–
elated, riverside oompah treat but very touristy. It has just
about as many rooms as tourists, though, and the TI has a
free room-finding service. All places I've listed here are an
easy walk from the train station and the town center. They
are used to travelers getting in after the Romantic Road bus
arrives (20:00) and will hold rooms for a telephone promise.

Hotels

Hotel Gasthaus zum Hechten offers all the modern conve-
niences in a traditional shell right under the Füssen castle in
the old-town pedestrian zone (D-90 DM, DB-100 DM-
110 DM; Ritterstrasse 6, tel. 7906, fax 39841). Adjacent this
gasthaus is "Infooday," a clever, modern self-service eatery
that sells its hot meals and salad bar by weight and offers lots
of English newspapers (10:30-18:30, closed Sunday, 7 DM/
filling salad).

   Gasthof Krone is a rare bit of pre-glitz Füssen also
in the pedestrian zone (dumpy halls and stairs but bright,
cheery, comfy rooms: S-50 DM, D-88 DM, T-132 DM,
10% less for 2-night stays, CC:MA; Schrannenplatz 17, tel.
7824, fax 37505, may renovate in '95).

   Bräustüberl (D-90 DM, T-135 DM; Rupprechtstrasse
5, a block from the station, tel. 7843, fax 38781, may renovate in '95) has clean and bright rooms in a musty old beer-
hall-type place.

Zimmer

Haus Peters (DB-70 DM, QB-120 DM; Augustenstrasse
5½, tel. 7171), Füssen's best value, is a comfy, smoke-free
home renting four rooms, 2 blocks from the station (toward
town, second left). Herr and Frau Peters are friendly, speak
English, and know what travelers like: a peaceful garden,
self-serve kitchen, and good prices. The funky old ornately
furnished **Pension Garni Elisabeth** (D-80 DM, DB-100,
showers-5 DM; Augustenstrasse 10, tel. 6275) in a garden
just across the street, exudes a chilling Addams-family friendliness. Floors creak and pianos are never played.

   Inexpensive farmhouse *Zimmer* abound in the Bavarian

countryside around Neuschwanstein and are a good value. Look for *Zimmer Frei* signs. The going rate is about 70 DM per double including breakfast; you'll see plenty of green "Vacancy" signs. For a *Zimmer* in a classic Bavarian home within walking distance of Mad Ludwig's place, try **Haus Magdalena** (SB-45 DM, D-70 DM, DB-81, extra bed-22 DM; free parking, Brumme Family; from the castle inter-section, about 2 blocks down the road to Schwangau at Schwangauerstrasse 11, 8959 Schwangau, tel. 08362/81126).

Youth Hostel

The excellent Germanly run **Füssen youth hostel** (4-bed rooms, 18 DM for B&B, 8 DM for dinner, 6 DM for sheets, the Bavarian age limit is not enforced here, laundry facilities; Mariahilferstrasse 5, tel. 7754) is a 10-minute walk from town, backtracking from the train station. You might rent a bike at the station to get there quick and easy.

Sleeping in Reutte, Austria
(11 AS = about $1, zip code: 6600, tel. code: 05672)
For less crowds, easygoing locals with a contagious love of life, and a good dose of Austrian ambience, homebase in Reutte. (To call Reutte from Germany, dial 0043-5672 and the local number.)

Hotels

Reutte is popular with Austrians and Germans who come here year after year for a one- or two-week vacation. The hotels are big and elegant, full of comfy carved furnishings and creative ways to spend so much time in one spot. They take great pride in their restaurants, and the owners send their children away to hotel management schools.

    Hotel Goldener Hirsch, a grand old hotel renovated to the hilt with a mod Tirolean Jugendstil flair, has sliding automatic doors, mini-bars, TV with cable in the room, and one lonely set of antlers. It's located right downtown (2 blocks from the station). For those without a car, this is the most convenient hotel (SB-490 AS, DB-820 AS, CC:VMA, a 3-minute walk from the station; 6600 Reutte-Tirol, tel. 2508 and ask for Helmut or Monika, fax 2508-100).

    Hotel Maximilian, up the river a mile or so in the vil-

see pg. 51! *maybe the same one if it's walking distance to the castle.*

I heard was great!

lage of Ehenbichl, is the best splurge. It includes the use of bicycles, ping-pong, a children's playroom, and the friendly service of the Koch family. Daughter Gabi speaks fine English. There always seems to be a special event here, and the Kochs host many Tirolean folk evenings (DB-840 AS, TB-1260 AS, cheaper for families, far from the train station in the next village but they may pick you up; A-6600 Ehenbichl-Reutte, tel. 2585, fax 2585-54).

Gasthof zum Schluxenhof gets the "remote old hotel in an idyllic setting" award (DB-700 AS, modern rustic elegance, A-6600 Pinswang-Reutte, between Reutte and Füssen in the village of Unterpinswang, tel. 05677/8903, fax 890323). **Gasthof Säuling**, also in Pinswang, is less idyllic (DB-600 AS, A-6600 Oberpinswang bei Reutte, tel. 05677/8698, fax 8153).

Gasthof-Pension Waldrast (550-650 AS per double; 6600 Ehenbichl, on Ehrenbergstrasse, a half-mile out of town toward Innsbruck, past the campground, just under the castle, tel. 05672/2443) separates a forest and a meadow and is warmly run by the Huter family. It has big rooms, like living rooms, many with a fine castle view, and it's a good coffee stop if you're hiking into town from the Ehrenberg ruins.

Zimmer

The tourist office has a list of over 50 private homes that rent out generally elegant rooms with facilities down the hall, a pleasant communal living room, and breakfast. Most charge 180 AS per person per night, don't like to rent to people staying less than three nights, and speak little if any English. Reservations are nearly impossible for a one- or two-night stay. But short stops are welcome if you just drop in and fill in available gaps. The TI can always find you a room when you arrive (free service).

The tiny village of Breitenwang is older and quieter than Reutte and has all the best central *Zimmer* (a 10-minute walk from the Reutte train station: at the post office roundabout, follow Plannseestrasse past the onion dome to the pointy straight dome, unmarked Kaiser Lothar strasse is the first right past this church). These four places are comfortable, quiet, and kid-friendly; accept one-nighters, have few stairs, speak some English, and are within 2 blocks of the

Breitenwang church steeple: **Maria Auer** (D-350 AS, minimum stay: 2 nights; Kaiser Lothar Strasse 25, tel. 29195), **Inge Hosp** (a more old-fashioned place with 360-AS doubles, a 190-AS single and antlers over the breakfast table; Kaiser Lothar Strasse 36, tel. 2401), across the street is her cousin **Walter Hosp** (D-350 AS; Kaiser Lothar Strasse 29, tel. 5377), and **Helene Haissl** (D-340 AS, 320 AS for a 2-night stay; Planseestrasse 63, tel. 41504).

Youth Hostels

Reutte has two excellent little youth hostels. If you've never hosteled and are curious, try one of these. They accept nonmembers of any age. The downtown hostel is clean, rarely full, and lacking in personality. It serves no meals but has a members' kitchen (80 AS per bed; a pleasant 10-minute walk from the town center, follow the Jugendherberge signs to the Kindergarten sign, 6600 Reutte, Prof. Dengelstrasse 20, Tirol, open mid-June to late August, tel. 71479).

The newly renovated **Jugendgastehaus Graben** (130-AS beds with breakfast; A-6600 Reutte-Höfen, Postfach 3, Graben 1; from downtown Reutte, cross the bridge and follow the road left along the river, about 2 miles from the station; tel. 2644, fax 5904) has 2-6 beds per room and includes breakfast, shower, and sheets. Frau Reyman, who keeps the place traditional, homey, clean, and friendly, serves a great dinner. No curfew, open all year, direct bus connection to Neuschwanstein Castle.

Eating in Reutte

Each of the hotels takes great pleasure in serving fine Austrian food at reasonable prices. Rather than go to a cheap restaurant, I'd order low on a hotel menu. For cheap food, the **Prima** self-serve cafeteria near the station (Mühler Strasse 20; Monday-Friday 8:00-18:30) and the **Metzgerei Storf Imbiss** (better but open only Monday-Friday 8:30-15:00), above the deli across from the Heimatmuseum on Untermarkt Street, are the best in town. For a late dinner in Reutte try **zum Mohren** on the main street (across from #31, tel. 2345).

BADEN-BADEN AND THE BLACK FOREST

Combine Edenism and hedonism as you explore this most romantic of German forests and dip into its mineral spas. Called the *Schwarzwald* in German, the Black Forest is a range of hills stretching 100 miles north-south along the French border from Karlsruhe to Switzerland. It's so thickly wooded that the people called it black. The poor farmland drove medieval locals to become foresters, glass-blowers, and great clock-makers. Today it's popular for its endless hiking possibilities, clean air, cuckoo clocks, cherry cakes, and

The Black Forest

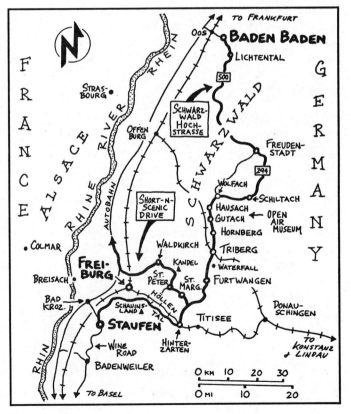

cheery villages. The area is impressively Catholic and traditional. On any Sunday, you'll find volks marches and traditional costumes coloring the Black Forest.

The two major (and very different) towns are Baden-Baden in the north and Freiburg in the south. Freiburg may be the Black Forest's capital, but Baden-Baden is Germany's greatest 19th-century spa resort. Stroll though its elegant streets and casino. Grin and bare it for a *kur* . . . sauna, massage, and utter restfulness.

Planning Your Time

Public transport and the local tourist industry expect that you'll make Baden-Baden your home base in the north and Freiburg your base for the south. I'd tour Freiburg, but spend the night in the charming and overlooked village of Staufen. By train the two big cities are easy, as is a short foray into the forest from either. With more time, do the small-town forest medley between the two. The region is best by car and with a car I'd do the whole cuckoo thing with a night in Staufen, a busy day touring north, and two nights and a relaxing day in Baden-Baden.

Baden-Baden

Of all the high-class resort towns I've seen, Baden-Baden is the easiest to enjoy in blue jeans and with a picnic. This was the playground of Europe's high-rolling elite 150 years ago. Royalty and aristocracy would come from all corners to take the *kur*—soak in the curative (or at least they feel that way) mineral waters—and enjoy the world's top casino. Today this town of 55,000 attracts a more middle-class crowd, both tourists in search of a lower pulse and Germans enjoying the fruits of their generous health care system.

Orientation (tel. code: 07221)

Baden-Baden is made for strolling with a poodle. The train station, in a suburb called Baden-Oos, is 8 kilometers from the center but city bus #1 zips you from the station downtown. Except for the station and a couple of hotels on the opposite side of town, everything is clustered within a 10-minute walk between the baths and the casino.

Baden-Baden

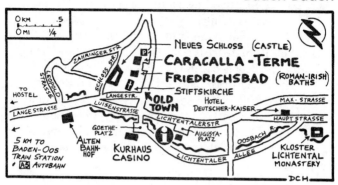

Tourist Information

The TI, in the center near the riverside park (Augustaplatz 8, 9:00-20:00, Sunday 10:00-20:00; tel. 275200), has enough recommended walks and organized excursions to keep even the most energetic vacationers happy.

Getting Around

Handy bus #1 runs straight through Baden-Baden, connecting its Oos train station, town center, and the far end of town (runs every 8 minutes, buy 2 DM 2-hour tickets or the 6 DM 24-hour ticket on the bus). It's important to embrace this wonderful bus and not struggle needlessly for parking downtown.

Sights-Sights—Baden-Baden

▲▲**Strolling**—Bestow a royal title on yourself and promenade down the famous Lichtentaler Allee, a pleasant lane through a park along a stream and past old mansions (lit until 22:00). Either walk the whole length and all the way back, or take city bus #1 one way (runs between downtown and Klosterplatz, near the monastery).

▲▲**Casino**—Even if you don't gamble, tour the casino. It's open for gambling from 14:00 to 2:00 (5 DM entry, 5 DM minimum bet, tie and coat required—and rentable). A third of those who go in just observe; you don't need to gamble. The casino gives dicey 30-minute German-language tours of its Versailles-rivaling interior every morning 9:30-12:00, 10:00-12:00 in winter (tours start on the half-hour, last one at 11:30, 4 DM, and no ties, tel. 07221/21060, call to see if there's a free-loadable English tour scheduled). The nearby "Old Bahnhof" is a simpler gaming place for those in need of a room full of one-armed bandits.

▲▲▲**The Roman-Irish Bath (Friedrichsbad)**—The high light of most Baden-Baden visits is a sober 2-hour ritual called the Roman-Irish Bath. Friedrichsbad, on Römerplatz 1, pampered the rich and famous in its elegant surroundings when it opened 120 years ago. Today, this steamy world of marble, brass columns, tropical tiles, herons, lily pads, and graceful nudity welcomes gawky tourists as well as locals.

For 38 DM, you get 3 hours and the works (28 DM without the 8-minute massage, hotels give a guest card for 10% discounts). The complex routine is explained in the blue English brochure and on the walls in English as you go. Follow the numbered arrows: take a shower; grab a towel and put on plastic slippers before hitting the warm air bath for 15 minutes; hot air bath for 5 minutes; shower; soap brush massage—rough, slippery, and finished with a spank; play Gumby in the shower; lounge under sunbeams and caryatids in one of several different thermal steam baths; glide like a swan under a divine dome in a royal pool; cold plunge; dry in warmed towels; wrapped like in a cocoon, lay clean and thinking prenatal thoughts on a bed for 30 minutes in the silent room.

All you need is money. You'll get a key, locker, and towel (daily except Sunday from 9:00-22:00, men and women together all day Wednesday and Saturday and from 16:00-22:00 on Tuesday and Friday, last admissions at 19:00 if you'll get a massage, at 19:30 otherwise, tel. 07221/275920). The dress code is always nude. During separate times, men and women use parallel and nearly identical facilities. "Mixed" is still mostly separate with men and women sharing only the "royal pool." Couples will do most of the regimen separated. Being your average American, I'm not used to nude. But naked, bewildered, and surrounded by beautiful people with no tan lines is a feeling Woody Allen could write a movie about.

You don't appreciate how really clean you are after this experience until you put your dirty socks back on. (Bring clean ones.)

Afterward, browse through the special exhibits and Roman artifacts upstairs in the Renaissance Hall, sip just a little terrible but "magic" water from the elegant fountain with old ladies who don't seem to be getting much out of it, and stroll down the broad royal stairway feeling, as they say, five years younger—or at least no older.

▲▲**Caracalla Therme**—For more of a glorified swimming pool experience, spend a few hours at the Baths of Caracalla (daily 8:00-22:00, last entry at 20:00), a huge palace of water, steam, and relaxed people, next to the Friedrichsbad.

Bring a towel (5 DM rental) and swimsuit (shorts are okay for men) pick up the blue English instruction sheet and buy a card (18 DM for the first 2 hours, 5 DM per half-hour after that), put the card in the locker to get a key, change, strap the key around your wrist, and go play. (Your key gets you into a poolside locker if you want money for a tan or a drink. Drivers can park under the *Thermen* for free for 2 hours if you validate your ticket at the Caracalla turnstile.)

It's an indoor/outdoor wonderland of steamy pools, waterfalls, neck showers, Jacuzzis, hot springs, cold pools, lounge chairs, exercise instructors, saunas, cafeteria, and bar. After taking a few laps around the fake river you can join the kinky gang for water spankings (you may have to wait a few minutes to grab a vacant waterfall). The steamy "inhalation" room seems like purgatory's waiting room, with six misty inches of visibility, filled with strange, silently aging bodies.

Climb the spiral staircase into a naked world of saunas, tanning lights, cold plunges, and sunbathing. There are three eucalyptus-smelling saunas: 80, 90, and 95 degrees. Read and follow the instructions on the wall. Towels are required, not for modesty but to separate your body from the wood that every other body sits on. The highlight for me was the arctic bucket in the shower room. Pull the chain. Only rarely will you feel so good. And you can do this over and over.

As you leave, take a look at the old Roman bath that Emperor Caracalla himself soaked in to conquer his rheumatism nearly 2,000 years ago.

Sleeping in Baden-Baden
(1.6 DM = about $1, zip code: 76530, tel. code: 07221)
Except for its hostel, rooms in Baden-Baden are expensive.
Doubles in small hotels or private homes start at 80 DM.
Rooms without private plumbing are a real deal. In Baden-
Baden, of all places, you should be able to manage without a
private bath. The TI can nearly always find you a room. The
only tight times are during the horse races (May 20-28,
August 25-September 3 in 1995). If you arrive at Baden-
Baden's Oos station, either stay near the station (see below),
or hop on wonderful bus line #1, which takes you to the
center of town (Augustaplatz, TI, baths, casino, hotels) and
continues to budget hotels on the east end of town.

Sleep code: **S**=Single, **D**=Double/Twin, **T**=Triple,
Q=Quad, **B**=Bath/Shower, **WC**=Toilet, **CC**=Credit Card (Visa,
Mastercard, Amex), **SE**=Speaks English (graded **A** through **F**).

Sleeping in the Center
There are five affordable hotels right in the nearly traffic-
free old town, 2 minutes from the TI, baths, and casino.

Hotel am Markt (S-48 DM, SB-70 DM, D-90 DM,
DB-115, TB-150 DM, cheap kids' beds available, CC:VMA;
Marktplatz 18, tel. 22747 or 22743, fax 391887, Herr und
Frau Bogner SE-A) is the best deal for a warm, small, family-
run hotel with all the comforts a commoner could want in a
peaceful, central location, 2 cobbled blocks from the baths.
The church bells blast charmingly through each room from
6:30 until 22:00. Otherwise, quiet rules. The daily menu
offers a good dinner deal (limited to guests only).

Around the corner, the **Hotel Bischoff** (DB-120 DM,
Römerplatz 2, tel. 29999, fax 38308) and a strange place
called **Bratwurstglocrel** (DB-120 DM, tel. 22968) embrace
the conformist values of private showers at all cost. But just
down the stairs, the funky **Gasthof Zum weissen Rössel**
(S-50 DM, SB-64 DM, D-83 DM, DB-93 DM, TB-122
DM; Baldreitstrasse 5, tel. 25582, Herr Granz SE-F), with
tidy rooms above the closest thing to a real bar you'll find
in downtown Baden-Baden, has enough character for a
"Wanted" poster.

Gästehaus Löhr (one tiny S-40 DM, several S-55 DM,
SB-60 DM, DB-90 DM, CC:VMA, SE-B; office at Café

Löhr at 19 Lichtentaler Strasse, on the main drag across from the TI, tel. 26204 or 31370) is basic, clean enough, and a good deal if you don't mind the Mickey-Mouse setup of the reception being in a café 2 blocks from the hotel. I'd prefer their cheap showerless rooms to the hostel.

Sleeping on Lichtentaler Allee

There are good budget beds, and easy parking, down Lichtentaler Allee on the east side of town. **Deutscher Kaiser** (S-48 DM, SB-73 DM, D-70 DM, DB-105 DM, down-the-hall showers cost 3 DM, CC:VMA; Hauptstrasse 35, Baden-Baden-Lichtental, tel. 72152, fax 72154, Mrs. Peter speaks English) offers some of the best rooms in town for the money. This big, traditional guest house is in a down-to-earth suburb town right on bus #1 line (stop: Eckerlestrasse) about a 15-minute walk down polite Lichtentaler Allee. **Gasthof Cäcilienberg** (S-49 DM, SB-59 DM, D-79 DM, DB-89 DM; Geroldsauer Strasse 2, tel. 72297) is comfortable and beautifully situated even farther out in a quiet area at the end of Lichtentaler Allee (bus #1, first stop after the Kloster Lichtental).

Sleeping near the Oos Train Station

Train travelers get only as close as the suburb of Oos. Those driving in from the autobahn will hit Oos first. Each of these places is on Ooser Hauptstrasse, with easy parking, just a few minutes' walk in front of the station. **Gasthof Adler** (SB-60 DM, D-100 DM, DB-105 DM, CC:VMA; Ooser Hauptstrasse 1, 7570 Baden-Baden Oos, tel. 61858 or 61811, fax 17145) is plain, comfortable, and friendly. **Hotel Goldener Stern** (SB-55 DM, DB-100 DM, CC:VA; Ooser Hauptstrasse 16, 7570 Baden-Baden, tel. 61509) has big, bright rooms.

Youth Hostel

Baden-Baden's great new **Werner Dietz Youth Hostel** (beds in 6-bed rooms, sheets and breakfast for 25 DM, 30 DM if you're over 27, add 6 DM if you have no hostel card; Hardbergstrasse 34, bus #1 to Grosse Dollenstrasse from the station or downtown, tel. 52223, 7:00-23:30, but doesn't answer phone in midday, SE-A) is your budget ace in the hole. They always save 25 beds to be doled out to "travelers" at 17:00, have an overflow hall when all beds are taken, give 4-DM discount coupons for both city baths, and serve cheap meals. (Drivers, turn left at the first light after the freeway into Baden-Baden ends, and follow the signs winding uphill to the big modern hostel next to a public swimming pool.)

Train Connections
Baden-Baden to: Freiburg (6/day, 60 min), **Triberg** (hrly, 60 min), **Strasbourg** (5/day, 45 min), **Heidelberg** (hrly, 60 min, catch Castle Road bus to Rothenburg), **Munich** (hrly, 5 hrs, with two changes), **Frankfurt** (every 2 hrs, 1½ hrs, with changes), **Koblenz** (2/hr, 2 hrs with change in Mannheim).

Freiburg
Freiburg's worth a quick look. The "sunniest town in Germany" feels like the university town it is (30,000 students). It feels like it had a chance to start all over and do it right (it was bombed almost flat in 1944). And it feels cozy, almost Austrian (it was Habsburg territory for 500 years). It's the "capital" of the Schwarzwald, surrounded by lush forests and filled with green (environmentally sensitive) people. Enjoy the pedestrian-only old center. Freiburg's trademark is its system of *Bächle*, tiny streams running down each street. A sunny day turns any kid into a puddle-stomper. Enjoy the ice cream and street-singing ambience of the cathedral square.

Tourist Information
The TI (between old center and station, 9:30-20:00, Sunday 10:00-12:00, less off-season, tel. 0761/3689090) offers a good 4-DM city guidebook, room-finding service, almost daily 8-DM English-language guided walks, and information on the entire Black Forest region. The train station is a short walk from the TI and center.

Sights—Freiburg
Church (Münster)—The church and its towering tower (not worth the 116-meter ascent) are impressive. A local guide or guidebook will point out the symbolism that gave the church's fine windows and sculpture meaning to its parishioners 600 years ago. Find the "mooning" gargoyle and wait for rain.

Augustiner Museum—This offers a good look at the local culture and medieval art including (downstairs) a close-up look at some of the Münster's medieval stained glass (4 DM, 9:30-17:00, closed Monday).

Schauinsland—Freiburg's own mountain offers the handiest quick look at the Schwarzwald for those without wheels. A gondola system, one of Germany's oldest, was designed for Freiburgers relying on public transportation. At the 4,000-foot summit are a panorama restaurant, pleasant circular walks, a tower on a nearby peak offering a commanding Black Forest view, and the Schniederli Hof—a 1592 farmhouse museum. About 25 DM gets you up and back including the tram ride from the town center.

Sleeping in Freiburg
(1.6 DM = about $1, tel. code: 0761)

I prefer to sleep in Staufen (see below), a pleasant small-town alternative to Freiburg. But if you're hosteling, Freiburg's your best bet. The big, modern **Freiburg Youth Hostel** (23 DM per bed with sheets and breakfast; Kartuserstrasse 151, tram #1 to Römerhof, tel. 0761/67656) is on the east edge of Freiburg on the recommended road into the Black Forest.

Train Connections

Freiburg to: Baden-Baden (6/day, 60 min), **Basel** (hrly, 60 min), **Bern** (3/day, 2 hrs, or hrly in 2½ hrs with change in Basel), **Interlaken** (3/day, 3 hrs), **Munich** (6/day, 4½ hrs changing in Karlsruhe), **Mainz** (6/day, 2½ hrs), **Staufen** (4/day, 30 min).

Staufen

Staufen makes a delightful home base for your exploration of Freiburg and the southern trunk of the Black Forest. A mini-Freiburg, it's a perfect combination of smallness and off-the-beaten-path-ness with a quiet pedestrian zone of colorful old buildings bounded by a happy creek that actually babbles. There's nothing to do here but enjoy the marketplace atmosphere. Hike through the vineyards to the ruined castle overlooking the town and savor a good dinner with local wine. A pub at the base of the castle hill offers *Winzergnossenshaft* (wine tasting).

Tourist Information

The TI, on the main square in the Rathaus, can help you find a room (Monday-Friday 8:00-16:30, closed Saturday afternoon and Sunday, tel. 07633/80536). Trains connect Staufen and Freiburg in 30 minutes. Staufen train info: 07633/5211.

Sights—Near Staufen

Wine Road (Badische Weinstrasse)—The wine road of this part of Germany staggers from Staufen through the tiny towns of Grunern, Dottingen, Sulzburg, and Britzingen, before sitting down in Badenweiler. If you're in the mood for some tasting, look for *Winzergnossenshaft* signs, which invite visitors in to taste and buy the wines, and often to tour the winery.

▲**Badenweiler**—If ever a town was a park, Badenweiler is it; an idyllic, poodle-elegant, and finicky-clean spa town known only to the wealthy Germans who soak there. Its *Markgrafenbad* (bath) is next to the ruins of a Roman mineral bath in a park of imported and exotic trees (including a California redwood). This prize-winning piece of architecture perfectly mixes trees and peace with an elegant indoor-outdoor swimming pool (8:00-18:00, Monday, Wednesday, and Friday until 20:00). The locker procedure combined with the language barrier makes getting to the pool more memorable than you'd expect (3 hours for 10 DM; towels, required caps, and suits are rentable). Badenweiler is a 20-minute drive south of Staufen.

Sleeping in Staufen
(1.6 DM = about $1, zip code: 79219, tel. code: 07633)

There's only one budget place in town, but for 30 more marks you'll get breakfasts and all the comforts. The TI has a list of private *Zimmer* (posted on the window after hours), but most don't like to take one-nighters.

Peewee Herman would enjoy **Gasthaus Bahnhof** (S-30 DM, D-70 DM, no breakfast; across from Shining Time Station, tel. 6190). This is the cheapest place in town, with a castle out back, self-cooking facilities, and one 12- to-14-SF dinner a day. It can seem a little depressing during the day, but at night, master of ceremonies Lotte makes it the squeezebox of Staufen. People come from miles around to party with Lotte. If you want to eat red meat in a wine barrel under a tree and still be low on the food chain, this is the place.

Gasthaus Hirschen (DB-100 DM, Haupstrasse 19 on the main pedestrian street, 7813 Staufen, tel. 5297), which has a storybook location in the old pedestrian center and a characteristic restaurant, is family-run with all the comforts. They also have a penthouse apartment for four.

Hotel Sonne (SB-70 DM, DB-100 DM; Albert-Hugard Strasse 1, tel. 7012, SE-B, family Stein), with eight rooms, is at the edge of the pedestrian center and also very comfortable.

Hotel Krone (SB-80 DM, DB-120 DM, TB-150, CC:VMA, Hauptstrasse 30, on the main pedestrian street, tel. 5840, fax 82903, SE-B) gilds the lily. Its restaurant (closed Friday and Saturday) appreciates vegetables and offers good splurge meals.

Sights—Staufen

▲▲**The Short and Scenic Black Forest Joyride**—This pleasant loop from Freiburg takes you through the most representative chunk of the area, avoiding the touristy and overcrowded Titisee. Leave Freiburg on Schwarzwaldstrasse (signs to Donaueschingen), which becomes scenic road 31 down the dark and fertile-with-fairy tales *Höllental* (Hell's Valley) toward Titisee. Turn left at Hinterzarten onto road 500, follow signs to St. Margen, then to St. Peter—one of the healthy, go-take-a-walk-in-the-clean-air places that doctors actually prescribe for people from all over Germany. There is a fine 7-km walk between these two towns, with regular buses to bring you back. St. Peter's TI (Monday-Friday 8:00-12:00, 14:00-17:00, tel. 07660/274), just next to the Benedictine abbey (closed to the public), can recommend a walk. If you're feeling like an overnight, the traditional old **Gasthof Hirschen** (DB-120 DM; St. Peter/ Hochschwarzwald, tel. 07660/204) is on the main square. **Pension Schwär** (D-70 DM; Schweighofweg 4, tel. 07660/219) is basic and friendly. Several morning and late-afternoon buses connect Freiburg and St. Peter.

From St. Peter, wind through idyllic Black Forest scenery up to Kandelhof. At the summit is the Berghotel

Kandel. You can park here and take a short walk to the 4,000-foot peak for a commanding view. Then the road winds steeply through a dense forest to Waldkirch, where a fast road takes you to the Freiburg Nord autobahn entrance. With a good car and no long stops, this route gets you from Freiburg to Baden-Baden in 3 hours.

▲▲**The Extended Black Forest Drive**—Of course, you could spend much more time in the land of cuckoo clocks and healthy hikes. For a more thorough visit, still connecting Freiburg and Baden-Baden, try this drive. As described above, drive from Freiburg down Höllental. After a short stop in St. Peter, wind up in Furtwangen, which has the impressive **Deutsches Uhrenmuseum** (German clock museum, 4 DM, daily April-October 9:00-17:00, less off-season, tel. 07723-656-117). More than a chorus of cuckoo clocks, this museum traces the development of time-keeping devices from the dark age to the space age. It has an upbeat combo of mechanical musical instruments as well.

Triberg—deep in the Black Forest, is famous for its Gutach Waterfall (a 500-foot fall in several bounces, 3 DM to see it, drivers can drop passengers at top and meet them at the 1.50 DM putt-putt golf course in town, a 15-minute downhill walk) and more important, the Heimat Museum (4 DM, daily 8:00-18:00, fewer hours off-season), which gives a fine look at the costumes, carvings, and traditions of the local culture. Touristy as Triberg is, it offers an easy way for travelers without cars to enjoy the Black Forest.

Black Forest Open-Air Museum (Schwarzwälder Freilichtermuseum)—offers the best look at this region's traditional folk life (north of Triberg, through Hornberg to Hausach/Gutach; 6 DM, April-October 8:30-18:00, last entry 17:00, tel. 07831/230). Built around one grand old farmhouse, the museum is a collection of several old farms filled with exhibits on the local dress and lifestyles. The surrounding shops and restaurants are awfully touristy, but this is a place you're sure to find plenty of the famous Schwarzwald Kirchetorte (Black Forest cherry cake).

Continue north, through Freudenstadt, the capital of the northern Black Forest, and onto the Schwarzwald-Hochstrasse, which takes you along a ridge through 30 miles of pine forests before dumping you right on Baden-Baden's back porch.

Route Tips for Drivers

Murten to the Black Forest (130 miles): From Murten (French Switzerland), follow signs to Bern, then Basel/ Zürich. Before Basel you'll go through a tunnel and come to Raststätte Pratteln Nord, a strange orange shopping mall that looks like a swollen sea cucumber laying eggs on the freeway. Take a break here for a look around one of Europe's greatest freeway stops. You'll find a bakery and grocery store for picnickers, a restaurant, showers, and a change desk open daily until 21:00 with rates about 2 percent worse than banks.

At Basel, follow the signs to Karlsruhe and Deutsch-land. Once in Germany (reasonable bank at the border sta-tion, daily 7:00-20:00), the autobahn will take you along the French border which, for now, is the Rhine River. Exit at Freiburg mitte. Park near TI and cathedral (single, tall, see-through spire). From Freiburg, signs lead south to Lörrach/road 3. In Bad Krozingen the yellow sign points to Staufen, on the left under the castle ruins. The dead-end road straight into town leaves you at a parking place near the pedestrian zone and your hotel.

ROTHENBURG AND THE ROMANTIC ROAD

From Munich or Füssen to Frankfurt, the Romantic Road takes you through Bavaria's medieval heartland, a route strewn with picturesque villages, farmhouses, onion-domed churches, Baroque palaces, and walled cities.

Dive into the Middle Ages via Rothenburg, Germany's best-preserved walled town. Countless renowned travelers have searched for the elusive "untouristy Rothenburg." There are many contenders (such as Michelstadt, Miltenberg, Bamberg, Bad Windsheim, and Dinkelsbühl), but none holds a candle to the king of medieval German cuteness. Even with crowds, over-priced souvenirs, Japanese-speaking night watchmen, and yes, even with schneeballs, Rothenburg is best. Save time and mileage, and be satisfied with the winner.

Planning Your Time

The best one-day look at the medieval heartland of Germany is the Romantic Road bus tour. Train travelers go free on the daily bus (Frankfurt to Munich or Füssen, or vice versa). Drivers can follow the route laid out in the tourist brochures. The only stop worth more than a few minutes is Rothenburg. Twenty-four hours is ideal for this town. Two nights and a day is a bit much unless you're actually relaxing on this trip.

Rothenburg in a day is easy. Four essential experiences: the Criminal museum, the wood carving in the church, the city walking tour, and a walk along the wall. With more time there are several mediocre but entertaining museums, walking and biking in the nearby countryside, and lots of cafés and shops. Make a point to spend at least one night. The town is yours after dark when the groups vacate and the town's floodlit cobbles wring some romance out of any travel partner.

Rothenburg

In the Middle Ages, when Frankfurt and Munich were just wide spots on the road, Rothenburg was Germany's second-largest free imperial city with a whopping population of 6,000. Today it's her best-preserved medieval walled town, enjoying tremendous tourist popularity without losing its

Rothenburg

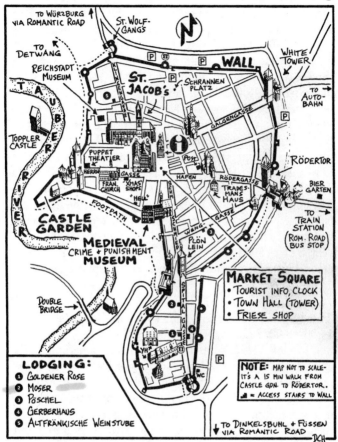

To Würzburg via Romantic Road

St. Wolfgang's

N

To Detwang

White Tower

Reichstadt Museum

P   P   P   **WALL**

To Autobahn

St. Jacob's

Schrannen Platz

T A U B E R

Galgengasse

Toppler Castle

R I V E R

Rödertor

Puppet Theater

Post

WC

Bier Garten

Herrn Gasse

Hafen

Rödergasse

Tradesman's Haus

Fran. Church

Xmas Shops

Heu

Castle Garden

Footpath

Gasse

To Train Station (Rom. Road Bus Stop)

Weng

Medieval
Crime + Punishment
Museum

Plön Lein

Spitalgasse

Market Square
• Tourist info, clock
• Town Hall (Tower)
• Friese Shop

Double Bridge

P

YH

WC

Lodging:
❶ Goldener Rose
❷ Moser
❸ Pöschel
❹ Gerberhaus
❺ Altfränkische Weinstube

Note: Map not to scale—it's a 15 min walk from Castle Gdn. to Rödertor.
▪ = access stairs to wall

↓ To Dinkelsbuhl + Füssen via Romantic Road

—DCH—

charm. Get medievaled in Rothenburg. Walk the wall, see the exquisitely carved altarpiece and the strangely enjoyable medieval crime-and-punishment museum. Be careful . . . this cobbled mall is Germany's best shopping town.

Orientation (tel. code: 09861)

To orient yourself in Rothenburg (ROE-ten-burg), think of the town map as a human head. Its nose—the castle garden—sticks out to the left, and the neck is the skinny lower part, with the youth hostel and my favorite hotels in the Adam's apple. You can walk across the town in 12 minutes.

During Rothenburg's heyday, from 1150 to 1400, it was the crossing point of two major trade routes: Tashkent-Paris and Hamburg-Venice. Most of the buildings you'll see were built by 1400. The city was born around its long-gone castle (today's castle garden; built in 1142, destroyed in 1356). You can see the shadow of the first town wall, which defines the oldest part of Rothenburg, in its contemporary street plan. A few gates from this wall survive. The richest and therefore biggest houses were in this central part. The commoners built higgledy-piggledy (read: picturesquely) farther from the center near the present walls. Today, the great trade is tourism; two-thirds of the townspeople are employed serving you. Too often, Rothenburg brings out the shopper in visitors before they've had a chance to appreciate the historic city. True, this is a great place to do your German shopping, but first see the town. While 2.5 million people visit each year, a mere 500,000 spend the night. Rothenburg is most enjoyable early and late when the tour groups are gone.

Tourist Information

The TI is on the market square (Monday-Friday 9:00-12:00, 14:00-18:00, Saturday 9:00-12:00, 14:00-16:00, closed Sunday, tel. 40492, after-hours board lists rooms still available). Pick up a map and the "sights worth seeing and knowing" brochure (a virtual walking guide to the town; read it all). The TI's free "Hotels and Pensions of Rothenburg" map has the most detail and names all streets. Confirm sightseeing plans and ask about the daily 13:30 walking tour and evening entertainment. The travel agency in the TI is a handy place to arrange train and couchette reservations. The best town map is available free at the Friese shop, two doors toward the nose. Rothenburg is a joy on foot. No sight or hotel is more than a 12-minute walk from the station or each other. Many hotels and guesthouses will pick desperate heavy packers up at the station.

Sights—Rothenburg

▲▲**Walk the Wall**—Just over a mile around, with great views, and providing a good orientation, this walk can be done by those under six feet tall in less than an hour and requires no special sense of balance. Photographers go through lots of film, especially before breakfast or at sunset when the lighting is best and the crowds are least. The best fortifications are in the Spitaltor (south end). Walk from there counterclockwise to the forehead. Climb the Rödertor in route. The names you see along the way are people who donated money to repair the wall after WWII.

▲**Rödertor**—The wall tower nearest the train station is the only one you can climb. It's worth the hike up for the view and a fascinating rundown on the bombing of Rothenburg in the last weeks of World War II (the northeast corner of the city was destroyed; photos, English translation, 1 DM, 9:00-17:00, closed off-season).

Walking Tours—The TI on the market square offers 90-minute guided tours in English (4 DM, daily May-October at 13:30 from the market square). The equally informative but more dramatic "night watchman's tour" leaves each evening at 20:00 (8 DM, April-October, in English). You can hire a private guide. For 50 DM, a local historian—who's usually an intriguing character as well—will bring the ramparts alive. Eight hundred years of history are packed between the cobbles. (Manfred Baumann, tel. 09861/4146, and Anita Weinzierl, tel. 09868/7993, are good guides.)

▲▲**Climb Town Hall Tower**—The best view of Rothenburg and the surrounding countryside and a closeup look at an old tiled roof from the inside (9:30-12:30, 13:00-17:00; off-season Saturday and Sunday 12:00-15:00 only) are yours for 1 DM and a rigorous (214 steps, 180 feet) but interesting climb. Ladies, beware: some men find the view best from the bottom of the ladder just before the top.

▲▲**Herrengasse and the Castle Garden**—Any town's Herrengasse, where the richest patricians and merchants (the *Herren*) lived, is your chance to see its finest old mansions. Wander from the market square down Herrengasse (past the old Rothenburg official measurement rods on the City Hall wall), drop into the lavish front rooms of a ritzy hotel or two. Pop into the Franciscan Church (from 1285, oldest in town, with a Riemenschneider altarpiece; free, 10:00-12:00, 14:00-16:00), continue on down past the old-fashioned puppet theater, through the old gate (notice the tiny after-curfew door in the big door and the frightening mask mouth from which hot tar was poured onto attackers) and into the garden that used to be the castle. (Great picnic spots and Tauber Riviera views at sunset.)

▲▲**Medieval Crime and Punishment Museum**—It's the best of its kind, full of fascinating old legal bits and *Kriminal* pieces, instruments of punishment and torture, even a special cage—complete with a metal gag—for nags. Exhibits are in English. (Fun cards and posters, 5 DM, daily 9:30-18:00, in winter 14:00-16:00).

▲**Toy Museum**—Two floors of historic *kinder* cuteness is a hit with many (just off the market square, downhill from the fountain, Hofbronneng 13; daily 9:30-18:00, 5 DM, 12 DM per family).

▲▲**St. Jacob's Church**—Here you'll find a glorious 500-year-old wooden altarpiece by Tilman Riemenschneider, located up the stairs and behind the organ. Riemenschneider was the Michelangelo of German wood-carvers. This is the one required art treasure in town (2 DM, daily 9:00-17:30, off-season 10:00-12:00, 14:00-16:00, free helpful English info sheet).

Meistertrunk Show—Be on the main square at 11:00, 12:00, 13:00, 14:00, 15:00, 20:00, 21:00, or 22:00 for the ritual gathering of the tourists to see the less-than-breathtaking reenactment of the Meistertrunk story. In 1631, the Catholic army took the Protestant town and was about to do its rape, pillage, and plunder thing when, as the story goes, the mayor said, "Hey, if I can drink this entire 3-liter tankard of wine in one gulp, will you leave us alone?" The invading commander, sensing he was dealing with an unbalanced people, said, "Sure." Mayor Nusch drank the whole thing, the town was saved, and the mayor slept for three days.

Hint: for the best show, don't watch the clock; watch the open-mouthed tourists gasp as the old windows flip open. At the late shows, the square flickers with flash attachments.

▲**Historical Vaults**—Under the town hall tower is a city history museum that gives a waxy but good look at medieval Rothenburg and a good-enough replica of the famous Meistertrunk tankard (well described in English, 2 DM, 9:00-18:00, closed off-season).

Museum of the Imperial City (Reichsstadt Museum)— This stuffier museum, housed in the former Dominican

Convent, gives a more scholarly look at old Rothenburg with some fine art and the supposed Meistertrunk tankard, labeled *"Kürfurstenhumpen"* (3 DM, 10:00-17:00, in winter 13:00-16:00).

St. Wolfgang's Church—This fortified Gothic church is built into the medieval wall at Klingentor (near the "forehead"). Explore its dungeon-like passages below and check out the shepherd's dance exhibit to see where they hot-oiled the enemy back in the good old days (2 DM, 10:00-13:00, 14:00-17:00, closed off-season).

Alt Rothenburger Handwerkerhaus—This 700-year-old tradesman's house shows the typical living situation of Rothenburg in its heyday (Alter Stadtgraben 26, near the Markus Tower; 3 DM, daily 9:00-18:00, closed off-season).

▲**Walk in the Countryside**—Just below the Burggarten (castle garden) in the Tauber Valley is the cute, skinny, 600-year-old castle/summer home of Mayor Toppler (2 DM, 13:00-16:00 on Friday, Saturday, and Sunday in summer only). Intimately furnished, it's well worth a look. On the top floor, notice the photo of bombed-out 1945 Rothenburg. Then walk on past the covered bridge and huge trout to the peaceful village of Detwang. **Detwang** is actually older than Rothenburg, with another Riemenschneider altarpiece in its church (from 968, the second oldest in Franconia). For a scenic return, loop back to Rothenburg through the valley along the river past a café with outdoor tables, great desserts, and a town view to match.

A Franconian Bike Ride—For a fun, breezy look at the countryside around Rothenburg, rent a bike from the train station (12 DM per day, 8 DM with a train pass or ticket, extra gears available for 1 DM each, 5:00-18:30). For a pleasant half-day pedal, bike south down to Detwang via Topplerschloss. Go north along the level bike path to Tauberscheckenbach, then huff and puff uphill about 20 minutes to Adelshofen and south back to Rothenburg.

Swimming—Rothenburg has a fine modern recreation center, with an indoor/outdoor pool and a sauna, a few minutes walk down the Dinkelsbühl Road (8:00 or 9:00-20:00, tel. 4565).

Franconian Open-Air Museum—Twenty minutes drive from Rothenburg in the undiscovered "Rothenburgy" town of Bad Windsheim is a small, open-air folk museum that, compared with others in Europe, isn't much. But it's trying very hard and gives you the best look around at traditional rural Franconia (5 DM, 9:00-18:00, closed off-season).

Shopping

Rothenburg is one of Germany's best shopping towns. Do it here, mail it home, and be done with it. Lovely prints, carvings, wineglasses, Christmas-tree ornaments, and beer steins are popular.

The Kathe Wohlfahrt Christmas trinkets phenomenon is spreading across the half-timbered reaches of Europe. In Rothenburg, tourists flock to the Kathe Wohlfahrt Kris Kringle Market and the Christmas Village (on either side of Herrengasse, just off the main square). This Christmas wonderland is filled with enough twinkling lights to require a special electric hookup, instant Christmas spirit mood music (best appreciated on a hot day in July), and American and Japanese tourists hungrily filling little woven shopping baskets with 5- to 10-DM goodies to hang on their trees. (Okay, I admit it, my Christmas tree dangles with a few KW ornaments.) Note: prices have hefty tour-guide kickbacks built into them.

The Friese shop (just off the market square, west of the tourist office on the corner across from the public WC) offers a charming contrast. Cuckoo with friendliness, it gives shoppers with this book tremendous service: a 10 percent discount, 14 percent tax deducted if you have it mailed, and a free Rothenburg map. Anneliese, who runs the place with her sons, Frankie and Berni, charges only her cost to ship things, changes money at the best rates in town with no extra charge, and lets tired travelers leave their bags in her back room for free.

For good prints, etchings, and paintings, 10 percent off marked prices with this book, and a free shot of German brandy, visit the Ernst Geissendörfer print shop where the main square hits Schmiedgasse.

Those who prefer to eat their souvenirs shop the *Bäckerei* (bakeries). Their succulent pastries, pies, and cakes are pleasantly distracting. Skip the good-looking but bad-tasting "Rothenburger Schneeballs."

Evening Fun and Beer Drinking

The best beer garden for balmy summer evenings is just outside the wall at the Rödertor (red gate). If this is dead, as it often is, go a few doors farther out to the alley (left) just before the Sparkasse for two popular bars and the hottest disco in town.

For a rare chance to mix it up with locals who aren't selling anything, bring your favorite slang and tongue-twisters to the English conversation club (Wednesdays, 20:00-24:00) at Mario's Altefränkische Weinstube. This dark and smoky pub is an atmospheric hangout any night but Tuesday, when it's closed (Klosterhof 7, off Klingengasse, behind St. Jacob's church, tel. 6404).

For mellow ambience, try the beautifully restored Alte Keller's Weinstube on Alterkellerstrasse under walls festooned with old toys. Wine lovers enjoy the Glocke Hotel's stube.

Sleeping in Rothenburg

(1.6 DM = about $1, zip code: 91541, tel. code: 09861)
Rothenburg is crowded with visitors, including probably Europe's greatest single concentration of Japanese tourists. But when the sun sets, most retreat to big-city high-rise hotels. Except for the rare Saturday night, room-finding is easy throughout the year. In fact, those who arrive by train may be greeted by the *Zimmer* skimmer trying to waylay those on their way to a reserved room. If you arrive without a reservation, try talking yourself into one of these more desperate B&B rooms for a youth hostel price.

My first five listings are at the south end of town, 15 minutes from station, a 7-minute (without shopping) walk downhill from the market square. Walk downhill on Schmiedgasse (*gasse* means lane) until it becomes Spitalgasse (Hospital Lane). Unless otherwise indicated, room prices include breakfast.

Sleep code: **S**=Single, **D**=Double/Twin, **T**=Triple, **Q**=Quad, **B**=Bath/Shower, **WC**=Toilet, **CC**=Credit Card (Visa, Mastercard, Amex), **SE**=Speaks English (graded **A** through **F**).

I stay in **Hotel Goldener Rose** (S-32 DM, D-60 DM, DBWC-80 DM-85)M in classy annex behind the garden, some triples, SE-B, ·id-friendly, EZ in annex, CC:VMA; Spitalgasse 28, tel. 4638, fax 86417, closed in January and

February) where scurrying Karin serves breakfast and stately Henni causes many monoglots to dream in fluent Deutsche. The hotel has only one shower for two floors of rooms and the streetside rooms can be noisy, but the rooms are clean and airy and you're surrounded by cobbles, flowers, and red-tiled roofs. The Favetta family also serves good, reasonably priced meals. Remember to keep your key to get in after they close (at the side gate in the alley).

For the best real, with-a-local-family, comfortable, and homey experience, stay with **Herr und Frau Moser** (30 DM per person, one double and one triple; Spitalgasse 12, tel. 5971). This charming retired couple speak little English but try very hard. Speak slowly, in clear, simple English.

Pension Pöschel (S-30 DM, D-60, T-90 DM, small kids free; Wenggasse 22, tel. 3430, SE-D) is also friendly, has 9 bright rooms, and is a little closer to the market square. Just across the street, the **Gastehaus Raidel** (D-64 DM, DB-84 DM; Wenggasse 3, tel. 3115) offers bright rooms with cramped facilities down the hall. It's run by grim people who make me want to sing the "Addams Family" theme song, but it works in a pinch.

Hotel Gerberhaus, a classy new hotel in a 500-year-old building, is warmly run by Ingra, who mixes modern comforts into bright and airy rooms while keeping the traditional flavor. Great buffet breakfasts, a guest's washer and dryer, and pleasant garden in back (DB-100 DM to 140 DM, no CC but takes personal checks, SE-B; Spitalgasse 25, tel. 3055, fax 86555).

Rothenburg's fine youth hostel, the **Rossmühle** (19 DM beds, 6 DM sheets, 8 DM dinners, tel. 4510, reception open 7:00-9:00, 17:00-20:00, 21:00-22:00, will hold rooms until 18:00 if you call, lockup at 23:30) has three to five double bunks per room and is often filled with school groups on weekdays. This droopy-eyed building is the old town horse-mill (used when the town was under siege and the river-powered mill was inaccessible). Here in Bavaria, hosteling is limited to those under 27, except for families traveling with children under 16. In 1995 Rossmuhle's newly renovated sister hostel will open (same phone number).

Gasthof Greifen is a big, traditional old place with all the comforts. It's family-run and creaks just the way you want it to (S-40 DM, SB-70DM, D-70 DM, DB-110 DM, T-100 DM, TB-150 DM, CC:VMA, half a block downhill from the Markt Platz at Obere Schmiedgasse 5 tel. 2281, fax 86374).

Right on the town square, **Gasthof Marktplatz** (S-35 DM, D-60 DM, DB-75 DM, DBWC-90 DM, T-81 DM, TB-100 DM; Grüner Markt 10, tel. 6722, Herr Rosner SE) has simple rooms and a cozy atmosphere. Its cheap rooms have sinks, but access to absolutely no shower.

Frau Guldemeister rents 2 simple and plain rooms (DB-60 DM-70 DM, breakfast in the room, SE-A, EZ-A; off the market square behind the Christmas shop, Pfaffleins-gasschen 10, tel. 8988).

Bohemians with bucks enjoy the **Hotel Altfränkische Weinstube am Klosterhof** (SB-65 DM, DB-90 DM-100 DM, TB-120 DM, CC:VM, kid-friendly, SE-A; behind St. Jacob's church, just off Klingengasse at Klosterhof 7, tel. 6404). A young couple, Mario and Erika, run this dark and smoky pub in a 600-year-old building. Upstairs they rent *gemütliche* rooms with upscale Monty Python atmosphere, TVs, modern showers, open-beam ceilings, and "*himmel* beds" (canopied four-poster "heaven" beds). Their pub is a candlelit classic, serving hot food until 22:00, closing at 1:00. You're welcome to drop by on Wednesday evenings (20:00-24:00) for the English conversation club.

If money doesn't matter, the **Burg Hotel** (DB-230 DM-300 DM, SE-A, CC:VMA; Klostergasse 1, on the wall near the castle garden, tel. 5037, fax 1487), with elegance almost unimaginable in a medieval building with a Tauber Valley view and a high-heeled receptionist, offers a good way to spend it.

In the modern world, a block from the train station, you'll find **Pension Willi Then,** run by a cool guy (Willi played the sax in a jazz band for seven years after the war and is a regular at the English language club) on a quiet street (D-65 DM, DB-75 DM, SE-A; across from a handy laundro-mat at 8 Johannitergasse, tel. 5177).

The town of Detwang, a 15-minute walk below Rothenburg, is loaded with quiet *Zimmer*. The clean, quiet, and comfortable old **Gasthof zum Schwarzen Lamm** in Detwang (D-80 DM, DB-98 DM, tel. 6727) serves good food, as does the popular and very local-style **Eulenstube** next door. **Gastehaus Alte Schreinerei** (8801 Bettwar, tel. 1541) offers good food and quiet, comfy, reasonable rooms a little farther down the road in Bettwar.

Eating in Rothenburg

Finding a reasonable meal (or a place serving late) in the town center can be tough. Most places serve meals only from 11:30-13:30 and 18:00-20:00. Galgengasse (Gallows Lane) has two cheap and popular standbys: **Pizzeria Roma** (19 Galgengasse, 11:30-24:00, 10-DM pizzas and normal schnitzel fare) and **Gasthof zum Ochsen** (26 Galgengasse, 11:30-13:30, 18:00-20:00, closed Thursday, decent 10-DM meals). **Zum Schmolzer** (corner of Stollengasse and Rosengasse) is a local favorite for its cheap beer and good food. If you need a break from schnitzel, the **Hong Kong China Restaurant**, outside the town near the train tracks (1 Bensenstrasse, tel. 7377), serves good Chinese food. There are two supermarkets near the wall at Rödertor (the one outside the wall to the left is cheaper).

Transportation Connections

A tiny train line from Rothenburg to **Steinach** (hrly, 15 min) connects Rothenburg to the rest of Germany. From Steinach, hourly trains go to **Wurzburg** (30 min), **Munich** (2 hrs) and **Frankfurt** (2 hrs, change in Wurzburg). Otherwise the Romantic Road bus tour takes you in and out each afternoon.

Romantic Road

The Romantic Road (Romantische Strasse) winds you past the most beautiful towns and scenery of Germany's medieval heartland. Once Germany's medieval trade route, now it's the best way to connect the dots between Füssen, Munich, and Frankfurt.

Wander through quaint hills and rolling villages, and stop wherever the cows look friendly or a town fountain beckons. My favorite sections are from Füssen to Landsberg and Rothenburg to Weikersheim. For ideas on planning your time see Rothenburg (above).

Getting Around

By car, you can simply follow the green *Romantische Strasse* signs.

Romantic Road

By train . . . take the bus. The Europa Bus Company runs buses daily between Frankfurt and Munich in each direction (April-October). A second route goes between Rothenburg and Füssen daily. Buses leave from train stations in towns served by a train. The 11-hour ride costs about $70 but is free with a Eurailpass. Each bus stops in Rothenburg (75-120 min) and Dinkelsbühl (50-105 min) and briefly at a few other attractions, and has a guide who hands out brochures and narrates the journey in English. While many claim Eva Braun survives as a Romantic Road bus-tour guide, there is no quicker or easier way to travel across Germany and get such a hearty dose of its countryside. Bus reservations are free but rarely necessary (except possibly on summer weekends; call 069/790 3256 one day in advance). You can start, stop, and switch over where you like.

Romantic Road Bus Schedule (Daily, April-October)

Frankfurt	8:15	
Wurzburg	9:45	
Arrive Rothenburg	12:30	
Depart Rothenburg	14:45	14:45
Arrive Dinkelsbuhl	15:30	15:25
Depart Dinkelsbuhl	16:20	16:20
Munich	19:30	—
Füssen		20:15
Füssen	8:00	
Arrive Wieskirche	8:30	
Depart Wieskirche	8:45	
Munich	—	9:00
Arrive Dinklesbuhl	12:20	12:00
Depart Dinkelsbuhl	—	13:45
Arrive Rothenburg	—	14:30
Depart Rothenburg	—	16:30
Wurzburg	—	18:15
Frankfurt	—	20:00

Sights—Along the Romantic Road (South to North)

Füssen—This town, the southern terminus of the Romantic Road, is 2 miles from the startlingly beautiful Neuschwanstein Castle, worthy of a stop on any sightseeing agenda. See the Bavaria and Tirol chapter.

▲▲**Wieskirche**—Germany's most glorious Baroque-Rococo church. In a sweet meadow. Newly restored. Heavenly! North-bound Romantic Road buses stop here for 15 minutes. See the Bavaria and Tirol chapter.

Rottenbuch—Impressive church, nondescript village in lovely setting.

▲**Dinkelsbühl**—Rothenburg's little sister is cute enough to merit a short stop. A moat, towers, gates, and a beautifully preserved medieval wall surround this town and its interesting local museum. Kinderzeche children's festival turns Dinkelsbühl wonderfully on end each mid-July. (TI tel. 09851/90240) You'll find 60-DM doubles at Haus Küffner, tel. 1247, and Zur Linde, tel. 3465, both on Neustädtlein.

▲▲▲**Rothenburg**—See opening of this chapter for more on Germany's best medieval town.

Herrgottskapelle—This peaceful church, graced with Tilman Riemenschneider's greatest carved altarpiece, is 1 mile from Creglingen and across the street from the fast and fun Fingerhut (thimble) museum. The south-bound Romantic Road bus stops here for 15 minutes, long enough to see one or the other (both open 8:30-18:00, 2 DM).

Weikersheim—Palace with fine baroque gardens (luxurious picnic spot), folk museum, and picturesque town square.

▲▲**Würzburg**—An historic city, though freshly rebuilt since World War II, Würzburg is worth a stop to see its impressive Prince Bishop's Residenz, bubbly baroque chapel (*Hofkirche*), and sculpted gardens. This is a Franconian Versailles with grand stairways, 3-D art, and a tennis-court-sized fresco by Tiepolo. Tag along with a tour if you can find one in English, or buy the fine little 4.50-DM guidebook (5 DM, April-September 9:00-17:00; October-March 10:00-15:30; closed Monday, last entry a half-hour before closing). Easy parking is available right there. The Residenz is a 15-minute walk from the train station.

The Würzburg TI offers English walks Tuesday through Saturday (11:00, 2 hours, 12 DM including the Residenz, TI tel. 0931/37335). For budget hotels between the train station and the palace, in ascending order of comfort and price, try **Pension Siegel** (S-50 DM, D-80 DM; just off Kaiserstrasse at Reisbrubengasse 7, tel. 0931/52941), **Hotel Schönleber** (DB-100 DM, CC:VMA, elevator; Theaterstrasse 5, tel. 0931/12068, fax 16012), or **Altstadt Hotel** (DB-110 DM, CC:VM; Theaterstrasse 7, tel. 0931/52204, fax 17317).

The Maypole—Colorfully ornamented Maypoles decorate town squares throughout Bavaria and throughout the year. Many are painted in Bavaria's colors, blue and white. The decorations that line each side of the pole symbolize the crafts or businesses to be found in that town or community.

Each May Day they are festively replaced. Traditionally, rival communities try to steal their neighbor's maypole. Locals will guard their new pole night and day as May Day approaches. Stolen poles are ransomed only with lots of beer for the clever thieves.

Frankfurt

Frankfurt is the northern terminus of the Romantic Road. While on few sightseeing targets, it's actually pleasant for a big city and offers a good look at today's no-nonsense urban Germany. For a quick look, pick up a city map at the TI in the train station (long hours, tel. 069/212-3-8849), walk down Kaiserstrasse past Goethe's house (great man, mediocre sight) to Römerberg, Frankfurt's lively market square. A string of museums is just across the river along Schaumainkai (10:00-17:00, closed Monday). Avoid driving or sleeping in Frankfurt. Pleasant Rhine or Romantic Road towns are just a quick train-ride or drive away.

If you must spend the night in Frankfurt, you can sleep near the station at **Hotel Goldener Stern** (D-75 DM, showers-4 DM, Karlsruherstrasse 8, tel. 069/233309), **Pension Becker** (S-40 DM, D-60 DM, showers-3 DM; near the Botanical Gardens, 15 minutes walk from the station or U-bahn to Westend, Mendelssohnstrasse 92, tel. 069/747992), or at the **youth hostel** (8-bed rooms, 24 DM per bed with sheets and breakfast for members of any age, bus #46 from station to Frankenstein Place, Deutschherrnufer 12, tel. 069/619058). For a quick meal in the station, find the Nordsee cafeteria.

Transportation Connections

Frankfurt to: Rothenburg: The 3-hour (hrly) train ride from Frankfurt requires a change in Würzburg and Steinach. The tiny Steinach-Rothenburg train often leaves from the "B" section of track, away from the middle of the station, shortly after the Würzburg train arrives. Don't miss it. Steinach has no tourism, for good reason. **Amsterdam** (8/day, 5 hrs), **Berlin** (8/day, 5 hrs), **Bern** (14/day, 4½ hrs, changes in Mannheim and Basel), **Bonn** (hrly, 2 hrs), **Brussels** (hrly, 5 hrs), **Freiburg** (hrly, 2 hrs, change in Mannheim), **Copenhagen** (6/day, 10 hrs), **Koblenz** (hrly, 1½ hrs), **Köln** (hrly, 2¼ hrs), **London** (5/day, 9½ hrs),

Milan (6/day, 9 hrs), **Munich** (hrly, 3½ hrs), **Paris** 4/day, 6½ hrs), **Wurzburg** (hrly, 1½ hrs).

Frankfurt's airport (Flughafen), just an 11-minute train ride from downtown (6/hr, 5 DM, ride included in the 6-DM all-day city transit pass), is efficient and user-friendly (with showers; baggage check; long-hours, fair-rates banks; a grocery store; a train station; a waiting lounge where you can sleep overnight; easy rental-car pickup; plenty of parking; a hard-to-miss, big green meeting point sign; an information booth; and even Mcbeer. McWelcome to Germany). Airport telephone directory: general information 069/690 30511, Lufthansa—690 71222, American Airlines—271 130, British Air—690 28831, Delta—664 1212, Northwest—666 6611, SAS—694 531, United—605 020.

Leaving the airport: Drivers heading for Rothenburg, follow autobahn signs to Wurzburg. Train travelers can validate Eurailpasses or buy tickets at the airport station and catch a train directly to Würzburg, connecting to Rothenburg via Steinach.

Flying home from Frankfurt: To get to the airport by autobahn, head toward Frankfurt and follow the little airplane signs to the airport (*Flughafen*), which is right on the autobahn. By train, it's even easier. The airport has its own train station, and many of the trains from the Rhine stop there on their way into Frankfurt (e.g., hrly 90-min rides direct from Bonn).

Route Tips for Drivers

Frankfurt to Rothenburg: The 3-hour drive from the airport to Rothenburg is something even a jet-lagged zombie can handle. The airport is on the Würzburg freeway. It's a 75-mile straight shot to Würzburg; just follow the blue (for autobahn) signs.

Leave the freeway at the Heidingsfeld-Würzburg exit. If you're going directly to Rothenburg, follow signs south to Stuttgart/Ulm/road 19, then to Rothenburg via a scenic slice of the Romantic Road. If stopping at Würzburg, follow "Stadtmitte" then "Residenz" signs from the same freeway exit. (*Wo ist* . . . ? means "Where is . . . ?") From downtown Würzburg follow Ulm/road 19 signs to Bad Mergentheim/Rothenburg.

Rothenburg to Füssen or Reutte, Austria: Get an early start to enjoy the quaint hills and rolling villages of what was Germany's major medieval trade route. After a quick stop, dead center, in Dinkelsbühl, cross the baby Danube River (*Donau* in German) and continue south along the Romantic Road to Füssen. Drive by Neuschwanstein Castle just to sweeten your dreams before crossing into Austria to get set up at Reutte.

If detouring past Oberammergau, you can drive through Garmisch, past Germany's highest mountain (the Zugspitze) into Austria via Lermoos and on to Reutte. Or you can take the small scenic shortcut to Reutte past Ludwig's Linderhof and along the windsurfer-strewn Plansee.

THE RHINE AND MOSEL VALLEYS

These valleys are storybook Germany, a fairy-tale world of Rhine legends and robber-baron castles. Cruise the most castle-studded stretch of the romantic Rhine as you listen for the song of the treacherous Loreley. For hands-on castle thrills, climb through the Rhineland's greatest castle, Rheinfels, above the town of St. Goar. Then for a sleepy and laid-back alternative, mosey through the neighboring Mosel Valley.

In the north, you'll find powerhouse cities of Köln and Bonn on an industrial stretch of the unromantic Rhine. Bonn is Germany's easy-going capital (until Berlin takes over) and Köln has Germany's greatest Gothic cathedral, best collection of Roman artifacts, a world-class art museum, and a good dose of German urban playfulness. These bustling cities merit a visit, but spend your nights in a castle-crowned village. On the Rhine, stay in St. Goar or Bacharach. On the Mosel, choose Zell.

Planning Your Time

The Rhineland does not take much time. The blitziest tour is 1 hour on the train. For a better look, cruise in, tour a castle, sleep in a medieval town, and train out. With limited time, cruise less and be sure to get into a castle. Ideally, spend two nights here, sleep in Bacharach, cruise the best hour of the river (from Bacharach to St Goar) and tour the Rhinefels castle. Those with more time could bike the riverside bike path. With two days, split your time between the Rhine and Mosel, seeing Berg Eltz and Cochem. With three days, add Bonn and/or Koln. Four days: add Trier and a sleepy night on the Mosel river valley.

The Rhine

Ever since Roman times, when this was the Empire's northern boundary, the Rhine has been one of the world's busiest shipping rivers. You'll see a steady flow of barges with 1,000- to 2,000-ton loads. Buses packed with tourists, hot train tracks, and highways line both banks.

Best of the Rhine

Many of the castles were "robber-baron" castles, put there by petty rulers (there were 300 independent little countries in medieval Germany) to levy tolls on all the passing river traffic. A robber baron would put his castle on, or even in, the river. Then, often with the help of chains and a tower on the opposite side of the river, he'd stop each ship and get his toll. There were ten customs stops between Mainz and Koblenz alone (no wonder merchants were early proponents of the creation of larger nation-states).

Some castles were built to control and protect settlements, and others were the residences of kings. As times changed, so did the lifestyles of the rich and feudal. Many castles were abandoned for more comfortable mansions in the towns.

Most of the Rhine castles were originally built in the 11th, 12th, and 13th centuries. When the pope successfully asserted his power over the German emperor in 1076, local princes ran wild over the rule of their emperor. The castles saw military action in the 1300s and 1400s as emperors began reasserting their control over Germany's many silly kingdoms.

The castles were also involved in the Reformation wars that saw Europe's Catholic and "protesting" dynasties fight it out using a fragmented Germany as their battleground. The Thirty Years War (1618–1648) devastated Germany. The outcome: each ruler got the freedom to decide if his people would be Catholic or Protestant, and one-third of Germany was dead.

The French destroyed most of the castles prophylactically (Louis XIV in the 1680s, the Revolutionary army in the 1790s, and Napoleon in 1806). They were often rebuilt in neo-Gothic style in the Romantic Age—the late 1800s—and today are enjoyed as restaurants, hotels, youth hostels, and museums.

Getting Around the Rhine

While the Rhine flows from Switzerland to Holland, the stretch from Mainz to Koblenz is by far the most interesting. Studded with the crenelated cream of Germany's castles, it bustles with boats, trains, and highway traffic. Have fun exploring with a mix of big steamers, tiny ferries, bikes, and trains.

While many travelers do the whole trip by boat, the most scenic hour is from St. Goar to Bacharach. Sit on the top deck with your handy Rhine map-guide and enjoy the parade of castles, towns, boats, and vineyards. Rhine boats cruise only from Easter through October. Off-season is so quiet that many hotels close down.

There are several boat companies, but most travelers sail on the bigger, more expensive and romantic Köln—Düsseldorf line (free with Eurail, otherwise about 15 DM per hour, tel. 0221/2088). Boats run daily in both directions (no express boat on Monday) from May through September with fewer boats off-season. Complete, up-to-date, and more complicated schedules are posted in any station, Rhineland hotel, TI, or current Thomas Cook Timetable. Purchase tickets at the dock 5 minutes before departure.

The boat is never full. (Confirm times at your hotel the night before.)

The smaller Bingen–Rüdesheimer line (tel. 06721/14140, Eurail not valid, buy tickets on the boat) is 25 percent cheaper than K-D with three 2-hour St. Goar–Bacharach trips daily in summer (departing St. Goar at 11:00, 14:10, and 16:10; departing Bacharach at 10:10, 12:30, 15:00; 11 DM one way, 14 DM round-trip).

Drivers have these options: (1) skip the boat; (2) take a round-trip cruise from St. Goar or Bacharach on the Bingen–Rüdesheimer line; (3) draw pretzels and let the loser drive, prepare the picnic, and meet the boat; (4) rent a bike, bring it on the boat (free), and bike back; or (5) take the boat one way and return by train (hourly milk-run trains down the Rhine hit every town: St. Goar–Bacharach, 12 min; Bacharach–Mainz, 30 min; Mainz–Frankfurt, 30 min).

You can rent bikes at the St. Goar TI or at Bacharach's Hotel Gelber Hof (10-speeds, 15 DM per day, 5 DM for child's seat). The best riverside bike path is from Bacharach to Bingen. The path is also good but closer to the highway

Lower Rhine

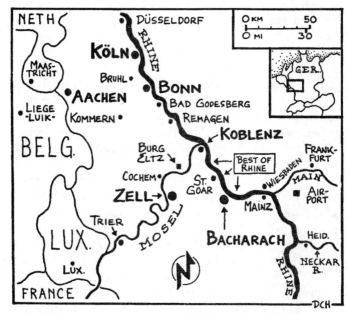

from St. Goar to Bacharach. Consider sailing to Bingen and biking back, visiting Rheinstein Castle (you're on your own to wander the well-furnished castle) and Reichenstein Castle (admittance with groups) and maybe even taking a ferry across the river to Kaub (where a tiny boat shuttles sightseers to the better-from-a-distance castle on the island). While there are no bridges between Koblenz and Mainz, several small ferries do their job constantly and cheaply.

Sights—The Romantic Rhine

(These sights are south to north, from Bingen to Koblenz.)
▲▲▲**Der Romantische Rhine Blitz Zug Fahrt**—One of Europe's great train thrills is zipping along the Rhine in this fast train tour. Here's a quick and easy, from-the-train-window tour (also works for car, boat, or bike) that skips the syrupy myths and the life story of Dieter von Katzeneln-bogen that fill normal Rhine guides.

For more information than necessary, buy the handy *Rhine Guide from Mainz to Cologne* (6-DM book with foldout map, at most shops). Sit on the right (river) side of the train going north from Bingen. While nearly all the castles listed are viewed from this side, clear a path to the left window for the times I yell, "Crossover."

You'll notice large black-and-white kilometer markers along the riverbank. I put those up years ago to make this tour easier to follow. They tell the distance from the Rhinefalls where the Rhine leaves Switzerland and becomes navigable. Now the river-barge pilots have accepted these as navigational aids as well. We're tackling just 36 miles of the 820-mile-long Rhine. Your Blitz Rhine tour starts near Mainz, Rüdesheim, and Bingen. If you're going the other direction, it still works. Just follow the kilometer markings.

Km 528: Niederwald monument—Across from the Bingen station on a hilltop is the 120-foot-high Niederwald monument, a memorial built with 32 tons of bronze in 1877 to commemorate "the reestablishment of the German Empire." A lift takes tourists to this statue from the famous and extremely touristic wine town of Rüdesheim.

Km 530: Ehrenfels Castle—Opposite the Bingerbrück station, you'll see the ghostly Ehrenfels Castle (clobbered by the Swedes in 1636 and by the French in 1689). Since it had no view of the river traffic to the north, it built the cute little *Mäuseturm* (Mouse Tower) on an island (the yellow tower you'll see near the train station today). Rebuilt in the 1800s in neo-Gothic style, today it's used as a Rhine navigation signal station.

Km 533: (cross to the other side of train)—**Burg Rheinstein** and (at km 534) **Burg Reichenstein** are some of the first to be rebuilt in the Romantic era (both are privately owned, tourable and connected by a pleasant trail, info at TI).

Km 538: (cross to other side of train)—**Castle Sooneck,** built in the 11th century, was twice destroyed by people sick and tired of robber barons.

Km 540: Lorch—This pathetic stub of a castle is barely visible from the road. Notice the small car ferry, one of several between Mainz and Koblenz, where there are no bridges.

Km 543: (cross to other side of train)—**Bacharach** is a great stop (see Sleeping, below) with 14th-century fortifications preserved throughout the town. One of the old towers is my favorite Rhine hotel. The train screams within 5 yards of Hotel Kranenturm. Perched above the town, the 13th-century Berg Stahleck is now a youth hostel. Bacharach, which once prospered from its wood and wine trade, is just a pleasant medieval town that misses most of the tourist glitz. Next to the K-D dock is a great park for a picnic (TI, Monday-Friday 9:00-12:00 and 14:00-17:00, tel. 06743/1297; look for "i" on the main street, then go through nearby door and follow signs to "Verkehrsamt" up the stairs, and down the squeaky hall). Some of the Rhine's best wine is from this town, whose name means "altar to Bacchus." The huge Jost beer stein "factory outlet," a block north of the church, carries everything a shopper could want (8:30-18:00, till 16:00 on Saturday, 11:00-15:00 on Sunday, 10% discount with this book).

Km 546: Burg Gutenfels (white painted "Hotel" sign) and the ship-shape **Pfalz Castle** (built in the river in the 1300s, notice the overhanging his-and-hers "outhouses") worked very effectively to tax medieval river traffic. The town of Kaub grew rich as Pfalz raised its chains when boats came and lowered them only when the merchants had paid their duty. Those who didn't pay spent time touring its

Bacharach

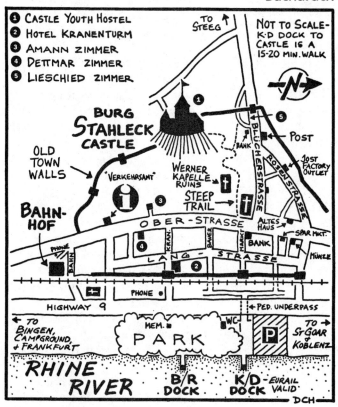

① Castle Youth Hostel
② Hotel Kranenturm
③ Amann zimmer
④ Dettmar zimmer
⑤ Lieschied zimmer

TO STEEG

NOT TO SCALE -
K·D DOCK TO
CASTLE IS A
15-20 MIN. WALK

BURG **STAHLECK** CASTLE

OLD TOWN WALLS

"Verkehrsamt"

BAHN-HOF

WERNER KAPELLE RUINS

STEEP TRAIL

BLÜCHERSTRASSE

ROSENSTRASSE

POST

BANK

JOST FACTORY OUTLET

OBER - STRASSE

ALTES HAUS

SPAR MKT.

BANK

MÜNZE

LANG - STRASSE

PHONE

PHONE

HIGHWAY 9

PED. UNDERPASS

← TO BINGEN, CAMPGROUND, & FRANKFURT

HEM.

PARK

WC

P

TO ST GOAR & KOBLENZ

RHINE RIVER

B/R DOCK

K/D DOCK - EURAIL VALID

DCH

fascinating prison, on a raft at the bottom of its well. In 1504, a pope called for the destruction of Pfalz, but a six-week siege failed. Pfalz is tourable but pretty empty, accessible by 3-DM ferry from Kaub on the other side (4 DM, 9:00-13:00, 14:00-18:00, tel. 06774/570).

Km 550: (cross to other side of train)—**Oberwesel** was Celtic town in 400 B.C., then a Roman military station, and has some of the best Roman wall-and-tower remains on the Rhine. Notice how many of the train tunnels have entrances designed like medieval turrets, built in the Romantic 19th century. Okay, back to the riverside.

Km 554: The Loreley—Steep a big slate rock in centuries of legend and it becomes a tourist attraction, the ultimate Rhinestone. The Loreley (two flags on top, name painted near shoreline) rises 450 feet over the narrowest and deepest point of the Rhine. (The fine echoes here were thought to be ghostly voices in the old days, fertilizing the legendary soil.)

Because of the killer reefs just upstream (at km 552, called the "Seven Maidens"), many ships never made it to St. Goar. Sailors (after days on the river) blamed their misfortune on a *wunderbar Fräulein* whose long blond hair almost covered her body. (You can see her statue at about km 555.) Heinrich Heine's *Song of Loreley* (the *Cliff Notes* version is on local postcards) tells the story of a count who sent his men to kill or capture this siren after his son was killed because of her. When the soldiers cornered the nymph in her cave, she called her father (Father Rhine) for help. Huge waves, the likes of which you'll never see today, rose out of the river and carried her to safety. And she has never been seen since.

But alas, when the moon shines brightly and the tour buses are parked, a soft, playful Rhine whine can still be heard from the Loreley. As you pass, listen carefully ("Sailors . . . sailors . . . over my bounding mane").

Km 556: Burg Katz—From the town of St. Goar, you'll see Burg Katz (Katzenelnbogen) across the river. Look back on your side of the river to see the mighty Rheinfels castle over St. Goar.

Together, Burg Katz (b. 1371) and Rheinfels had a clear view up and down the river and effectively controlled traffic. There was absolutely no duty-free shopping on the medieval Rhine. Katz got Napoleoned in 1806 and rebuilt around 1900; today it's a convalescent home.

Km 557: St. Goar and Rheinfels Castle—The pleasant town of St. Goar was named for a sixth-century hometown monk. It originated in Celtic times (really old) as a place where sailors would stop, catch their breath, send home a postcard, and give thanks after surviving the seductive and treacherous Loreley crossing.

St. Goar is worth a stop (see Sleeping, below) to explore its **Rheinfels Castle**. Sitting like a dead pit-bull above St. Goar, this mightiest of Rhine castles rumbles with ghosts from its hard-fought past. Burg Rheinfels (b. 1245) withstood a siege of 28,000 French troops in 1692, but was creamed by the same team in 1797. It was huge, the biggest

St. Goar

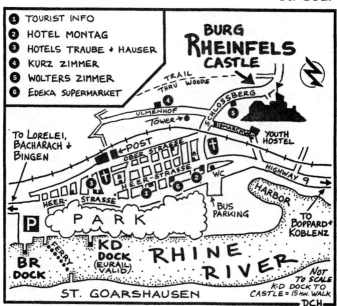

on the Rhine, then used as a quarry. Today it's a hollow but interesting shell and offers your best single hands-on castle experience on the river. Follow the castle map with English instructions (.50 DM from the ticket window). If you follow the castle's perimeter, circling counterclockwise and downward, you'll find an easy-to-explore chunk of the several miles of spooky tunnels. Bring your flashlight (and bayonet). These tunnels were used to lure in and entomb enemy troops. You'll be walking over the remains (from 1626) of 300 unfortunate Spanish soldiers. The reconstruction of the castle in the museum shows how much bigger it was before Louis XIV destroyed it. Climb to the top for the Rhine view (5 DM, daily 9:00-18:00, in October until 17:00; winter, Saturday and Sunday only; form a group of ten English-speaking tourists to get a cheaper ticket and a free English tour; tel. 383; a 15-minute steep hike up from St. Goar, you can call a taxi at tel. 430 for a 7-DM lift from the boat dock to the castle, 10 DM for a mini-bus).

The St. Goar TI (daily 8:00-12:30, 14:00-17:00; Saturday 9:30-12:00; closed Sunday and earlier in winter, tel. 06741/383) now functions as the town's train station with free left-luggage service and 10-DM-per-day bike rentals (50 DM or a passport deposit). They have information on which local wineries do English-language tours and tastings for individuals.

St. Goar has good shops (steins and cuckoo clocks, of course) and a waterfront park hungry for a picnic. The small supermarket (EDEKA) on Main Street is fine for picnic fixings. The friendly and helpful Montag family in the shop under the Hotel Montag has Koblenz-to-Mainz Rhine guidebooks, fine steins, and copies of this guidebook. And across the street, you'll see what must be the biggest cuckoo clock in the world.

Km 559: Burg Maus got its name because the next castle was owned by the Katzenelnbogen family. In the 1300s, it was considered a state-of-the-art fortification . . . until Napoleon had it blown up in 1806 with state-of-the-art explosives. It was rebuilt true to its original plans around 1900.

Km 567: The "Hostile Brothers" castles (with the white square tower)—Take the wall between Burg Sterrenberg and Burg Liebenstein (actually designed to improve the defenses of both castles), add two greedy and jealous brothers and a fair maiden, and create your own legend. They are restaurants today.

Km 570: Boppard—Once a Roman town, Boppard has some impressive remains of fourth-century walls. Notice the Roman tower just after the Boppard's train station and the substantial chunk of Roman wall just before.

Boppard is worth a stop. Just above the market square are the remains of the Roman wall. Below the square is a fascinating church. Notice the carved Romanesque crazies at the doorway. Inside, to the right of the entrance, you'll see Christian symbols from Roman times. Also notice the painted arches and vaults. Originally, most Romanesque churches were painted this way. Down by the river, notice the high water (*Hochwasser*) marks on the arches from various flood years. (Throughout the Rhine and Mosel valleys you'll see these flood marks.)

Km 580: Marksburg (with the three modern chimneys behind it) is the best-looking of all the Rhine castles and the only surviving medieval castle on the Rhine. Because of its commanding position, it was never attacked. It's now open as a museum with a medieval interior second only to the Mosel's Burg Eltz (10:00-17:00, by 7-DM tour only, tours generally in German, worth a visit only if you can tag along with a rare English tour, call ahead, tel. 02627/206).

Km 585: Burg Lahneck—This castle (above the modern autobahn bridge over the Lahn river) was built in 1240 to defend local silver mines, ruined by the French in 1688, and rebuilt in the 1850s in neo-Gothic style. Burg Lahneck faces the yellow Schloss Stolzenfels (out of view above the train, open for touring, a 10-minute climb from the tiny car park, closed Monday).

Km 590: Koblenz—The Romantic Rhine thrills and the Blitz Rhine tour ends at Koblenz. Not a nice city, it was really hit hard in World War II, but its place as the historic *Deutsches-Eck* (German corner)—the tip of land where the Mosel joins the Rhine—gives it a certain magnetism. "*Koblenz*," Latin for "confluence," has Roman origins. Walk through the park, noticing the blackened base of what was once a huge memorial to the Kaiser. Across the river, the yellow Ehrenbreitstein Castle is now a youth hostel. It's a 30-minute hike from the station to the Koblenz boat dock.

Sleeping on the Rhine in Bacharach and St. Goar (1.6 DM = about $1)

The Rhine is an easy place for cheap sleeps. *Zimmer* and *Gasthäuser* abound, offering beds for 25 DM-30 DM per person (and *Zimmer* normally discount their prices for longer stays). Several exceptional Rhine-area youth hostels offer even cheaper beds. Each town's helpful TI is eager to set you up, and finding a room should be easy any time of year (except for wine-festy weekends in September and October). St. Goar and Bacharach, the best towns for an overnight stop, are about 10 miles apart, connected by milk-run trains, river boats, and a riverside bike path. Bacharach is less touristic; St. Goar has the famous castle.

Sleep Code: **S**=Single, **D**=Double/Twin, **T**=Triple, **Q**=Quad, **B**=Bath/Shower normally with a WC, **CC**=Credit Card (Visa, Mastercard, Amex). Breakfast included unless otherwise noted. All hotels speak some English. Most *Zimmer* do not.

Sleeping in Bacharach (zip code: 55422, tel. code: 06743)

Bacharach's **youth hostel, Jugendherberge Stahleck**, is a 12th-century castle on the hilltop high above Bacharach with a royal Rhine view (IYHF members of all ages welcome, 20 DM dorm beds with breakfast, 5 DM for sheets, normally places available but call and leave your name, they'll hold a bed until 18:00, tel. 1266, English spoken, easy parking). This is a gem but very much a youth hostel—with six to eight beds per room. A 15-minute climb on the trail from the town church, it's warmly and energetically run by Evelyn and Bernhard Falke (FALL-kay), who serve hearty, cheap meals.

Hotel Kranenturm gives you the feeling of a castle without the hostel-ity or the climb. This is my choice for the best combination of comfort and hotel privacy with *Zimmer* warmth, central location, and medieval atmosphere (DB-80 DM with this book, discounts for staying several nights, kid-friendly, family rooms available, Rhine views come with train noise, the back side is quieter, CC:VMA, easy reservations by phone, SE-A; Langstrasse 30, tel. 1308, fax 1021, closed January and February). Run by hardworking Kurt Engel and his intense but friendly wife Fatima, this hotel is actually part of the medieval fortification. Its former *Kranen* (crane) towers are now round rooms. When the riverbank was higher, cranes on this tower loaded barrels of wine onto Rhine boats. Hotel Kranenturm is 5 yards from the train tracks (just under the medieval gate at the Frankfurt end of town), but a combination of medieval sturdiness, triple-pane windows, and included ear plugs make the riverside rooms sleepable. The Kranenturm really stretches it to get toilets and showers in each room. Kurt, a great cook, serves fine inexpensive dinners. His big-enough-for-three Kranenturm ice-cream special may ruin you (9 DM). For a quick trip to Fiji in a medieval German cellar, check out his tropical bar.

Frau Amann (D-50 DM; Oberstrasse 13, in the old center on a side lane a few yards off the main street, tel. 1271) rents two rooms in her quiet, homey, traditional place. Guests get a cushy living room, a self-serve kitchen, and the free use of bikes. You'll laugh right through the language barrier with this lovely woman.

Annelie and Hans Dettmar (DB-50 DM, TB-70 DM, QB-100 DM; Oberstrasse 8, on the main drag in the center, tel. 2661 or 2979, SE-A, kid-friendly) are a young entrepreneurial couple who rent four smoke-free rooms (one is a huge family-of-four room, several have kitchenettes) in a modern house above their craft shop. Breakfast is served in their shop with knickknacks dangling everywhere.

Frau Erna Lieschied (D-60 DM, Blucherstrasse 39, tel. 1510, speaks German fluently) shares her ancient, higgledy-piggledy, half-timbered house, 3 blocks uphill from the church, next to the medieval town gate. The rooms are very comfortable.

Ursula Orth rents out two rooms in her home next to the Dettmars' in the town center (a bit musty, DB-50 DM, Spurgasse 3, tel. 1557).

For inexpensive and atmospheric dining in Bacharach, try the **Hotel Kranenturm** or **Altes Haus** (the oldest building in town). For a little wine tasting, drop in on entertaining Fritz Bastian's **Weingut zum Brunen Baum** winestube (just past the Altes Haus, tel. 1208). He's the president of the local vintners club.

Sleeping in St. Goar (zip code: 56329, tel. code 06741)

Hotel Montag (SB-70 DM, DB-130 DM, price can drop if you arrive late or it's a slow time, CC:VMA; Heerstrasse 128, tel. 1629, fax 2086) is just across the street from the world's largest free-hanging cuckoo clock. Mannfred Montag, his wife Maria, and son Misha speak New Yorkish. Even though Montag gets a lot of bus tours, it's friendly, laid back, and comfortable. Check out their adjacent crafts shop (heavy on beer steins).

Hotel Hauser (S-42 DM, D-84 DM, DB-98 DM, DB with Rhine view balconies-110 DM to 130 DM, show this book and plead poverty and you'll get a view room for the low price if available, cheaper in off-season, CC:VMA, Heerstrasse 77, tel. 333, fax 1464, telephone reservations easy), very central and newly redone with solid beds, is warmly run by Frau Velich.

Hotel am Markt, big, well-run by another Frau Velich, and rustic with all the modern comforts, features a hint of antler with a pastel flair and bright rooms in the center of town (DB-100 DM, QB-140 DM, CC:VMA, Am Markt 1, tel. 1689, fax 1721).

St. Goar's best *Zimmer* deal is the home of **Frau Kurz**, with a breakfast terrace, fine view, easy parking, and all the comforts of a hotel (S-34 DM, D-60 DM, DB-70 DM, showers-5 DM, minimum two nights; Ulmenhof 11, 5401 St. Goar/Rhein, tel. 459, 2-minute walk above the station).

The Germanly run **St. Goar hostel** (18 DM beds with breakfast, 28 DM if you're over 28, Bismarckweg 17, tel. 388 morning and after 17:00), the big beige building under the castle, is a good value with cheap dorm beds, a few smaller rooms, a 22:00 curfew, and hearty 8-DM dinners.

Transportation Connections

Milk-run trains stop at all Rhine towns each hour. **Koblenz, Boppard, St. Goar, Bacharach, Bingen**, and **Mainz** are each about 15 minutes apart. From Koblenz to Mainz takes 75 minutes. To get a big train go to Mainz or Koblenz. From Mainz regular trains go to **Frankfurt** (40 min), **Frankfurt airport** (20 min), **Köln** (1½ hrs), **Munich** (4 hrs), **Baden-Baden** (2½ hrs, changing in Mannheim), **Cochem** (1½ hrs, changing in Koblenz).

Mosel Valley

The misty Mosel is what many visitors hoped the Rhine would be—peaceful, sleepy, romantic villages slipped between the steep vineyards and the river, fine wine, a sprinkling of castles, and lots of friendly *Zimmer*. Boat, train, and car traffic here is a trickle compared to the roaring Rhine. While the swan-speckled Mosel moseys from France to Koblenz, where it dumps into the Rhine, the most scenic piece of the valley lies between the towns of Bernkastel-Kues and Cochem. I'd savor only this section.

Getting Around the Mosel

For sightseeing along the Mosel, Eurailers have some interesting transportation options. While the train can take you along much of the river, the K-D (Köln–Düsseldorf) line sails once a day in each direction (May through mid-October, Koblenz to Cochem 10:00-14:30, or Cochem to Koblenz 15:50-20:10, free with Eurail). You can also rent bikes at some stations and leave them at others, or rent a bike in Cochem from the K-D line kiosk at the dock or from Kreutz at Ravenestrasse 7. If you find yourself stranded, hitching isn't bad.

Sights—Mosel Valley

Cochem—With a majestic castle and picturesque medieval streets, Cochem is the touristic hub of this part of the river. The Cochem TI has a free town history and a walking tour brochure. The pointy Cochem castle is the work of over-imaginative 19th-century restorers (March-October, 9:00-17:00, German language—with written English explanation—tours on the hour, 5 DM). Consider a boat ride from Cochem to Zell (3 hours, 2 per day) or Beilstein (1 hour, 4 per day, 17 DM round-trip). The Beilstein-Cochem bus takes 15 minutes (4 DM). The Cochem TI (Monday-Friday 10:00-13:00, 14:00-17:00; summer Saturdays 10:00-15:00; Sundays 10:00-12:00, tel. 02671/3971) books rooms and keeps a thorough 24-hour listing in its window. Many train travelers end up sleeping in Cochem. **Gästezimmer Götz** (7 big 60-DM doubles, 1 family apartment, CC:MA, Ravenestrasse 34, next to the station, tel. 02671/8438, ground floor rooms, speaks some English) is a good and handy value that welcomes one-night stays.

Throughout the region on summer weekends and during the fall harvest time, wine festivals with oompah bands, dancing, and colorful costumes are powered by good food and wine. ▲▲▲**Burg Eltz**—My favorite castle in all of Europe lurks in a mysterious forest, left intact for 700 years, and furnished

Mosel River Valley

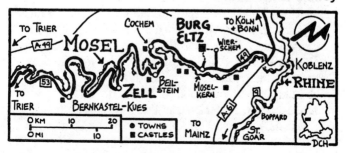

throughout as it was 500 years ago. Burg Eltz is still owned by the aristocratic family Eltz. The countess arranges for new flowers in each room weekly. Unless you happen to visit when an English-speaking group is scheduled, the only way to tour the castle is by hour-long German-only tours (depart every 15 minutes, English fact sheets provided). It's worth a phone call to see if there's an English-language group scheduled that you could tag along with (8 DM, daily April-October 9:30-17:30, tel. 02672/1300, constant 1.50-DM shuttle bus service from car park).

Reaching Burg Eltz by train, walk 1 (steep) hour from Moselkern station (midway between Cochem and Koblenz) through a pine forest where sparrows carry crossbows, and maidens, disguised as falling leaves, whisper "watch out." Driving to Burg Eltz, leave the river at Hatzenport following the white "Burg Eltz P&R" sign. More signs will direct you past Wiersheim to the castle car park, a 10-minute walk from the castle. (It seems like a long way, but I promise it's worth it.) There are three "Burg Eltz" parking lots. Only this one is close enough for an easy walk.

▲**Beilstein**—Farther downstream is the quaintest of all Mosel towns. (For accommodations, see Sleeping, below.) Beilstein is Cinderella land. Check out the narrow lanes, ancient wine cellar, resident (and very territorial) swans, and ruined castle. (TI open daily in summer 7:00-19:00, tel. 02673/1417.)

▲**Zell**—This is the best Mosel town for an overnight stop (see Sleeping, below). It's peaceful, with a fine riverside promenade, a pedestrian bridge over the river, plenty of *Zimmer*, and a long pedestrian zone filled with colorful shops, restaurants, and winestubes. (TI open 8:00-12:30, 13:30-17:00, tel. 06542/4031 or 70122).

▲▲**Trier**—Germany's oldest city lies at the head of the scenic Mosel Valley, near the Luxembourg border. Founded by Augustus in 15 B.C., it was 80,000 strong when Emperor Constantine used the town as the capital of his fading western Roman Empire. A short stop here offers you a look at Germany's oldest Christian church, the *Dom*, or cathedral, which houses the "Holy Robe" of Christ (found by Constantine's mother, St. Helena, and only very rarely on display, next showing in 1996). Connected to the Dom is the

Liebfrau church from 1235, which claims to be the oldest Gothic church in Germany (7:00-18:00). Communists can lick their wounds at Karl Marx's house (15-minute film at 20 past each hour, 10:00-18:00, Monday 13:00-18:00).

Trier has some epic Roman ruins. The basilica is the largest intact Roman building outside of Rome. It's now a church, but you can still imagine Constantine giving audiences from his altar-like throne. From the basilica a fragrant garden leads to the remains of a Roman bath and a 25,000-seat amphitheater. On the other side of town, next to the TI, is the famous and huge Porta Nigra (best Roman fortifications in Germany, climb-able). Skip the city museum in the adjacent courtyard.

The Hauptmarkt square is a people-filled swirl of fruit stands, flowers, painted facades, and fountains—with a handy public WC. Trier's tourist office, next to the Porta Nigra (9:00-18:30, Sunday 9:00-15:30, less off-season, tel. 0651/978080) organizes 2-hour, 9-DM town walks in English daily at 14:00. (For accommodations, see Sleeping, below.)

Sleeping on the Mosel
(1.6 DM = about $1)

Sleeping in Zell (zip code: 56856, tel. code: 06542)
If the Mosel charms you into spending the night, do it in Zell. By car, this is a natural. By train, you'll need to go to Bullay (from Cochem or Trier) where the hourly 10-minute bus ride takes you to little Zell. Its hotels are a disappointment, but its private homes are great. The owners speak almost no English and discount their rates if you stay more than one night. My favorites are on the south end of town, a 2-minute walk from the town hall square and the bus stop.

The comfortable and modern home of **Fritz and Susanne Mesenich** is quiet, friendly, clean, central, and across from a good winestube (D-60 DM, 50 DM if you stay two nights, Oberstrasse 3, tel. 4753). Frau Mesenich can find you a room if her place is full. Herr Mesenich can take you into his cellar for a look at the *haus* wine. Notice the flood marks on the wall across the street and flood photos in her breakfast room and hope it doesn't rain.

Gästhaus Gertrud Thiesen (S-35 DM, D-60 DM for 1 night, 50 DM for 2 nights; Balduinstrasse 1, tel. 4453) is across the street, just as much fun but classier, with a TV-living-breakfast room and a river view. The Thiesen house has big, bright rooms and is on the town's first corner over-looking the Mosel from a great terrace.

The cheapest beds in town are in the simple but comfortable home of **Natalie Huhn** (D-40 DM for 1 night, 35 DM for 2; near the pedestrian bridge behind the church at Jakobstrasse 32, tel. 41048).

If you're looking for room service, a sauna, pool, and elevator, sleep at **Hotel Grüner Kranz** (DB-140 DM with Mosel views, CC:VMA, elevator, tel. 4549 or 4276, fax 4311).

Weinhaus Mayer, a classy old pension next door, is perfectly central with Mosel-view rooms (13 rooms, DB-120 DM, CC:V, Balduinstrasse 15, tel. and fax 4530).

Sleeping in Beilstein (zip code: 56814, tel. code: 02673)

Cozier and farther north, Beilstein is very small and quiet, with no train nearby but plenty of Cochem bus connections.

Hotel Haus Lipmann (5 rooms, DB-120 DM-150 DM, tel. 1573) is your chance to live in a medieval mansion with hot showers and TVs. A prize-winner for atmosphere, it's been in the Lipmann family for 200 years. The creaky wooden staircase and the elegant dining hall with long wooden tables surrounded by antlers, chandeliers, and feudal weapons will get you in the mood for your castle sightseeing but the riverside terrace may mace your momentum.

The half-timbered, river-front **Altes Zollhaus Gäst-zimmer** (DB-95 DM, 15 DM more on Friday and Satur-day, tel. 1574 or 1850, open March-October) has crammed all the comforts into tight, bright and modern rooms.

Gasthaus Winzerschenke an der Klostertreppe (DB-60 DM, tel. 1354) is comfortable and a great value, right in the tiny heart of town. There are cheaper rooms in Beilstein's gaggle of private homes.

Sleeping in Trier (tel. code: 0651)

For reasonable beds near the train station, try **Hotel Monopol** (S-60 DM-90 DM, D-110 DM, DB-120 DM-

150 DM, CC:VM, buffet breakfast; Bahnhofsplatz 7, tel. 714090) or **Hotel Kurfürst Balduin** (S-55 DM, D-95 DM, DB-120 DM, CC:VMA; Theodor Heuss Allee 22, tel. 25610). To sleep in a near-palace that tries too hard to be cute and antique, check into **Fassbender's Central Hotel** (DB-140 DM, CC:VMA; Sichelstrasse 32, tel. 978780, fax 9787878). The best value in town is the Catholic Church-run **Kolpinghaus Warsberger Hof** (25 DM per bed with sheets and breakfast in two- to six-bed dorm rooms or 35 DM per person in the S, D, or T hotel rooms, no private showers; 1 block off the market square, Dietrichstrasse 42, tel. 75131, fax 74696). This place is super-clean, well-run, and serves inexpensive meals in its open-to-anyone restaurant. On the same street, **Hotel Frankenturm** (S-60 DM, D-80 DM, DB-130 DM, CC:VMA, Dietrichstrasse 3, tel. 45712, fax 9782449) is plain, comfortable and simple, above a classy saloon.

The Unromantic Rhine

Romance isn't everything. Bonn and Köln are urban Jacuzzis that keep the Rhine churning. The small town of Remagen had a bridge that helped defeat Hitler in WWII and unassuming Aachen (near the Belgian border) was once the capital of Europe.

Getting Around

Fast and frequent super-trains connect Bonn, Köln, Trier, Koblenz, and Frankfurt. All major sights are within a reasonable walk from each city's train station. The only frustrations you'll deal with are the rare departures in the small riverside towns and bus connections between the smallest Mosel towns.

Sights—Unromantic Rhine

▲▲▲**Köln (Cologne)**—A big, no-nonsense city, Germany's fourth largest, Köln has a compact and lively center. The Rhine was the northern boundary of the Roman Empire and 1700 years ago Emperor Constantine (the first Christian emperor) made "Colonia" the seat of a bishop. Five hundred years later, under Charlemagne, it became the seat of an archbishop. With 40,000 people living within its walls, it was an important cultural and religious center throughout the

Middle Ages. To many, the city is most famous for its toilet water. "Eau de Cologne" was first made here by an Italian chemist in 1709. Even after World War II bombs destroyed 95 percent of it, Köln has remained, after a remarkable recovery, a cultural and commercial center as well as a fun, colorful, and pleasant-smelling city. And it couldn't be easier to visit: Köln's three important sights cluster within 2 blocks of its train station and TI (opposite church entry, open daily 8:00-22:30, until 21:00 in winter, has a list of reasonable private guides, tel. 0221/221 3345). This super pedestrian zone is a constant carnival of people. If you drive to Köln, follow signs to Zentrum and then to the huge Dom/Rhein pay lot under the cathedral.

The Gothic **Dom**, or cathedral, is far and away Germany's most exciting church (100 yards from the station, open 7:00-19:00). Inside, under its 500-foot-tall spire, don't miss the amazingly realistic and way-ahead-of-its-time "Gero Crucifix," sculpted in 976. The "Shrine of the Magi" is a lavish gold altarpiece containing the "bones of the three kings," which, by some stretch of medieval Christian logic, justified the secular power of the local king. These important relics, acquired in the 12th century, made Köln a big enough stop on the pilgrimage trail to merit the construction of this magnificent cathedral.

Next to the Dom is the outstanding **Römisch-Germanisches Museum**, Germany's best Roman museum (5 DM, Tuesday-Friday 10:00-16:00, Saturday and Sunday 11:00-16:00). Cheapskates can view its prize piece, a fine mosaic floor, free from the front window. Proudly, the museum offers not a word of English among its elegant and fascinating display of Roman artifacts (fine glassware, jewelry, and mosaics). Next door (and, I think, more enjoyable), the **Wallraf-Richartz and Ludwig Museum** offers a world-class collection of medieval, northern Baroque, Impressionist, and 20th-century painting, thoughtfully described in English. (8 DM, Tuesday-Friday 10:00-18:00, Saturday-Sunday 11:00-18:00, closed Monday; buy the .50 DM guide/map, great cafeteria with a salad bar, tel. 0221/2212372.)

▲**Bonn**—Bonn was chosen for its sleepy, cultured, and peaceful nature as a good place to plant Germany's first post-Hitler government. Now that Germany is one again, Berlin will retake its position as capital. Apart from the tremendous cost of switching the seat of government, more than 100,000 jobs are involved, and lots of Bonn families will have some difficult decisions to make. Exactly when the move will happen is not clear.

Today Bonn is sleek, modern, and by big-city standards, remarkably pleasant and easygoing. Stop here not to see Beethoven's house (10:00-17:00, Sunday 10:00-13:00, 5 DM, tel. 0228/635188) but to come up for a smoggy breath of the real world after the misty, romantic Rhine. The TI is directly in front of the station (open 8:00-21:00, Sunday 9:30-12:30, tel. 0228/773466, free room-finding service).

The pedestrian-only old town stretches out from the station and makes you wonder why the United States can't trade in its malls on real, people-friendly cities. The market square and Münsterplatz are a street-musician-filled joy. People-watching doesn't get much better.

Hotels are expensive in Bonn. **Hotel Eschweiler Taco** (S-72 DM, SB-82 DM, SBWC-95 DM, D-108 DM, DB-118 DM, DBWC-135 DM; Bonngasse 7, tel. 0228/631760 or 631769, fax 694904) is plain but well-located, just off the market square on a pedestrian street next to Beethoven's place above a taco joint (7-minute walk from the station).

▲**Remagen**—Midway between Koblenz and Köln, you'll find what little remains of the Bridge at Remagen, of World War II fame. But the memorial and the bridge stubs are enough to stir the emotions of Americans who remember when it was the only bridge that remained, allowing the Allies to cross the Rhine and race to Berlin in 1945. The small museum tells the bridge's fascinating story in English (2.50 DM, daily March-October 10:00-17:00). It's located on the west bank of the Rhine. Follow the "Brücke von Remagen" signs through the town of Remagen.

▲**Aachen (Charlemagne's Capital)**—This city was the capital of Europe in A.D. 800, when Charles the Great (Charlemagne) called it Aix-la-Chapelle. The remains of his rule include an impressive Byzantine/Ravenna-inspired church with his sarcophagus and throne. The city also has a headliner newspaper museum and great fountains including a clever arrange-'em-yourself version.

Sightseeing Lowlights

Heidelberg—This famous old university town attracts hordes of Americans. Any surviving charm is stained almost beyond recognition by commercialism. It doesn't make it in Germany's top 20 days.

Mainz, Wiesbaden, Rüdesheim, and Frankfurt—These towns are all too big or too famous. They're not worth your time. Mainz's Gutenberg Museum is also a disappointment.

Train Connections

Trains cover this area quickly and easily: **Cochem-Köln** (every 2 hrs, 80 min), **Bacharach** or **St. Goar-Köln** (hrly, 90 min with one change), **Koblenz-Köln** (2/hr, 60 min), **Köln-Bonn** (2/hr, 30 min), **Koblenz-Trier** (hrly, 75 min), **Cochem-Trier** (hrly, 45 min), **Koln-Trier** (9/day, 2½ hrs), **Koln-Aachen** (2/hr, 60 min).

BERLIN

No tour of Germany is complete without a look at its historic and newly united capital, Berlin. Enjoy the thrill of walking over what was The Wall and through Brandenburg Gate. Crossing "into the East" is now like stepping on a dead dragon, no longer mysterious and foreboding—just ugly. That thrill is gone.

Berlin has shut the door on a tumultuous 50-year chapter in its 750-year history. It was flattened in World War II, then divided by the Allied powers, with the American, British, and French sectors being West Berlin and the Russian sector, East Berlin. The division was set in stone when the East built the Berlin Wall in 1961. In 1989 the Wall fell, and in 1990 Germany was formally reunited. Today the city is like a man who had a terrible accident and half the body was given the best of care and the other was denied therapy. But Dr. Capitalism has arrived and the east is healing quickly.

The new right-wing city government is eager to charge forward with little nostalgia for anything that was "eastern." Big corporations and the national government have moved in and the dreary swath of land that was the Wall will soon again be the city center. The entire area is a construction zone, its skyline a nest of cranes as city planners are boldly taking the reunification of the city and the return of the national government (in the year 2000) as a good opportunity to make Berlin a great capital once again.

Planning Your Time

Because of its location, on a quick trip I'd spend either one or two days in Berlin and sleep in and out on the train. On a three-week trip through Germany, Austria and Switzerland, I'd give Berlin two days and spend them this way:

Day 1: Arrive early on the overnight train, visit TI and check into hotel, visit memorial church and KaDeWe, do the complete Bus #100 orientation tour with a visit to the Reichstag and Brandenburg Gate (or take the Guide Friday tour). After lunch near Alexanderplatz, tour the Pergamon Museum, spend the afternoon strolling Kurfurstendamm.

Day 2: Check out of hotel, leave bags there. Subway to Hermannplatz and ride bus #129 through Kreuzberg to Haus am Checkpoint Charlie. Tour the museum, see remains of the Wall, tour the Topography of Terror exhibit. Divide rest of day between the paintings of the Gemaldegalerie, the Egyptian museum, and Charlottenburg Palace. Depart on an overnight train.

Orientation (tel. code: 030)

The tourist's Berlin can be broken into chunks: (1) The area around the Bahnhof Zoo and the grand Kurfürstendamm boulevard (transportation, information, hotel, shopping, and nightlife hub), (2) former downtown East Berlin (Brandenburg Gate, Unter den Linden boulevard, Pergamon Museum, Wall-related sights), (3) the museums and palace at Charlottenburg, and (4) the museums at Dahlem. Chunks 1 and 2 can be done on foot or with bus #100. Catch the U-Bahn to chunks 3 and 4.

Arriving by Train

Berlin's central station is called Bahnhof Zoo because it's near Berlin's famous zoo. Berlin has three stations. "Zoo" is for most of Western Europe. Hauptbahnhof is for most eastbound and southbound trains. And Lichtenberg is for eastbound and northbound trains. All trains are connected by subway. Train info: tel. 19419.

Most travelers arrive at the "Zoo Bahnhof." There's no clear front of the station, but eventually you'll end up on Hardenbergplatz (filled with city buses). Tip-toe through the riff-raff to the big intersection on the right. Looking down Hardenbergstrasse, past the close skyscraper with the giraffe on it, you'll see the black bombed-out hulk of the Kaiser-Wilhelm Memorial Church. The TI is behind that, in the Europa Center (with the Mercedes symbol spinning on its roof). Facing the church, most of the hotels I recommend are to your right. Just ahead amidst the traffic is the BVG transport information kiosk. (Buy the 24-hour 13-DM pass here, pick up a free subway map and maybe the 2-DM transit map.) From here, walk to the TI, descend into the subway system, and catch bus #100 for the intro tour.

Tourist Information

The main TI office is 5 minutes from the Berlin Zoo train station, in the Europa Center (with Mercedes symbol on top, enter outside to the left, on Budapesterstrasse, 8:00-22:30, 9:00-21:00 on Sunday, tel. 030/262-6031). Their free *Berlin Berlin* magazine has good reading on Berlin and lists the latest location and hours of major sights. The *Berlin Program*, a 3-DM German language monthly, lists upcoming events. The transit map is worth 2 DM only if you'll be riding a lot of buses. Get the free metro map. Smaller TIs: Zoo Bahnhof (8:00-23:00, closed Sunday, tel. 313-9063), Hauptbahnhof (daily 8:00-20:00, tel. 279-5209), and Brandenburg Gate (may be in business in 1995).

Getting Around Berlin

Berlin is miserable on foot. Use Berlin's fine public-transit system. The U-Bahn, S-Bahn, and all buses are now one "BVG" system operating conveniently on the same tickets. (The S-Bahn is free with a Eurailpass.) A basic buy-as-you-board or buy-from-machines (Erwachsene Normaltarif) 3.50 DM ticket gives you 2 hours of travel on buses or subways. For a single short ride (a distance of six bus stops or three subway stations, with one transfer) get the "Einzelfahrschein" ticket (2.30 DM). A "Sammelkarte" gives you four of either of these tickets at a small discount. The 13-DM "Berlin Ticket" is a great deal, giving you the works for 24 hours. The many police escorting cheaters out of the subway make you happy you're not taking advantage of this honor system. The double-decker buses are a joy to ride, and the subway is a snap. Right from the start, commit yourself to public transit in Berlin. Taxis are expensive.

Bus #100 Do-It-Yourself Orientation Tour

Berlin's bus #100 is made to order for sightseers (Bahnhof Zoo, Europa Center/Hotel Palace, Siegessaüle, Reichstag, Brandenburg Gate, Unter den Linden, Pergamon Museum, to Alexanderplatz). If you have the 30 DM and 90 minutes for a Guide Friday tour, take that. But this 3.50-DM, 30-minute tour is a winning intro to the city. Buses leave from Hardenbergplatz in front of the Zoo station (or near the Europa Center TI, in front of the Hotel Palace). Get out when you like. Buses come every 10 minutes and tickets are good for 2 hours. Climb aboard, stamp your ticket (giving it a time) and grab a front seat on top. If you have the TI's fun free pictorial "Kurfurstendamm to Alexanderplatz" map, use it to follow the route (and tell me the giraffe's not doing what I think he's doing). Major sights are mentioned here and described in more depth below (listed in the order bus #100 hits them).

• (On right, before descending into the tunnel) The bombed-out hulk of the Kaiser-Wilhelm Memorial Church, with its new sister church (described below).

• (Stop: in front of the Hotel Palace) On the left, the Berlin Zoo entrance and its aquarium (described below).

• (Driving down Kurfurstenstrasse, turning left into Tiergarten) The 60-meter-tall Victory Column or Siegessaüle (described below).

West Berlin

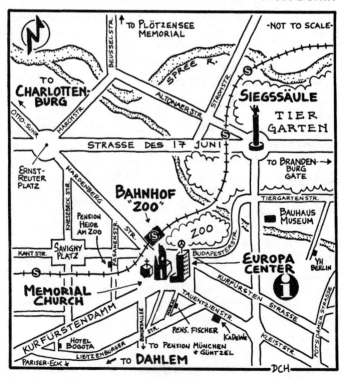

• (On the left immediately after leaving the Siegessäule) The 18th-century late-rococo Bellevue Palace is the new German "White House," the residence of the federal president. If the flag's flying, he's home.

• (Driving along the Spree River) This park area was a residential district before WWII. Soon it will be filled with the buildings of the new national government. Construction has already started. Floating in front of the slope-roofed "House of World Cultures" (left side) is a Henry Moore sculpture. The modern tower (next on left) is a Carillon with 68 bells (1987).

• (Big, black, flag-waving building on left) The Reichstag building is as full of history as its bullet-riddled and patched up complexion suggests (described below).

• (Immediately around the corner, on left) Brandenburg Gate (described below) was the center of old Berlin. As you

East Berlin

drive under it look left and right. That was all important government buildings, bombed to smithereens, and later the Wall. Behind you on the right is the Siegessaüle and a grand 10-mile-long boulevard leading from Charlottenburg, through the Brandenburg Gate, up Unter den Linden, to the heart of old imperial Berlin and what was the palace of the Prussian emperor, Frederick the Great.

• (Driving up Under den Linden straight toward the TV tower in the distance) In the 15th century this was a horse-way leading from the palace to the hunting lodge. In the 17th century, Hohenzollern princes and princesses moved in, building their palaces here to be near the Prussian emperor. Linden trees still give it a pleasant strolling ambiance. This was the most elegant street of Prussian Berlin, and the main drag of East Berlin.

• (First big building on right) The Russian embassy is not quite as important now as it was a few years ago. It flies the Russian white, blue, and red. Next to it is the Russian airline, Aeroflot.

• (The large equestrian statue in the street ahead) On the horse is Frederick II ("the Great"). Most of the buildings around you were from his governmental center. His palace would have been just ahead. Behind the statue is the Humboldt University (formerly one of Europe's greatest, Marx and Lenin—not the brothers or the sisters—studied here). The Greek temple-like building next on the left is the "New Watch" (from the early 1800s) which is now a national memorial for the German dead of both great wars.

• (Crossing the bridge) You're now on the "Museum Island," home of Germany's first museums and today famous for its Pergamon Museum (described below). The museum complex starts with the Neoclassical facade on the left. The huge church is the 100-year-old Berlin Cathedral, or "Dom" (inside, the great reformers stand around the dome like stern saints guarding their theology). Immediately across the street (right) is the "Palace of the People," the grand center and international showcase of East Berlin. Debate rages over whether or not to tear it down. It sits on the spot of the original palace of the Prussian emperor.

• (Crossing another bridge, you leave the Museum Island) On your right are the pointy twin spires of the Nikolai church.

This was medieval Berlin (not worth a visit). The huge red-brick building is the city hall, built after the revolution of 1848 and arguably the first democratic building in the city. Next to this were the DDR presidential palace and head-quarters of the Communist party. The much closer church, the Marien church, dates back to 1270.

• (Under the TV tower) Alexanderplatz, under the tracks on the right, was the commercial heart of East Berlin (described below).

• This is the end of the tourist's bus #100 route. There are plenty of handy eateries and a subway station here. Stay on the bus to ride through workaday eastern Berlin, with its Lego-hell apartments (30 minutes round-trip). Are the people different? They are politically free. Are they economically free? How's the future? (At the end of the line, get out. At the same stop, in a few minutes, another bus will take you back to Alexanderplatz, or even back to the start at Zoo.)

Sights—Near Bahnhof Zoo

▲**Kurfürstendamm**—In the 1850s, when Berlin became a wealthy and important capital, Berlin's new rich chose Kurfurstendamm as their street. Bismarck made it Berlin's Champs-Elysees. In the 1920s it became a chic and fashionable drag of cafés and boutiques. During the Third Reich, as home to the international community of diplomats and journalists, it enjoyed more freedom than the rest of Berlin. Throughout the Cold War, economic subsidies from the West made sure that capitalism thrived on Ku'damm, as west Berlin's main drag is popularly called. And today, while much of the old charm has been hamburgerized, Ku'damm is still the place to feel the pulse of the city and enjoy its most elegant shops (around Fasanenstrasse) and department stores. Ku'damm, starting at Kaiser Wilhelm Memorial Church, does its commercial can-can for over 2 miles.

Europa Center—This shiny high-rise shopping center, where you'll find the city Tourist Information and lots of shops and restaurants, was built as a showcase of Western capitalism during the cold war. If you arrive in Berlin before the TI opens, the Deli French (ground floor, open at 7:00, 8:00 Sunday) is a more pleasant place to brush your teeth and start your day than the seedy Bahnhof Zoo.

▲**Kaiser Wilhelm Memorial Church
(Gedächtniskirche)**—Originally a memorial to the first
emperor of Germany, who died in 1888, this is now a
memorial to the destruction of Berlin in WWII. The
charred and gutted ruins of this bombed-out church (free,
Tuesday-Saturday 10:00-16:00) have great ceiling mosaics
and an interesting photo exhibit about the bombing. Next to
it, a new church (1961) offers a world of 11,000 little blue
glass windows.

▲**Kaufhaus des Westens (KaDeWe)**—The "department
store of the West" is the biggest department store in Europe.
It takes a staff of more than 3,000 to help you find and purchase what you need from the vast selection of more than
200,000 items. You can get everything from a haircut and
train ticket to souvenirs (fourth floor). The sixth floor is a
world of taste treats. This biggest selection of deli and exotic
food in Germany offers plenty of free samples and classy
opportunities to sit down and eat. Or, better, ride the glass
elevator to the seventh floor's glass-domed Le Buffet
self-service cafeteria (9:30-18:30, Saturday until 14:00,
Thursday until 20:30, closed Sunday, tel. 21210, U-Bahn:
Wittenbergplatz).

The Berlin Zoo—1,500 different kinds of animals call
Berlin's famous zoo home (or so the zookeepers like to think,
10 DM, 9:00-18:30, feeding times posted at entry, morning
is the best visiting time, enter near TI in front of Hotel
Palace, tel. 254010).

Tiergarten/Siegessaüle—Berlin's "Central Park" stretches
about 2 miles from the Zoo train station to the Brandenburg
Gate. Its centerpiece, the Siegessaüle (Victory Column), was
built to commemorate the Prussian defeat of France in 1870.
The pointy-helmeted Germans rubbed it in, decorating the
tower with French cannon and paying for it all with francs
received as war reparations. Statues of Moltke and other
German military greats goose-step around the angel at night.
You can climb its 285 steps for a fine Berlin-wide view
(1.50 DM, 9:00-18:00, Monday 13:00-18:00, bus #100).
From the tower the grand Strasse des 17 Juni leads to the
Brandenburg Gate (via a thriving flea-market each Saturday
and Sunday).

Sights—East Berlin

▲▲Brandenburg Gate—The historic Brandenburg Gate was the symbol of Berlin and then the symbol of divided Berlin. It sat, part of a sad circle dance called the Wall, for over 25 years. Now a free little photo exhibit in the gate and postcards all over town show the ecstatic day—December 23, 1989—when the world enjoyed the sight of happy Berliners jamming the gate like flowers on a parade float. A carnival atmosphere continues as tourists stroll, past hawkers with "authentic" pieces of the wall, DDR flags and military paraphernalia, to the traditional rhythm of an organ-grinder. Step aside for a minute, and think about struggles for freedom—past and present. Ebertstrasse leads from Brandenburg Gate to Potsdamer Platz, formerly the busiest square in all of Europe, then for decades a vacant lot. Sony and Mercedes are busy making Potsdamer Platz once more a vibrant center of commerce.

▲The Reichstag—It was from this old Parliament building that the German republic was proclaimed in 1918. Hitler burned this symbol of democracy to frame the Communists in 1933. And it was in here that the last 1,500 Nazis made their last stand, extending WWII in Europe by four days. For its 101st birthday, in 1995, the Bulgarian artist Cristo will wrap it up. The Reichstag houses a modern German history exhibit, "Questions on German History" (free, 10:00-17:00 Tuesday-Sunday, enter from side opposite the bus #100 stop, cheap cafeteria, lots of free literature on the German government). Nothing is explained in English but you can follow a good, socio-economico-meaty and exhausting 45-minute tape-recorded tour for 2 DM. In a few years this collection will move, as the Reichstag resumes its real function as Germany's Parliament building. On the Brandenburg Gate side of the building, the garden of crosses is a memorial to those killed trying to cross The Wall.

▲▲Under den Linden and Alexanderplatz, the heart of East Berlin—In Berlin's good old days, Unter den Linden was one of Europe's grand boulevards. Walk or catch bus #100 from Brandenburg Gate to Alexanderplatz. The "Bus #100 tour" above describes the sights along the way. The 1,200-foot-tall Fernsehturm TV tower (built 1969, 6 DM, 9:00-24:00) offers a fine view from 600 feet at the deck and café. Farther east, pass under the train tracks into Alexanderplatz, formerly the DDR's consumer paradise.

▲▲▲**The Museum of the Wall (Haus am Checkpoint Charlie) and a surviving chunk of The Wall**—The 100-mile "Anti-Fascist Protective Rampart," as it was called by the DDR, was erected almost overnight in 1961. It was 13 feet high with a 16-foot tank ditch, 160 feet of no-man's-land, and 300 sentry towers. In its 28 years there were 1,693 cases when border guards fired, 3,221 arrests, 5,043 documented successful escapes (565 of these were DDR guards), and 80 deaths.

The fascinating **Haus am Checkpoint Charlie** museum tells the gripping history of The Wall and the many ingenious escape attempts. A visit includes plenty of video and film coverage of those heady days when people-power tore it down (U-Bahn to Kochstrasse, 7.50 DM daily, 9:00-22:00). Formerly up against the wall and on nearly worthless land, the rent here has skyrocketed and the museum may have to move.

The gate of **Checkpoint Charlie**, the famous American military border crossing, stands permanently raised as a memorial. When the Wall fell, it was literally carried away by the euphoria. Little remains. From Checkpoint Charlie, Zimmerstrasse leads to a small surviving stretch. Walk the length of this bit. Then look left to see the "Topography of Terror" exhibit.

The **Topography of Terror**, built atop the recently excavated air-raid shelter next to what was the Gestapo headquarters, shows the story of Nazism in Germany (English translation 1 DM, free, 10:00-18:00, closed Monday). Between this building and Checkpoint Charlie is a park with English descriptions of this once-formidable center of tyranny. **The German Resistance Memorial Centre**—This center tells the story of the German resistance to Hitler. "The Benderblock" was a military headquarters where an ill-fated conspiracy to assassinate Hitler was plotted and its instigators executed. There is a memorial and rooms explaining Germany's struggles against its Fuhrer (9:00-18:00, Saturday and Sunday 9:00-13:00, just south of the Tiergarten at Stauffenbergstrasse 11, tel. 2654 2202).

▲▲**Pergamon Museum**—Many of Berlin's top museums cluster on the Museuminsel (Museum Island), just off Unter den Linden, in East Berlin. Only the Pergamon Museum, with the fantastic Pergamon Altar, the Babylonian Ishtar Gate, and many ancient Greek and Mesopotamian treasures, is of interest to the normal tourist. (Walk along the canal, passing the first bulky Neoclassical building on your right, to a bridge that leads to a second bulky Neoclassical building, 4 DM, 9:00-17:00, closed Monday, free Sunday). Take advantage of the free 30-minute tape-recorder tours of the museum's highlights.

Sights—Around Charlottenburg Palace

Schloss Charlottenburg—This only surviving Hohenzollern Palace is Berlin's top baroque palace (8 DM, Tuesday-Friday 9:00-17:00, Saturday and Sunday 10:00-17:00, U-1 to Sophie-Charlotte Platz and a 10-minute walk, or bus #121, bus #145, or bus #204 direct from Bahnhof Zoo). If you've seen the great palaces of Europe, this one comes in at about tenth place, especially since its center is tourable only with a German guide. For a quick look, the Knöbelsdorff Wing (3 DM) is set up to let you wander on your own, a substantial hike through restored-since-the-war, gold-crusted white rooms filled with Frederick the Great's not-so-great collection of baroque paintings. Ahhh, skip it all together.

▲▲**The Egyptian Museum**—Across the street from the palace is a fine little museum filled with Egyptian treasures. It offers one of the great thrills in art appreciation—gazing into the still-young and beautiful face of 3,000-year-old Queen Nefertiti, the wife of King Akhenaton (4 DM, Monday-Thursday 9:00-17:00, Saturday and Sunday 10:00-17:00, Schlossstrasse 70).

▲**The Bröhan Museum** is like walking through a dozen beautifully furnished Art Nouveau (Jugendstil) and Art Deco living rooms. If you're tired, the final rooms are not worth the six flights of stairs (6 DM, 10:00-18:00, closed Monday, next to the Egyptian Museum, across the street from the Charlottenburg Palace).

Other Berlin Sights

▲▲**Dahlem Gemälde-galerie**—Dahlem is actually a cluster of important museums that, one by one over the next decade, will be moved to the new museum complex in the Tiergarten. The *Gemälde-galerie* (picture gallery), Dahlem's essential stop, may be moved as early as 1995. Check at the TI before heading out. It has more than 600 canvases by the likes of Dürer, Titian, Botticelli, Rubens, Vermeer, and Bruegel, and one of the world's greatest collection of Rembrandts. The *Man with the Golden Helmet*, recently determined not to have been painted by Rembrandt, still shines (4 DM, free on Sunday, Tuesday-Friday 9:00-17:00, Saturday and Sunday 10:00-17:00, closed Monday, U-Bahn to Dahlem-Dorf).

Kreuzberg—This poorer district along the Wall, with old restored and unrestored buildings and plenty of student and Turkish street life, offers the best look at melting-pot Berlin in a city where original Berliners are as rare as old buildings. Berlin is the fourth-largest Turkish city and this is its "downtown." But to call it a little Istanbul insults the big one. You'll see mothers wearing scarves, *doner kebap* stands, and spray-paint decorated shops. For a dose of Kreuzberg without getting your fingers dirty, you can joyride on bus #129. (Take U8 to Hermannplatz, you'll ascend through the Karstadt department store's great cafeteria, #129 buses wait immediately outside its door, leaving every 5 minutes. After leaving Kreuzberg, they stop right at the Checkpoint Charlie Museum and go all the way to KaDeWe and Ku'damm.) For a walk, wander the area between the Kottbusser Tor and Schlesisches Tor subway stops, ideally on Tuesday and Friday afternoons when a Turkish Market sprawls along the bank of the Maybachufer River (U-Bahn: Kottbusser Tor, 12:00-18:00).

East Side Gallery—The biggest remaining stretch of the Wall is now "the world's longest art gallery," stretching for about a mile and completely covered with murals painted by artists from around the world, mostly in celebration of the Wall's demise. While not overly impressive, and in dire need of restoration, it does make for a thought-provoking walk. From Schlesisches Tor (end of Kreuzberg) walk across the river on the pedestrian bridge, turn left, follow the Wall to the Berlin Hauptbahnhof (a train station two stops from Alexanderplatz).

Käthe-Kollwitz Museum—This local artist (1867-1945), who experienced much of Berlin's most tumultuous century, conveys some powerful and mostly sad feelings through the black-and-white faces of her art (6 DM, 11:00-18:00, closed Tuesday; off Ku'damm at Fasanenstrasse 24).

Museum of Natural History (Museum für Naturkunde)— Worth a visit just to see the largest dinosaur skeleton ever assembled. While you're there meet "Bobby," the stuffed ape. (3 DM, open 9:30-17:00, closed Monday; U-6 to Zinnowitzer Strasse, at Invalidenstrasse 43).

City Bus Tours—Several companies do quick, 1- to-2-hour, 15- to-30-DM orientation bus tours. I'm a Guide Friday bus-tour fan. They are established throughout Britain and now have hop-on-and-hop-off, 90-minute, fast-talking tours of Berlin (30 DM, buses every half-hour, in German and English). These do the basic predictable circle (east, west, and out to Charlottenburg) and, on a sunny day when the double-decker buses go topless, they are a photographer's delight. They're fairly competitive with several companies doing short and long tours, mostly departing from the Ku'damm (Severin & Kühn, Ku'damm 216, tel. 883 1015, BVB buses, doing quicker tours, from Ku'damm 225). The TI has all the brochures.

City Walking Tours—Walking tours give a more intimate glimpse of the city. Several companies do short, inexpensive, English-only walks: a general walk (2½ hrs, 10 DM, tel. 611-7425) and more specialized Third Reich and Wall Nostalgia walks (2 hrs, around 20 DM, tel. 211-6663). Both give student discounts. Since Nazi sights are so hard to find and really understand, the Third Reich walk is the best way to cover this slice of Berlin. Raymond Huygelen is a good freelance city guide (tel. 261-6625).

Late-Night Berlin

Zitty and *Tip* (sold at kiosks) are the top guides to youth and alternative culture. The TI's *Berlin Program* lists the nonstop parade of concerts, plays, exhibits, and cultural events. Berlin's top night spots are near Ku'damm. If you just wander around Savignyplatz, Olivaerplatz, Leninerplatz, and Ludwigskirchplatz, you'll find plenty of action. Contributing to Berlin's wild late-night scene is the fact that while the rest of Germany must close down at midnight or 1:00, Berlin night spots must close for only one hour a day.

Sleeping in Berlin
(1.6 DM = about $1, tel. code: 030)
Since reunification, costs in Berlin have skyrocketed: 32-DM hostel beds; 70-DM dumpy hotel doubles; 100-DM pleasant, small, pension doubles; 200-DM "normal" hotel doubles. Because of the cost of lodging and the distance necessary to travel to Berlin, I sleep on the train in and sleep on the train out.

Discount Business Hotels
For the most comforts at the least cost, arrive without a reservation (ideally in the morning) and let the TI book you a room in a fancy hotel on their push list. As in so many cities, business hotels over-built and when there are no conventions or fairs, rather than go empty, they rent rooms through the TI to lowly tourists for around half price. June, July, and August are dead for business travel. During these months hotels are empty and you can expect to land a modern, all-the-comforts, 200-DM business hotel double with a buffet breakfast within walking distance of the TI for around 100 DM. That's the price you'll pay for a tattered but comfortable room in the struggling little pensions recommended below. (They can't afford to play the discount game.)

My listings are a 5- to 15-minute walk from the Zoo Bahnhof, near the Ku'damm, in decent and comfortable neighborhoods. Most cluster conveniently around subway stops. Nearly all are a couple of flights up in big, run-down buildings. But inside they are clean, quiet, and big enough so that their well-worn character is actually charming. Most rooms are thoughtfully appointed, big with high ceilings, and on relatively quiet streets. Rooms in the back are on quiet courtyards. Unless otherwise noted, hallway showers are free, breakfast is included, they speak English, and take no credit cards.

Sleep code: **S**=Single, **D**=Double/Twin, **T**=Triple, **Q**=Quad, **B**=Bath/Shower, **WC**=Toilet, **CC**=Credit Card (**V**isa, **M**astercard, **A**mex), **SE**=Speaks English (graded **A** through **F**).

Sleeping Between Zoo Station and Savingyplatz
Pension Heide am Zoo (S-85 DM, SB-110 DM, D-130 DM, DB-150 DM; Fasanenstr. 12, from Zoo Bahnhof walk

down Kant Strasse, left on Fasanenstrasse, 10623 Berlin, tel. 3130496, fax 3130497), run by friendly Frau Bäumer, is stylish but homey on a quiet street a 5-minute walk from the station. Call first; no rooms are given to drop-ins. Farther down the same street, **Hotel-Pension Funk** (S-60 DM to 70 DM, SB-75, D-100, DB-120, DBWC-135 DM; Fasanenstrasse 69, tel. 8827193, fax 8833329) is the former home of a 1920s silent-movie star, offering 14 elegant, richly furnished old rooms for a great price. **Alpenland Hotel** (D-110 DM, DBWC-180 DM, CC:VM, their prices may be soft in summer, just off colorful Savignyplatz on a quiet street, Carmerstrasse 8, D-10623 Berlin, tel. 312-3970, fax 313-8444) is a classy hotel with a fine restaurant which has a handful of great value shower-less doubles. Many are on the fourth floor and there's no elevator. But the rooms are big, bright and clean and there are plenty of showers on the hall. Down the same street, **Hotel-Pension Bialas** (S-70 DM, SB-100 DM, D-100 DM, DB-155 DM, T-140 DM, TB-210 DM, Carmerstrasse 16, tel. 312 5025, fax 312 4396) feels a bit like a hostel with 30 big, bright, airy rooms.

Sleeping at Augsburgerstrasse U-Bahn Stop
Hotel-Pension Nürnberger Eck (SB-75 DM, DB-120 DM, extra bed 45 DM, Nürnberger Strasse 24a, D-10789 Berlin, tel. 2185371, fax 2141540) has 8 big, plush rooms. Just upstairs, **Pension Fischer** (S-50 DM, D-70 DM-80 DM, DB-90 DM, 35 DM for third or fourth person, breakfast 7 DM, tel. 218 6808, fax 2134225) is run-down, simple, and the best I found in its price range.

Sleeping at Güntzelstrasse U-Bahn Stop (three stops from Zoo on U9)
Hotel Pension München (S-56 DM-60 DM, D-75 DM-95 DM, DBWC-115 DM-130 DM, 35 DM extra for third or fourth person, breakfast 9 DM, elevator; Güntzelstrasse 62, 10717 Berlin, tel. 857-9120, fax 853 2744) is bright, cheery, and filled with modern art. At the same address, **Pension Güntzel** (SB-90 DM, DB-110 DM-130 DM, DBWC-130 DM-150 DM, 35 DM for third person, tel. 857 9020, fax 853 1108) rents 8 fine rooms. **Pension Finck** (D-100 DM, DB-110 DM, 50 DM for third person, elevator,

Guntzelstrasse 54, tel. 861-2940, fax 861-8158) has 12 big, bright rooms in a more traditional building.

Hotel Bogota (S-68 DM, SB-95 DM, D-110 DM, DB-140 DM, DBWC-180 DM, 45 DM for third person, CC:VMA, elevator, Schlüterstr. 45, 10707 Berlin, tel. 881 5001, fax 883 5887) has big, bright, modern rooms in a spacious old building half a block off Ku'damm. The service is brisk and hotelesque. This is the best no-nonsense hotel-type listing.

Youth hostels feature small rooms and are open to all. While many are often packed with West German school groups field-tripping to Berlin, the TI has a long list of places renting dorm beds. **Jugendgastehaus Berlin** (35-DM beds with sheets and breakfast in 4- to 6-bed rooms; Kluckstrasse 3, take bus #129 from the Europa Center or the Ku'damm U-Bahn stop, tel. 261 1097 or 261 1098; over 400 beds but often filled with groups, so call up to two weeks in advance and leave your name; non-members pay 6 DM extra, 9 DM lunches and dinners) is most central. The **Studenten Hotel Berlin** (35-39 DM per bed in doubles and quads with sheets and breakfast; Meiningerstrasse 10, tel. 784 6720, near the City Hall on JFK Platz or U-Bahn to Rathaus Schoneberg) is also decent.

Eating in Berlin

Berlin has plenty of fun food places, both German and imported. If the *kraut* is getting *wurst*, try one of the many Turkish, Italian, or Balkan restaurants. **Wertheim** department store (at Ku'damm U-Bahn) has cheap basement food counters and a fine self-service cafeteria up six banks of escalators with a view. **KaDeWe's** sixth-floor deli food department is a picnicker's nirvana. Drool your way through more than 1,000 kinds of sausage and 1,500 types of cheese. You can even get peanut-butter here! Put together a picnic and grab a sunny bench. For cheap and substantial *kebabs*, eat Turkish in Kreuzberg.

The local pubs, called *Kneipe*, are colorful places to get a light meal and to try out the local beer, Berliner Weiss. Ask for it *mit Schuss* and you'll get a shot of syrup in your suds.

Train Connections

Berlin to: Amsterdam (8/day, 9 hrs), **Budapest** (5/day, 13 hrs), **Frankfurt** (8/day, 5 hrs), **Copenhagen** (4/day, 8 hrs), **Köln** (hrly, 6½ hrs), **London** (4/day, 15 hrs), **Munich** (8/day, 8½ hrs), **Paris** (6/day, 13 hrs), **Prague** (10/day, 4½ hrs), **Warsaw** (4/day, 8 hrs), **Vienna** (5/day, 12 hrs), **Zurich** (12/day, 10 hrs). Berlin is connected by easy overnight trains from **Bonn, Köln, Frankfurt, Munich, Vienna,** and **Copenhagen.** A *Liege-platz,* or bunk bed, on the train is money well spent (26 DM for a place in a six-bed cabin, 40 DM in the same cabin with two beds left empty). The beds are the same for first- and second-class tickets. Trains are rarely full, but get your bed reserved a few days in advance from any travel agency or train station.

AUSTRIA (ÖSTERREICH, THE KINGDOM OF THE EAST)

- 32,000 square miles (the size of South Carolina, or two Switzerlands).
- 7.6 million people (235 per square mile and holding, 85 percent Catholic).
- About 11 AS = $1. Figure a dime each.

During the grand old Habsburg days, Austria was Europe's most powerful empire. Its royalty built a giant kingdom of more than 50 million people by making love, not war (having lots of children and marrying them into the other royal houses of Europe).

Today this small, landlocked country does more to cling to its elegant past than any other in Europe. The waltz is still the rage. Austrians are very sociable; it's important to greet people in the breakfast room and those you pass on the streets or meet in shops. The Austrian's version of "Hi" is a cheerful *Grüss Gott* (may God greet you). You'll get the correct pronunciation after the first volley—listen and copy.

While they speak German and talked about unity with Germany long before Hitler ever said *"Anschluss,"* the Austrians cherish their distinct cultural and historical traditions. They are not Germans. Austria is mellow and relaxed

Austria

compared to Deutschland. *Gemütlichkeit* is the local word for this special Austrian cozy-and-easy approach to life. It's good living—whether engulfed in mountain beauty or bathed in lavish high culture. The people stroll as if every day were Sunday, topping things off with a visit to a coffee or pastry shop.

It must be nice to be past your prime—no longer troubled by being powerful, able to kick back and celebrate life in the clean, untroubled mountain air. While the Austrians make less money than their neighbors, they enjoy a short work week and a long life span. Austria was a neutral country throughout the cold war. Now, of course, it's free to join its western neighbors.

The Austrian schilling (S or AS) is divided into 100 groschen. Divide prices by ten to get approximate costs in dollars (e.g., 420 AS is $42). About 7 AS = 1 DM. While merchants and waiters near the border are happy to accept DM, you'll save money if you use schilling.

Austrians eat on about the same schedule we do. Treats include *Wiener Schnitzel* (breaded veal cutlet), *Knödel* (dumplings), *Apfelstrudel*, and fancy desserts like the *Sachertorte*, Vienna's famous chocolate cake. Service is included in restaurant bills.

Shops are open from 8:00-17:00 or 18:00. Banks keep roughly the same hours but usually close for lunch.

VIENNA (WIEN)

Vienna is a head without a body. Built to rule the once-grand Habsburg Empire— Europe's largest—she started and lost World War I, and with it her far-flung holdings. Today, you'll find a grand capital of 1.7 million people (20 percent of Austria's population) ruling a small, relatively insignificant country. Culturally, historically, and from a sightseeing point of view, this city is the sum of its illustrious past. The city of Freud, Kafka, Brahms, a gaggle of Strausses, Maria Theresa's many children, and a dynasty of Holy Roman emperors, is right up there with Paris, London, and Rome.

Planning Your Time

Vienna is worth two days and two nights. It's not only packed with great sights, but it's a joy to kill time in. It seems like it was designed to help people simply meander through a day. To be grand tour efficient, you could sleep in and sleep out on the train (Berlin, Venice, the Swiss Alps, Paris, and the Rhine are each handy night-trains away). But then you'd miss the Danube and Melk. I'd come in from Salzburg via Hallstatt, Melk, and the Danube and spend two days this way:

Day 1:
 9:00 Orientation tour by tram around the Ring (as explained below, or the night before with a stop at the Kursalon for Strauss).
10:00 Stroll Karntnerstrasse (take care of TI and ticket needs).
11:00 Tour the Opera.
12:00 Browse the Naschmarkt, lunch there.
14:00 Kunsthistorisches Museum.
17:00 Coffee at the Kursalon for Strauss concert.
19:00 Choose classical music, Heuringer wine garden, Prater amusement park, or an Opera performance. Spend some time wandering the old center.

Day 2:
 9:00 St. Stephen's Cathedral.
10:00 Tour Hofburg, Neue Burg, Treasury.
13:00 Schonbrunn Palace (possibly, if by car, on way out of town before 5-hour drive to Hall near Innsbruck).

Orientation

(tel. code within Austria: 0222, from outside: 1)

Vienna, or *Wien* ("veen") in German, is bordered on three sides by the Vienna woods (*Wienerwald*) and the Danube (*Donau*). To the southeast is industrial sprawl. The Alps, which arc across Europe from Marseilles, end at Vienna's wooded hills. These provide a popular playground for walking and new-wine drinking. This greenery's momentum carries on into the city. You'll notice over half of Vienna is park land, filled with ponds, gardens, trees, and statue memories of Austria's glory days.

Think of the city map as a target. The bull's-eye is the cathedral, the first circle is the Ring and the second is the Gürtel. The old town snuggles around towering St. Stephan's Cathedral south of the Donau, bound tightly by the Ringstrasse. The Ring, marking what was the city wall, circles the first district (or "*Bezirk*"). The Gürtel, a broader ring road, contains the rest of downtown (Bezirke 2 through 9).

Greater Vienna

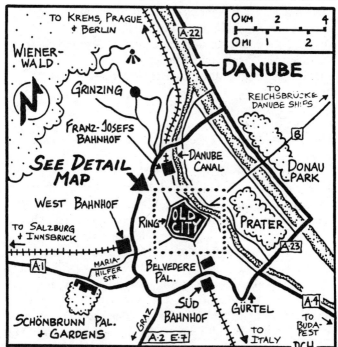

Addresses start with the Bezirk followed by street and street number. Any address higher than the ninth Bezirk is beyond the Gürtel, far from the center. The middle two digits of Vienna postal codes show the district, or Bezirk. The address "7, Lindengasse 4" means in the seventh district, #4 on Linden Street. Its postal code would be 1070. Nearly all your sightseeing will be done in the core first district or along the Ringstrasse. As a tourist, concern yourself only with this small old center, and sprawling Vienna suddenly becomes manageable.

Arriving by Train at the West Station

Most train travelers arrive at the Westbahnhof. To get situated, walk across the street from the station to the tram/metro station. At a VOR-Fahrkarten machine, push the yellow 24 *stunden* button, the window says 50 AS, put in 50 AS, and get your 24-hour ticket. (The Tobacco shop around the corner also has tickets.) To get to the center (and very likely, your hotel), go down the escalator to line U3. Down two levels (on the left) is an information desk. Ask for a free city map. One more level down takes you to the U3 tracks. Catch a train in the direction U3-Erdberg. Ride five stops to "Stephansplatz," escalate in the exit direction "Stephansplatz," and you hit the cathedral. The TI is a 5-minute stroll down the busy Karntnerstrasse pedestrian street.

Tourist Information

The "tourist offices" at the stations are really hotel agencies. Vienna's real tourist office, behind the Opera House at Kärntnerstrasse 38 (daily 9:00-19:00, later in the stations, tel. 0222/513 8892 or 211140) is excellent. Stop here first with a list of needs and questions, to confirm your sightseeing plans, and to pick up the free (and essential) city map, the museum brochure (listing hours, telephone numbers, and handicap accessibility), the monthly program of concerts, and the fact-filled *Youth Scene* magazine. Consider investing in the handy 50-AS *Vienna from A to Z* book. Every important building has a numbered flag banner that keys into this guidebook. *A to Z* numbers are keyed into the TI's city map. When lost, find one of the "famous-building flags" and match its number to your map. If you're at a "famous building" check the map to see what other key numbers are nearby, then check the *A to Z* book to see if you want to drop by. Many of my recommended accommodations keep enough tourist maps and brochures on hand to make a trip to the TI unnecessary.

Trains
The Westbahnhof serves most of Europe and the Süd-bahnhof serves Italy, the former Yugoslavia, and Greece. Subway line U3 connects the Westbahnhof with the center, tram D takes you from the Südbahnhof downtown, and tram #18 connects the two stations. Trains to Krems and the Wachau Valley leave from a third station, the Franz Josef Bahnhof. For train information, call 1717.

Getting Around Vienna
To take simple and economical advantage of Vienna's fine transit system of buses, trams, and sleek, easy subways, buy the 24-hour (50 AS) or 72-hour (130 AS) subway/bus/tram pass at a station machine or Tabak shops near any station. Take a moment to study the eye-friendly city center map on metro station walls to internalize how the metro and tram system can help you. I use it mostly to zip along the Ring (tram #1 or #2). The 15-AS transit map is overkill. The necessary routes are listed on the free tourist city map. Without a pass, blocks of five tickets for 85 AS are cheaper than the 20-AS individual tickets (each good for one journey with necessary changes) you can buy from the driver. Eight-strip 8-day, 265-AS transit passes can be shared (for instance, four people for two days each, a 33% savings over the cheap 24-hour pass). Stamp your pass as you enter the system or tram (which puts a time on it). Vienna's comfortable, honest, and easy-to-flag-down taxis start at 24 AS and mount quickly; you'll pay about 60 AS for a 5-minute ride.

Note that Vienna's telephone code changes: 0222 (from inside Austria) and 1 (from outside Austria).

Sights—Vienna
▲▲▲**Ringstrasse Tour**—In the 1860s, Emperor Franz Josef had the city's ingrown medieval wall torn down and

replaced with a grand boulevard 190 feet wide, arcing nearly 3 miles around the city's core. The road pre-dates all the buildings that line it. So what you'll see is neo-Gothic, Neoclassical, and neo-Renaissance. One of Europe's great streets, it's lined with many of the city's top sights. Trams #1 and #2 circle the whole route and so should you.

In fact, start your Vienna visit with this do-it-yourself, 20-AS, circular, 30 minute tour. "Tours" leave every 5 min utes. Tram #1 goes clockwise, tram #2 counterclockwise. Since most of the sights are on the outside of the Ring, tram #2 is best (sit on the right). Ideally, catch it at the Opera house (but anywhere will do). With a 24-hour ticket, you can jump on and off as you go. This is great, since trams come so often. With no ticket, give the driver 20 AS as you board (good for only one ride). All described sights on this tour are on the right unless I say "on left." For more information on many of the sights, see individual descriptions later in the chapter. Let's go:

• Just past the Opera (on left), the city's main pedestrian drag, Karntnerstrasse, leads to the zigzag roof of St. Stephan's Cathedral. This tour makes a 360-degree circle, staying about this far from that spire.

• (At first corner, look towards tall fountain) Schwartzen-berg Platz, with its equestrian statue of Prince Charles Schwartzenberg who battled Napoleon, leads to the Russian monument (behind the fountain). This monument was built in 1945 as a forced thanks to the Soviets for liberating Austria from the Nazis. Formerly a sore point, now it's just ignored.

• (Going down Schubertring) The white and yellow concert hall behind the trees is the Kursalon, opened in 1867 by the Strauss brothers who directed many waltzes here. (See below for free concert times.) The huge Stadtpark (city park) hon-ors 20 great Viennese musicians and composers with statues.

• (Immediately after next stop) The gilded statue of Waltz King Johann Strauss shows him holding his violin as he did when he conducted his orchestra

• (While at next stop at end of park) On the left, a green and white statue of Dr. Karl Lueger honors the popular man who was mayor of Vienna until 1910.

• (At next bend in road) The quaint building with military helmets decorating each window was the Austrian ministry of war, back when that was a serious operation. Field Marshal Radetzky, a military big shot in the 19th century under Franz Joseph, still sits on his high horse.

• (At next corner) The white domed building is the Urania, Franz Joseph's 1910 observatory. Lean forward and look behind it for a peek at the huge red cars of the huge 100-year-old Ferris wheel in Vienna's Prater Park.

• Now you're rolling along the Danube Canal. The actual Danube is father to the right. This was the site of the original Roman town, Vindobona. In three blocks on the left (opposite the Mobile station) you'll see the ivy-covered walls and round romanesque arches of St. Ruprechts, the oldest church in Vienna (built on a bit of Roman ruins). By about 1200 Vienna had grown to fill the area within this ring road.

• (Leaving the canal, turning up Schottenring, at first stop)

Vienna

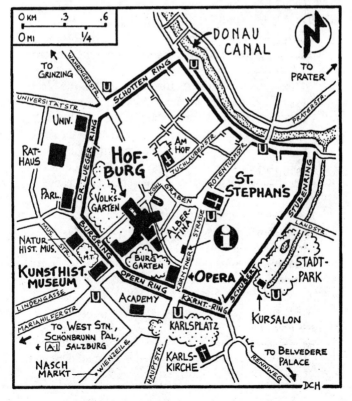

On the left, the pink and white neo-Renaissance temple of money, the Borse, is Vienna's stock exchange.

• (Next stop, at corner) The huge frilly neo-Gothic church is a "votive church" built in 1853 as a thanks to God when an assassination attempt on Emperor Franz Joseph failed. Ahead on the right is the Vienna University building which faces (on the left, behind the gilded angel) a bit of the old city wall.

• (At next stop) The neo-Gothic City Hall, flying the flag of Europe, towers over Rathaus Platz, a festive site of outdoor movies and concerts. Immediately across the street (on left) is the Hofburg Theater.

• (At next stop) The neo-Greek temple of democracy houses the Austrian Parliament. The lady with the golden helmet is Athena, the goddess of wisdom. Across the street (on left) is the Volksgarten.

• (At next stop) Ahead on the right is the first of Vienna's huge twin museums. Empress Maria Theresa sits as a mother of 13 should between the two. On her left is the city's great-est collection of paintings, the Kunsthistorisches Museum. She is facing (on your left) the grand gate to the Hofburg, the emperor's palace. Of the five arches, only the emperor used the center.

• (50 yards after the next stop, through a gate in the black iron fence) On the left is the much-adored statue of Mozart in the Burggarten, which until 1880 was the private garden of the emperor. A few yards later (on the left) Goethe sits in a big thought-provoking chair playing trivia with Schiller (on your right). Behind the statue of Schiller is the Academy of Fine Arts. Vienna had its share of intellectual and creative geniuses.

• Hey, there's the Opera again. Jump out and see the rest of the city. (In front of the Opera, there's a person who'd love to take you on a bus tour of what you just did . . . for 220 AS.)

▲▲▲**St. Stephan's Cathedral**—Stephansdom is the Gothic needle around which Vienna spins. Hundreds of years of his-tory are carved in its walls and buried in its crypt (open at various times, tel. 515 52 526). Tours of the church are in German only, the 50-minute daily mass is impressive (sched-ule near the entry), and the crowded lift to the north tower (daily 9:00-18:00) shows you a big bell but a mediocre view. A great view is only 343 tightly wound steps away, up the spiral staircase to the watchman's lookout, 246 feet above the postcard stand (south tower, daily 9:00-17:30). From the top, figure out the town, using your *Vienna from A to Z* to locate the famous sights. The church is nearly always open. The Cathedral Museum (Dom und Diözesan Museum, 10:00-16:00, Thursday until 18:00, Sunday until 13:00, closed Monday) is at Stephansplatz 6. Downstairs in the Stephansplatz subway stop you can peer into the 13th-century Virgilkapelle.

▲**Stephansplatz**—The atmosphere of the church square is colorful and lively. And at the nearby *Graben* (ditch) street, topnotch street entertainment dances around an exotic plague monument. It was common for cities, when they survived their plague ordeal, to thank God with a monument. Vienna's is one of the grandest plague monuments.

Remains of the Habsburgs—Visiting the remains is not as easy as you might imagine. These original organ donors left their bodies in the Kaisergruft (Capuchin Crypt, a block behind the Opera on Neuer Markt, daily 9:30-16:00, 30 AS, 5-AS map with a Habsburg family tree and a chart locating each coffin), their hearts in St. George Chapel in the church of the Augustinian friars (near the Hofburg, Augustinerstrasse 3, church open daily but to see the goods you'll have to talk to a priest), and their entrails in the crypt below the cathedral. Don't tripe. Rather than chasing down all these body parts, remember that the magnificence of this city is the real remains of the Habsburgs. Pan up. Watch the clouds glide by the ornate gables of Vienna.

▲▲**Hofburg**—The complex, confusing, imposing Imperial Palace with 640 years of architecture, demands your attention (and with so many turnstiles, a lot of your money). The winter residence of the Habsburg rulers until 1918, it's still the home of the Spanish Riding School, the Vienna Boys' Choir, the Austrian president's office, and several important museums. The *A to Z* book sorts out this time-blackened, jewel-stained mess. Or, if overwhelmed, tour the Imperial Apartments first where you can buy a glossy, four-language, 50-AS Hofburg guidebook with a fine map and great photos While you could lose yourself in its myriad halls and courtyards, I suggest you focus on three things:

▲▲**The Imperial Apartments**—These lavish, Versailles-type "wish I were God" royal rooms are a small, downtown version of the grander Schönbrunn Palace. Tour one palace or the other. If rushed, these suffice. (40 AS, 65 AS with a German tour, Monday-Saturday 8:30-12:00, 12:30-16:00, Sunday 8:30-12:30, entrance from courtyard under the dome of St. Michael's Gate, Michaelerplatz, tel. 587 555 4515.) For any information, you'll have to spring for the 50-AS book.

▲▲Treasury—The Weltliche and Geistliche Schatzkammer (secular and religious treasure room) is expensive, but if you want historic and lavish jewels, these are by far the best on the Continent. Reflect on the glitter of ten rooms filled with scepters, swords, crowns, and orbs. Doubleheaded eagles, gowns, dangles, and gem-studded bangles. Remember that these were the Holy Roman Emperor's— the divine monarch's. The highlight is Room 11 with the 11th-century Reichskrone—the crown of the Holy Roman Emperor—and two cases of Karls des Grossen (Charlemagne) riches. (60 AS, 10:00-18:00, closed Tuesday; follow Schatzkammer signs through the Swiss Courtyard; you can rent a 30-minute Walkman tour for 30 AS or 40 AS for two).

▲The Neue Burg, or new palace, is the last (from this century, built for Franz Ferdinand but never used) and most impressive addition to the palace. Its grand facade arches around Heldenplatz (the horse-and-buggy depot). The palace houses three museums: an armory, historical musical instruments, and classical statuary from ancient Ephesus. The musical instruments are particularly entertaining, with the free radio headsets which play appropriate music in each room. Wait at the orange dots for the German description to finish and you'll often hear the instruments you're seeing. Stay tuned in, as graceful period music accompanies your wander through the neighboring halls of medieval weaponry—a killer collection of crossbows, swords, and armor. An added bonus is the chance to just wander all alone among those royal Habsburg halls, stairways, and painted ceilings (30 AS for all three collections, 10:00-18:00, closed Tuesday, almost no tourists).

▲▲▲Opera—The Staatsoper facing the Ring, just up from Stephansdom and next to the TI, is a central point for any visitor. While the critical reception of the building 130 years ago led the architect to commit suicide, and it's been rebuilt since the World War II bombings, it's a dazzling place.

(Visits by 40-minute tour only, daily in English, July and August at 10:00, 11:00, 13:00, 14:00, 15:00, and often at 16:00; other months, afternoons only; 40 AS. Tours are often canceled for rehearsals and shows, so check the posted schedule or call 51444-2613.)

The **Vienna State Opera**, with the Vienna Philharmonic Orchestra in the pit, is one of the world's top opera houses. There are performances almost nightly, except in July and August, with expensive seats and shows normally sold out. Unless Pavarotti is in town, it's almost always easy to get one of 500 *Stehplatz* (standing-room spots, which are 20 AS-30 AS; the downstairs spots are best). Join the *Stehplatz* lineup at the Abendkasse side door where the number of available places is posted. The ticket window opens an hour before each performance. Buy your place at the padded leaning rail. If your spot isn't numbered, tie your belt or scarf to it and you can slip out for a snack and return to enjoy the performance. If less than 500 people are in line, don't line up early.

▲▲▲**The Kunsthistorisches Museum**—This exciting museum showcases the great Habsburg collection of work by Dürer, Rubens, Titian, Raphael, and especially Brueghel. There's also a fine display of Egyptian, classical, and applied arts, including a divine golden salt shaker by Cellini. If you forgot to pack the chapter from *Mona Winks*, the museum sells a pamphlet on the top 21 paintings and offers English tours (usually at 11:00 and 15:00) The paintings are hung on one floor, and clear charts guide you (Tuesday-Sunday 10:00-18:00, Thursday until 21:00, closed Monday, tel. 52177-0489; 100 AS, 50 AS for students and seniors over 60).

Natural History Museum—In the twin building facing the art museum, you'll find moon rocks, dinosaur stuff, and the Venus of Willendorf—at 30,000 years old, the world's eldest sex symbol.

▲**Academy of Fine Arts**—This small but exciting collection includes works by Bosch, Botticelli, and Rubens, a Venice series by Guardi, and a self-portrait by 15-year-old Van Dyck (3 minutes from the Opera at Schillerplatz 3, Tuesday, Thursday, and Friday 10:00-14:00, Wednesday 10:00-13:00 and 15:00-18:00, Saturday and Sunday 9:00-13:00, tel. 5881-6225).

▲**Belvedere Palace**—The elegant palace of Prince Eugene of Savoy (the still-much-appreciated conqueror of the Turks), and later home of Franz Ferdinand, houses the Austrian Gallery of 19th- and 20th-century art. Skip the lower palace and focus on the garden and the top floor of the upper palace (*Oberes Belvedere*) for a winning view of the city and a fine collection of Jugendstil art, Klimt, and Kokoschka (30 AS, Tuesday-Sunday 10:00-17:00, entrance at Prince Eugen Strasse 27, tel. 784-1580). Your ticket includes the Austrian baroque and gothic art in the Lower Palace.

▲▲▲**Schönbrunn Palace**—Schloss Schönbrunn, the Habsburg's summer residence, is second only to Versailles among Europe's palaces. Located 7 kilometers from the center, it was the Habsburgs' summer residence. It is big—1,441 rooms—but don't worry, only 40 rooms are shown to the public. (95 AS for 40 rooms with guided tour, 80 AS to romp unattended through 22 rooms; 8:30-17:00, until 16:30 off-season, Saturday and Sunday are most crowded; 12:00 to 14:00, and after 16:00 are least crowded, call to confirm English tour times, tel. 8111-3238.) Nearby is an impressive coach museum (30 AS, Wagenburg). The sculpted gardens and Gloriette Park above the palace are open until dusk and free. The long walk to Gloriette earns you only a fine city view.

▲**Jugendstil**—Vienna gave birth to its own curvaceous brand of Art Nouveau around the turn of the century. Jugendstil art and architecture is popular around Europe these days, and many come to Vienna solely in search of it. The TI has a brochure laying out Vienna's 20th-century architecture. The best of Vienna's scattered Jugendstil sights are in the Belvedere Palace collection, the Karlsplatz subway stop, and the clock on Höher Market.

KunstHausWien—This "make yourself at home" modern art museum, opened in 1990, is a real hit with lovers of modern art. It features the work of local painter/environmentalist Hundertwasser (daily 10:00-19:00, 3, Weissgerberstrasse 13, tel. 7120491). Nearby, the one-with-nature **Hundertwasserhaus** is a complex of 50 lived-in apartments. This was built in the 1980s as a breath of architectural fresh air in a city of blocky, suicidally predictable apartment complexes. It's not open to visitors but worth visiting for its fun-loving exterior and the Hundertwasser festival of shops across the street, and just to annoy its residents (third district, at Löwengasse and Kegelgasse).

▲**City Park**—Vienna's Stadtpark is a waltzing world of gardens, memorials to local musicians, ponds, peacocks, music in bandstands, and local people escaping the city. Notice the Jugendstil entry at the Stadtpark subway station. The Kursalon orchestra plays Strauss waltzes daily in summer 16:00-18:00 and 19:45-22:35. You can buy an expensive cup of coffee for a front row seat or join the local senior citizens and ants on the grass for free.

▲**Prater**—Vienna's sprawling amusement park tempts any visitor with its huge (220-foot-high, 9:00-23:00 in summer), famous, and lazy Ferris wheel called the Riesenrad; endless food places; and rides like the roller coaster, bumper cars, and Lilliputian Railroad. This is a fun, goofy place to share the evening with thousands of Viennese (subway: Praterstern). For a family local-style dinner, eat at Schweizerhaus or Wieselburger Bierinsel.

▲**Naschmarkt**—Vienna's ye olde produce market bustles daily, near the Opera along Wienzeile Street. It's likeably seedy and surrounded by sausage stands, cafés, and theaters. Each Saturday it's infested by a huge flea market (Monday-Friday 6:00-18:30, Saturday 6:00-13:00). For a picnic park, walk one block down Schleifmuhlgasse.

City Tours—Vienna offers many organized city tours. Of its many guided walks, only a few are in English (90 min, 120 AS, tel. 51450, brochure at TI). The 75-minute "Getting Acquainted" German/English bus tour (220 AS, daily from the Opera at 10:30, 11:45, 15:00, and in summer, 16:30, no reservations necessary, tel. 712 46 830) is essentially what I covered above in the Ring Tour with a detour to and stop at the Upper Belvedere palace. While pricey, it's intensely informative and a good introduction if you're lazy. Cut out at the palace (which is near the end) if you'd like to see its collection of Klimt and Art Nouveau. The TI has a booklet listing all city tours. Eva Prochaska (tel. 513 5294, 1, Weihburggasse 13-15) is an excellent private guide who charges 1,100 AS for a half-day.

Sunbathing—Like most Europeans, the Austrians, worship the sun. Their lavish swimming centers are as much for tanning as for swimming. The Krapfenwaldbad, in the high-class 19th district, is renowned as the gathering point for the best-looking topless locals. For the best man-made island beach scene, head for the "Danube Sea," Vienna's 20 miles of beach along the Danube Island (subway: Donauinsel).

▲▲**Music**—Vienna is Europe's music capital. It's music *con brio* from October through June, with things reaching a symphonic climax during the Vienna Festival each May and June. Sadly, in July and August, the Boys' Choir, the Opera, and many more music companies are—like you—on vacation. But the "Summer of Music" festival (special brochure at TI, tel. 4000-8410 for information, tickets at the Wien Ticket pavilion on Karntnerstrasse next to the Opera House) assures that even in the summer you'll find lots of top-notch classical music.

Music is becoming a tourist trap in Vienna. Powdered, wigged Wolfgang Mozarts are peddling tickets in the streets at all the sights. Every night 400-AS-a-seat Mozart and Strauss concerts are put on for the flash-in-the-pan classical fans. And anything booked in advance or through a box office comes with a stiff 25 percent booking fee. (There's a handy box office next to the TI behind the Opera.)

But you can get great classical music at fair prices (150 AS-250 AS). Get the TI's monthly program. If a show comes to you, be wary. The Summer of Music pavilion (mentioned above) sells tickets to its shows at net prices. If you call a concert hall directly, they can advise you on the availability of (cheaper) tickets at the door. Vienna takes care of its starving artists (and tourists) by offering lots of standing-room places to top-notch music and opera nearly free. And remember, the Philharmonic plays at each opera in a great setting with easy-to-get nearly free standing rooms tickets. But anyone with a yen for classical music can get good tickets virtually any day of the year upon arrival in Vienna. Ask about the free opera films in front of the Opera (festive young atmosphere).

If you opt for the touristy Wiener Mozart Konzerte concert, it is a fun trip back into Vienna's glory days of music. The orchestra, clad in historic costumes and looking better than it sounds, performs Mozart's greatest hits, including his famous opera arias.

The Vienna Boys' Choir—The boys sing (heard but not seen, from a high balcony) at mass in the Imperial Chapel of the Hofburg (entrance at Schweizerhof) at 9:15 Sundays except from July through mid-September. Seats (50 AS-220 AS) must be reserved at least two months in advance but standing room is free and open to the first 60 or 70 who line up. Concerts (on stage in the Vienna Concert Hall) are also given Fridays at 15:30 in May, June, September, and October (320 AS-400 AS, fax 011-43-1-5871268 from U.S.A.). They're nice kids, but for my taste, not worth all the commotion.

Spanish Riding School—Performances are usually sold out in advance, but training sessions in a chandeliered baroque hall are open to the public (February-June and September-October, Tuesday-Saturday 10:00-12:00, 70 AS at the door; Josefsplatz in the Hofburg; long line; if you don't like horses, not worth the trouble).

▲**Wine Gardens**—The Heurige is a uniquely Viennese institution celebrating the *Heuriger*, or new wine. It all started when the Habsburgs let Vienna's vintners sell their own wine tax-free for 300 days a year. Several hundred families opened up Heurigen wine-garden restaurants clustering around the edge of Vienna, and a tradition was born. Today they do their best to maintain their old village atmosphere, serving the homemade new wine (the last vintage, until November 11th) with light meals and strolling musicians. For the whole story and a complete listing with maps and descriptions of each district, get the TI's *Heurige in Wien* brochure.

Of the many Heurigen suburbs, Grinzing is the most famous and touristy. **Neustift am Walde** (bus #35A) is a local favorite with plenty of tourists but much of its original charm intact. **Weinbau Wolff** (on the main street at Rathstrasse 46, tel. 442335) has a great buffet spread, hundreds of outdoor tables, and the right ambience. **Haus Zimmermann** (bus #35A to Mitterwurzergasse 20, tel. 441207) is a local favorite, more remote, low key, and without music. For more crowds and music with your meal, visit Beethoven's home in Heiligenstadt (tel. 371287, tram #37 to last stop and walk 10 minutes to Pfarrplatz). At any of these places you'll fill your plate at a self-serve cold-cut buffet. Waitresses will then take your wine order (30 AS per quarter-liter). Many locals claim it takes several years of practice to distinguish between Heuriger and vinegar. For a near-Heurigen experience right downtown, drop by **Gigerl Stadtheuriger** (see Eating, below).

▲**The Viennese Coffeehouse**—In Vienna, the living room is the coffeehouse down the street. This tradition is just another example of the Viennese expertise in good living. Each of Vienna's many long-established (and sometimes even legendary) coffeehouses has its individual character. They offer newspapers, pastries, sofas, elegance, and a "take all the time you want" charm, for the price of a cup of coffee. You may want to order *brauner* (with a little milk) rather than *schwarzer* (black).

Some of my favorites are: **Café Hawelka** (1, Dorotheergasse 6, closed Tuesday, just off the Graben) with a rumpled "brooding Trotsky" atmosphere, paintings on the walls by struggling artists who couldn't pay, a saloon wood flavor, chalkboard menu, smoked velvet couches, international selection of newspapers, and a phone that rings for regulars; the **Central** (1, Herrengasse 14, Jugendstil decor, great *topfen strudel*); the Jugendstil **Café Sperl** (6, Gumpendorfer 11, just off Naschmarkt); and the basic, untouristy **Café Ritter** (6, Mariahilferstrasse 73, near several of my recommended hotels).

Honorable Mention—There's much, much more. The city museum brochure lists everything. If you're into Esperanto, undertakers, tobacco, clowns, firefighting, or the homes of dead composers, you'll find them all in Vienna. Several good museums that try very hard but are submerged in the greatness of Vienna include: Historical Museum of the City of Vienna (Karlsplatz, Tuesday-Sunday 9:00-16:30); Folkloric Museum of Austria (8, Laudongasse 15, tel. 43 89 05); and the Museum of Military History (Heeresgeschichtliches Museum, at 3, Arsenal, Objekt 18, 10:00-16:00, closed Friday, one of Europe's best if you like swords and shields). The Jesuit Church (9 on your city map, on Dr. Ignaz Seipel Platz) has a fascinating false dome painted on its ceiling. Mariahilferstrasse, with over 2,000 shops, is the best-value shopping street. For a walk in the Vienna Woods, catch the U-4 subway to Heiligenstadt, then bus #38A to Kahlenberg for great city views, woodsy restaurants, and plenty of trails.

Nightlife

If old music or new wine isn't your thing, Vienna has plenty of alternatives. For an up-to-date rundown on fun after dark, get the TI's free *Youth Scene* magazine. An area known as the Bermuda *Dreieck* (Triangle), north of the cathedral between Rotenturmstrasse and Judengasse, is the hot local nightspot with lots of classy pubs or *Beisles* (such as Krah Krah, Salzamt, and Roter Engel) and popular music spots (such as the disco P1 at Rotgasse 3, tel. 535 9995, and Jazzland at Franz Josefs-Kai 29, tel. 533 2575). **Tunnel**, popular with local students, features live music and cheap meals (daily 11:00-02:00, a 10-minute walk behind the Rathaus at 8, Florianigasse 39, tel. 423465). Most lively on a balmy summer evening is the scene at the Danube Island.

Sleeping in Vienna
(11 AS = about $1, tel. code within Austria: 0222, from outside: 1)

Plan to spend 150 AS for a hostel bed or 550 AS for the cheapest pension or hotel double with breakfast. I list two places well worth the 1,200-AS splurge. Beds in central private homes are cozier but no cheaper than simple pensions. In the summer, call a few days in advance. All places listed speak some English. Most will hold a room without a deposit if you promise to arrive before 17:00. I've chosen two handy and central locations. Unless otherwise noted, prices include a sparse continental breakfast. (Street addresses start with the district. Postal code is 1XX0 with XX being the district.)

Sleep code: **S**=Single, **D**=Double/Twin, **T**=Triple, **Q**=Quad, **B**=Bath/Shower and usually a toilet, **WC**=Toilet (used only when some rooms are bath only), **CC**=Credit Card (**V**isa, **M**astercard, **A**mex), **SE**=Speaks English (graded **A** through **F**).

Sleeping Between the Westbahnhof and the Opera

Lively Mariahilferstrasse connects the West Station with the center. The U3 subway line goes from the Westbahnhof, down Mariahilferstrasse to the Cathedral. (For the step-by-step, see Orientation, above.) The first three listings are near the train station. The next five are about halfway between the station and the opera (two stops from the station down subway U3 to Neubaugasse). The rest are scattered mostly north of Mariahilferstrasse and equally close to the center. Mariahilferstrasse is an attraction in itself for east Europeans who come to shop. While most places are on stern and quiet no-nonsense side roads, the nearby Mariahilferstrasse is a comfortable and vibrant area filled with local shops, cafés, and Viennese being very Viennese.

Pension Funfhaus (D-540 AS, DB-620 AS, T-810 AS, TB-900 AS; 2-bedroom apartments-1,080 AS; Frau Susi Tersch promises these prices through 1995 if you book direct with this book; no elevator, free and easy street parking, closed mid-November through February; Sperrgasse 12, tel. 892-3545 or 892-0286) is big, clean, stark, and quiet with 100 beds split between the main building and an annex. Just a 7-minute walk behind the station (leaving, turn right, and right again on Mariahilferstrasse, go 7 blocks to Sperrgasse), this place is an exciting value, especially the spacious, bright DB rooms.

Hotel Stiegelbrau (DB-1,200 AS, with buffet breakfast, CC:VMA, free parking, 5 minutes' walk behind the station following directions for Funfhaus, at Mariahilferstrasse 156, tel. 892-3335, fax 892-3221-495), for my rich and lazy readers, is a fine value with all the comforts and a restaurant that spills into its breezy, laid-back garden.

Hospiz CVJM (S-360 AS, SB-400 AS, D-640 AS, DB-700 AS, T-900 AS, TB-1,020 AS, Q-1,160 AS, QB-1,320 AS, CC:VM; WC always on the hall, no elevator, free parking; leaving the Westbahnhof, walk 2 blocks left and 1 block right to 7, Kenyongasse 15, tel. 523-1304, fax 523-1304-13) is 47 beds big, sterile, quiet, old-institutional and well-run, as you'd expect a YMCA to be.

Privatzimmer F. Kaled (D-500 AS, DB-600 AS, T-750 AS, 150 AS for extra bed, optional 50-AS breakfast in bed, prices promised through 1995 if you book direct, stay two nights, and have this book; 7, Lindengasse 42, tel. 523-9013, fax 526-2513, credit-card number secures reservation, try to arrive before 14:00), is lovingly run by Tina, Fred, and Freddie. It's bright, airy, homey, quiet, and has TVs (with CNN) in each of the four rooms. Hardworking Tina is a mini tourist information service. (Being Hungarian, she has good contacts for people visiting Budapest.)

Pension Lindenhof (S-350 AS, SBWC-450 AS, D-580 AS, DB-800 AS, showers 20 AS; 7, Lindengasse 4, tel. 523-0498, fax 523-7362) is well-worn but clean, filled with plants, and run with Bulgarian strictness.

Pension Hargita (S-400 AS, SB-450 AS, D-550 AS, DB-650 AS, DBWC-800 AS, TBWC-1,000 AS, QBWC-1,100 AS, breakfast-40 AS, cheaper in winter, corner of Mariahilferstrasse and Andreasgasse, 7, Andreasgasse 1, tel. 526-1928, fax 526-0492), with 19 generally small, bright, and tidy rooms, is a bit overpriced but very handy (right at the Neubaugasse U3 stop).

Pension Quisisana (S-300 AS, SB-370 AS, D-500 AS, DB-600 AS, DBWC-700 AS, third person-270 AS, prices promised through 1995 with book; simple doubles are small with head-to-toe twin beds—it's worth going DB; no elevator; a block south of Mariahilferstrasse at Windmuhlgasse 6, 1060 Vienna, tel. 587-7155, fax 587-7156-33), whose name is Latin for "Don't Worry, Be Happy," is old and ramshackle, but with comfortable rooms and a great value.

Privatzimmer Hilde Wolf (S-395 AS, D-540 AS, T-790 AS, Q-1,025 AS, with a big, friendly, family-style breakfast; 20-AS showers; prices promised through 1995; 4, Schleifmühlgasse 7, A-1040 Vienna, tel. 586 5103, reserve by telephone and credit-card number), 3 blocks off Naschmarkt near U2-Karlsplatz, is a homey place one floor above an ugly entry, with four huge rooms like old libraries. Hilde loves her work, offers free use of her washing machine, and even offers to babysit if traveling parents need a break. Her helpful husband, Otto, speaks English. From West Station: tram # four stops to Eichenstr, tram #62 six stops to Paulinergasse. For a real home in Vienna, this is my best listing.

Jugendherberg Myrthengasse/Neustiftgasse (IYHF hostel, 150 AS with sheets and breakfast in 4- or 6-bed rooms, plus 40 AS for non-members; 7, Myrthengasse 7, tel. 523-6316, fax 523-5849) is actually two hostels side by side. Both are new, cheery, and well-run, have a 1:00 curfew, will hold a rooms until 16:00, and offer 60-AS meals. June and September are the tightest because of visiting school groups.

Across the street is **Believe It Or Not** (160 AS per bed, 110 AS November-April; Myrthengasse 10, no sign, ring apt #14, tel. 526 4658), a friendly and basic place with one big coed dorm for ten travelers. Run by an entrepreneurial and charming Pole named Gosha. Locked up 10:30-12:30; kitchen facilities; no curfew; snorers sleep here at their own risk.

Pension Wild (D-560 AS, T-790 AS, Q-1,000 AS, with plenty of showers and WCs on the floor, CC:VMA, near U2: Rathaus, at Langegasse 10, 1080 Vienna, tel. 406-5174, fax 402-2168) has 14 fine rooms and a good, "keep it simple and affordable" attitude. There are plenty of handy extras, like full kitchen facilities on each floor and cheap passes to health club downstairs.

Pension Andreas (SB-600 AS, DB-820 AS, DBWC-890 AS, big DBWC-990 AS, CC:MA, elevator; near U2: Rathaus, at 8, Schlösselgasse 11, tel. 405-3488, fax 405-3488-50) is run by a gracious woman named Sevil; this well-located, classy, quiet place is a worthwhile splurge.

Turmherberge "Don Bosco" (65-AS dorm beds, 25 AS for sheets, 40 AS extra for those without IYHF cards; 3, Lechnerstrasse 12, tel. 713 1494) is far away but I stayed there in 1973 and it's still the cheapest place in Vienna (with some of the same staff)—Catholic-run, closed 12:00-17:00, open to people of any sex from March-November. Take tram #18 to Stadionbrucke from south station, and U3 to Kardinal Nagl Platz from the west station.

Sleeping Within the Ring, in the Old City Center

These places offer less room per schilling but are comfortable, right in the town center, with elevators and a straight shot by subway from the west station. (For the step-by-step, see Orientation, above.) All are popular and take easy telephone reservations, so call well ahead. The first three are in the shadow of St. Stephan's Cathedral, on or near the Graben where the elegance of Old Vienna strums happily over the cobbles. The last two listings are near the Opera (Subway: Karlsplatz) just off the famous Kärntnerstrasse, near the tourist office and 5 minutes from the cathedral.

At **Pension Nossek** (SB-600 AS, SBWC-770 AS, DBWC-950 AS-1,050 AS; 1, Graben 17, tel. 533 7041, fax 535 3646) an elevator takes you above any street noise into a

Frau Bernad's world where the dog and children seem to be placed among the lace and flowers by an interior designer. Street musicians, a pedestrian mall filled with cafés, and the plague monument are just outside your door. This is the best value of these first three.

Pension Aclon (S-450 AS, SB-500 AS, SBWC-700 AS, D-800 AS, DB-1,060 AS, T-1,130 AS, TB-1,460, Q-1,430, QB-1,810; CC:VMA, elevator only goes up; 1, Dorotheergasse 6-8, tel. 512 79 400, fax 513 8751) is quiet, elegant, sternly-run, a block off the Graben, above a classic Vienna café.

Pension Pertschy (DB-1,080 AS-1,280 AS depending on the size, third person-300 AS, CC:VM; 1, Habsburgergasse 5, tel. 53449, fax 5344949) is more hotelesque than the others, with more energy put into the lobby than its rooms. Its big rooms are huge (ask to see a few); those on the courtyard are most quiet.

Pension Suzanne (SB-750 AS, DB-930 AS-1,130 AS, third person-300 AS; push doorbell with caution; 1, Walfischgasse 4, tel. 513 2507, fax 5132500), as baroque and doily as you'll find in this price range, is wonderfully located a few yards from the Opera. Suzanne is professional and quiet, with pink elegance bouncing on every bed.

Hotel zur Wiener Staatsoper (SB-900 AS, DB-1,200 AS, TB-1,450 AS, buffet breakfast, CC:VMA; 1, Krugerstrasse 11, tel. 513 1274, fax 513 1274-15) is quiet, rich, and hotelesque. Its rooms come with high ceilings, chandeliers, and fancy carpets on parquet floors, a great value for this locale and ideal for people whose hotel taste is a cut above mine.

Eating in Vienna

The Viennese appreciate the fine points of life, and right up there with the waltz is eating. The city has many atmospheric restaurants. As you ponder the menus, remember that Vienna's diverse empire may be gone but its flavor lingers. You'll find Slavic and Eastern European specialties here along with wonderful desserts and local wine.

On nearly every corner you can find a colorful *Beisl* (Viennese tavern) filled with poetry teachers and their students, couples loving without touching, housewives on their way home from cello lessons, and waiters who thoroughly enjoy serving hearty food and good drink at an affordable price. All my recommended eateries are within a 5-minute walk of the cathedral.

These **Wine Cellars** are fun, touristic but typical, in the old center of town with painless prices and lots of smoke. **Esterhazykeller** is an inexpensive, rowdy, smoky, self-service cellar (16:00-21:00, at Haarhof near Am Hof, off Naglergasse). **Augustinerkeller** is fun, inexpensive, and, like the Esterhazykeller, touristy (10:00-24:00, next to the Opera under the Albertina Museum on Augustinerstrasse). **Figlmüller** is a popular Beisl famous for its giant schnitzels (one can easily feed two) near St. Stephan's Cathedral (just down the 6 Stephansplatz alley at Wollzeile 5). **Zu den Drei Hacken** is famous for its local specialties (indoor/outdoor, 1, Singerstrasse 28, closed Saturday and Sunday). The less touristy **Pürstner** restaurant (indoor/outdoor, 150-AS meals, a block away at Riemergasse 10, tel. 512-6357, nightly) is pleasantly drenched in Old World atmosphere. **Melker Stiftskeller**, the least touristy, is a deep and rustic cellar with hearty, inexpensive meals and new wine (17:00-24:00, closed Sunday and Monday, halfway between Am Hof and the Schottentor subway stop at Schottengasse 3, tel. 5335530).

For a near "Heuriger" experience (a la Grinzing, see above) without leaving the center, eat at **Gigerl Stadtheuriger** (indoor/outdoor, near the cathedral, a block off Kärntner-strasse, a few cobbles off Rauhensteingasse on Blumenstock, tel. 5134431). Just point to what looks good (cold cuts, spinach strudel, good salads, all sold by the weight, around 150 AS/plate) and choose from many local wines.

Brezel-Gwölb, a wonderfully atmospheric wine cellar with outdoor dining on a quiet square, serves delicious, mod-erately priced light meals, fine Krautsuppe, and local dishes. It's ideal for a romantic late glass of wine (daily 11:30-1:00, Ledererhof 9, off Am Hof). Around the corner, **Zum Scherer Sitz u. Stehbeisl** (Judenplatz 7, near Am Hof, Monday-Saturday 11:00-1:00, Sunday 17:00-24:00) is just as untouristy, with indoor or outdoor seating, a soothing woody atmosphere, intriguing decor, and local specialties.

For a fast, light and central lunch: **Rosenberger Markt Restaurant** is a popular highway chain that opened an ele-gant super branch a block toward the cathedral from the

Opera. This place, while not cheap, is brilliant: friendly and efficient, with special theme rooms to dine in, offering a fresh and healthy cornucopia of food and drink and a cheery break from the heavy, smoky, traditional eateries (lots of fruits and vegetables, 11:00-23:00, Maysedergasse 2, just off Kärntner Strasse). The Billa supermarket (2 blocks down Walfischgasse from the Opera) is picnic-friendly.

Buffet Trzesniewski is justly famous for its elegant and cheap finger sandwiches (8 AS) and small beers (9 AS). Three sandwiches and a *kleines Bier* (Pfiff) make a fun, light lunch (just off the Graben, across from the brooding Café Hawelka, on Dorotheergasse, Monday-Friday 9:00-19:30, Saturday 9:00-13:00).

Naschmarkt, 5 minutes beyond the Opera, is Vienna's best Old World market (6:30-18:00, Saturday until 13:00, closed Sunday), with very fresh produce, plenty of cheap eateries, cafés, and sausage stands. For about the cheapest hot meal in town, lunch at the nearby **Technical University's Mensa** (cafeteria) in the huge, modern, light-green building just past Karlsplatz at Wiedner Hauptstrasse 8-19, second floor (Monday-Friday 12:00-14:00). Anyone is welcome to eat here with a world of students. The snack bar is less crowded but the bigger mensa on the same floor has a more interesting selection.

Wherever you're eating, some vocabulary will help. Three interesting drinks to try are *Grüner Veltliner* (dry, white wine, any time), *Traubenmost* (a heavenly grape juice on the verge of wine, autumn only, sometimes just called *Most*), and *Sturm* (barely fermented most, autumn only). The local red wine (called "Portuguese") is pretty good. Since the Austrian wine is often very sweet, remember the word *Trocken* (German for dry). You can order your wine in a quarter-liter (*viertel*) and an eighth-liter (*achtel*). Beer comes in a *Krugel* (.5 liter) or *Seidel* (.3 liter).

Train Connections
Vienna to: Melk (hrly, 75 min), **Krems** (10/day, 1 hr), **Salzburg** (hrly, 3 hrs), **Innsbruck** (9/day, 5½ hrs), **Budapest** (9/day, 3½ hrs), **Prague** (4/day, 5½ hrs), **Munich** (10/day, 4½ hrs), **Berlin** (5/day 12 hrs), **Zurich** (5/day, 9 hrs), **Rome**

(3/day, 14 hrs), **Venice** (4/day, 9 hrs), **Frankfurt** (7/day, 7½ hrs), **Amsterdam** (4/day, 13 hrs).

Vienna and Eastern Europe: Vienna is the natural springboard for a quick trip to Prague and Budapest. Vienna is 3½ hours by train from **Budapest** (520 AS round-trip, free with Eurail) and 5 hours from **Prague** (600 AS round-trip, less with Eurail). Visas are not required. Train tickets are purchased easily at any travel agency. Intropa, next to the TI on Kärntnerstrasse sells train tickets, as well as one-day 1,400-AS tours.

DANUBE VALLEY

The Danube at its romantic best is just west of Vienna. Mix a cruise with a bike ride through the Danube's Wachau Valley, lined with ruined castles, glorious abbeys, small towns, and vineyard upon vineyard. After a look at the glorious abbey of Melk, take an intermission from fairy-tale Austria for a pilgrimage to the powerful Mauthausen concentration camp.

Planning Your Time

For a day-trip from Vienna: catch the early train to Melk, tour the abbey, lunch in Melk, split afternoon trip along the river from Melk to Krems by boat and rented bike. From Krems, catch train back to Vienna. Remember, the boat is dreadfully slow upstream (going west). While this region is a logical day-trip from Vienna with good train connections to both Krems and Melk, spending a night in Melk is a winning idea. Melk is on the main Munich/Salzburg/Vienna train line. Mauthausen, farther away, should be seen en route to or from Vienna. On a three-week trip through Germany, Austria, and Switzerland, I'd see only one concentration camp. Mauthausen is more powerful than the more convenient Dachau.

Danube Cruise

By car, bike, or boat, the 38-kilometer stretch of the Danube between Krems and Melk is as pretty as they come. The boat goes four times daily in season (see below). Those without a car can take advantage of the boat line's generous bike-and-cruise program: 35-AS bike rentals; you can pick them up and drop them at different docks and take your bike onto the boat. The bikes are usually one-speeds; you may get better bikes at the train station. Pedal along the north bank (just off the main road; the "bike in a red border" signs mean "no biking") following the TI's "Cycle Track" brochure. It's about a 3-hour pedal from Krems to Melk, where you can drop the bike. You can go half and half by trading in the boat for a bike or vice versa at the Spitz or Durnstein docks.

Boats run between Krems and Melk (3/day in each direction, May-September, 238 AS, free with Eurailpass),

Danube Valley

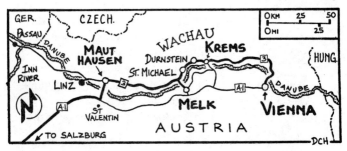

departing from Melk at 11:10, 14:00, and 14:55 (1½-hour ride, upstream, because of the 6-knot flow of the Donau, it's 3 hours for the same trip). To confirm these times, call the DDSG boat-company office, 0732/771090 in Linz or 0222/72750 in Vienna, the Melk TI (02752/2307), or Krems TI (02732/82676). Some boats start or end in Vienna, if you'd like a longer cruise.

The cruise takes you along Danube's wine road and you'll see wine gardens all along the river. Those hanging out a wreath of straw or greenery are inviting you in to taste. St. Michael has a small wine garden and an old tower you can climb for a view. In local slang, someone who's feeling his wine is "blue." Blue Danube?

Sights—Danube Cruise

Krems—A gem of a town. From the boat dock, walk a few blocks to the TI (pick up a town map). Then walk into the traffic-free, shopper's-wonderland old town. If nothing else, it's a pleasant 20-minute stroll from the dock to the train station (hourly trains, a 60-minute ride into Vienna's Franz Josef Bahnhof). The local TI (8:00-18:00, less on weekends and in winter, tel. 02732/82676) can find you a cheap bed in a private home (D-400 AS, DB-500 AS) if you decide to side-trip into Vienna from this small-town alternative. Melanie Stasny Gastezimmer (next to dock at Steiner Landstrasse 22, tel. 02732/82843) is good.

Durnstein—This touristic flypaper lures hordes of visitors with its traffic-free quaintness and its one claim to fame (and fortune): Richard the Lion-Hearted was imprisoned here in 1193. You can probably sleep in his bedroom.

Willendorf—Known among art buffs as the town where the oldest piece of European art was found. A few blocks off the river (follow the signs to Venus) you can see the monument where the well-endowed, 30,000-year-old fertility symbol, the Venus of Willendorf, was discovered. (She's now in Vienna's Natural History Museum.)

▲**Melk**—Sleepy and elegant under its huge abbey that seems to police the Danube, the town of Melk offers a pleasant stop. The helpful TI (9:00-19:00, less off season, tel. 02752/2307), near the traffic-free main square, has ideas for sightseeing in the area (nearby castle, bike rides along the river, and so on).

▲▲**Melk Abbey (Benediktinerstift)**—The newly restored abbey beaming proudly over the Danube Valley is one of Europe's great sights. Freshly painted and gilded throughout, it's a Baroque dream, a lily alone. Its lavish library, church, palace rooms, and the great Danube view from the abbey balcony are the highlights of the 45-minute tour. German tours are available constantly, English tours only with groups of 20 or more (45 AS, 55 AS with a tour, daily 9:00-18:00, last entry 17:00). Call 02752/2312 to find out when the next English group is scheduled; there are often English tours at 15:00, and you are welcome to tag along. The abbey garden, café, and charming village below make waiting for a tour pleasant.

Sleeping in Melk
(11 AS = about $1, tel. code: 02752)
Melk makes a fine overnight stop. **Hotel Fürst** (DB-600 AS; Rathausplatz 3-5, A-3390 Melk, tel. 2343) is a fluffy, creaky old place with 15 rooms, run by the Madar family, right on the traffic-free main square with a fountain out your door and the abbey hovering overhead. **Gasthof Goldener Stern** (D-460 AS, cheaper 3- to 5-bed rooms; Sterngasse 17, A-3390, Melk, tel. 2214, SE-D) is traditional and also quiet and cozy on a pedestrian street in the center. **Gasthof Baumgartner** (D-350 AS, across from the station, tel. 2419) is pretty dumpy but cheap. The modern **youth hostel** (145-AS beds in quads with sheets and breakfast, easygoing about membership, tel. 2681) is a few minutes' walk from the station.

Train Connections

Melk is on the autobahn and the main Salzburg-Vienna train line with hourly trains to **Vienna** (60 min) and **Salzburg** (2 hrs). Train also go hourly to **St. Valentin** (for **Mauthausen**, 75 min with one change).

Mauthausen Concentration Camp

More powerful and less tourist-oriented than Dachau, this slave-labor and death camp functioned from 1938 to 1945 for the exploitation and extermination of Hitler's opponents. Over half of its 206,000 quarry-working prisoners were killed here. Set in a strangely beautiful setting next to the Danube, in a now-still and overgrown quarry, Mauthausen is open daily 8:00-18:00 (15 AS, last entry at 17:00, closes mid-December through January and at 16:00 off-season, tel. 07238/2269, TI tel. 07238/2023).

The camp barracks house a museum (at the far end on the right; some English labels, but the 20-AS English guide-book gives a complete translation) and shows a graphic 45-minute movie (top of each hour; ask for an English showing; if necessary gather a group of English-speaking visitors; if it's running, don't wait for the next showing, just slip in). The most emotionally moving rooms and the gas chamber are downstairs. The spirits of the victims of these horrors can still be felt. Outside the camp each victim's country has erected a gripping memorial. Many yellowed photos sport fresh flowers. Walk to the barbed-wire memorial overlooking the quarry and the "stairway of death."

By visiting a concentration camp and putting ourselves through this emotional wringer, we heed and respect the fervent wish of the victims of this fascism—that we "never forget." Many people forget by choosing not to know.

Train Connections

Most trains stop at St. Valentin, midway between Salzburg and Vienna, where hourly trains make the 15-minute ride to Mauthausen (3 miles from camp, get map from station attendant, camp is #9; free baggage check; 50-AS bike rental; 120-AS minibus taxi, or 60-minute hike). The local bus goes to the base of the hill a mile from the camp, where it's easy to hitch a ride up. **St. Valentin-Salzburg** or **Vienna** (hrly, 1½ hrs).

Route Tips for Drivers

Hallstatt to Vienna, via Mauthausen, Melk, and Wachau Valley (210 miles): Forget easygoing Austria—today is very demanding (unless you can splice in an extra day, which Hallstatt and the Wachau Valley could easily gobble up). Drivers leave Hallstatt early. Follow scenic route 145 through Gmunden to the autobahn and head east. After Linz, take exit #155, Enns, and follow the Mauthausen signs (8 km from the freeway). Go quickly through the village of Windpassing, cross the Donau (Danube, hum "dut duh da da da, dee dee, doo doo"), go through Mauthausen town, and follow signs to Ehemaliges KZ-lager. From Mauthausen, the speedy route is the autobahn to Melk, but the curvy, scenic route 3 along the river is worth the nausea.

This region, from Persenbeug to Melk, is Nibelung-engau, the fourth- and fifth-century home of the legendary Nibelung tribe, dramatized in Wagner's opera. Next stop: Melk's great abbey. Cross the bridge and follow the signs not into town (Zentrum Melk) but to Stift Melk, the *Benediktinerstift* (Benedictine abbey).

The most scenic stretch of the Donau is the Wachau Valley, lying between Melk and Krems. From Melk (get a Vienna map at the TI), cross the river again (signs to Donaubrucke) and stay on route 3. After Krems, it hits the autobahn (A22), and you'll barrel right into Vienna's traffic.

Navigating in Vienna, if you understand the Ring and Gürtel, isn't bad. Study the map and see the two ring roads looping out from the Donau. As you approach the city from Krems, you'll cross the North Bridge and land right on the Gürtel, or outer ring. You can continue along the Danube canal to the inner ring, called the Ringstrasse (clockwise traffic only). Circle around either thoroughfare until you reach the "spoke" street you need.

Vienna west to Hall in Tirol (280 miles): To leave Vienna, follow the signs past the Westbahnhof to Schloss Schönbrunn, which is directly on the way to the West A-1 autobahn to Linz. The king had plenty of parking. Leave by 15:00, beating rush hour, and follow the autobahn signs to West A-1, passing Linz and Salzburg, nipping through Germany, turning right onto route 93 in the direction of Kufstein, Innsbruck, and Austria at the *Dreieck* Inntal (autobahn intersection). Crossing back into Austria, you'll follow the scenic Inn River valley, stopping 5 miles east of Innsbruck at Hall in Tirol. There's an autobahn tourist information station just before Hall (10:00-22:00 daily in season, working for the town's hotels but still helpful). This 5-hour ride is nonstop autobahn all the way. Gasthof Badl is just off the autobahn one stop before Innsbruck in Hall.

SALZBURG AND WEST AUSTRIA

Enjoy the sights and sounds of Salzburg, Mozart's hometown, then commune with nature in the Salzkammergut, Austria's *Sound of Music* Country. Amid hills alive with the *S.O.M.*, you'll find the tiny town of Hallstatt, as pretty as a postcard (and about the same size). On the far western border of Austria, the Golden Roof of Innsbruck glitters, but you'll strike it rich in neighboring Hall, which has twice the charm and none of the tourist crowds.

Salzburg

With a well-preserved old town, gardens, churches, and lush surroundings, set under Europe's biggest intact medieval castle, its river adding an almost seaside ambiance, Salzburg is forever smiling to the tunes of Mozart and *The Sound of Music*. This town knows how to be popular. Eight million tourists crawl its cobbles each year. That's a lot of Mozart balls.

Planning Your Time

Salzburg is the best single stop in Austria. While Vienna measures much higher on the Richter scale of sightseeing thrills, Salzburg is simply a joy. A touristy joy, but a joy nevertheless. If you're going into the nearby Salzkammergut lake country, you don't need to take the *Sound of Music* tour. But this tour kills a nest of sightseeing birds with one ticket (city overview, *S.O.M.* sights, a luge ride, and a fine drive through the lakes). If you're not planning a detour through the lakes, allow half a day for this tour. That means a minimum of two nights and a busy day for Salzburg. Of course, the nights are important for concerts and swilling beer in atmospheric local gardens. The actual town sights are mediocre—it's the town itself that you should enjoy, like the body of your lover the first time you saw it naked. If you like things slow, bike down the river or hike across the Monchsberg.

Orientation (tel. code: 0662)

Salzburg, a city of 150,000 (Austria's fourth largest) is divided into old and new. The old town, sitting between the Salzach

Greater Salzburg

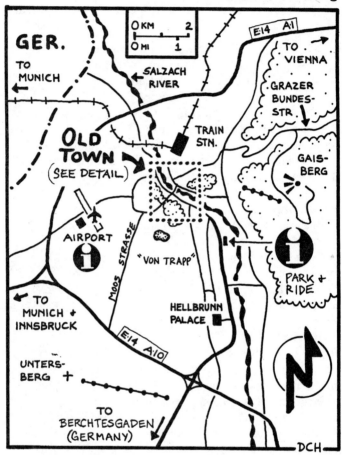

River and the 1,600-foot-high hill called Mönchsberg, is a bundle of Baroque holding all the charm and most of the tourists.

Tourist Information

Salzburg's helpful tourist offices (at the train station, on Mozartplatz in the old center, and on the freeway entrance to the city, tel. 847568 or 88987) know who butters the local bread. Each is equally helpful. Ask for a city map, the "hotel plan" map, a transit map, a list of sights with current hours, and a schedule of events. Book a concert upon arrival.

The Salzburg Station makes getting set up easy. The TI is at track 2A. Downstairs is the place to leave bags, rent bikes, buy tickets, and get train information. This lower street level faces the bus station (where buses numbers 1, 2, 5, 6, 51, and 55 go to the old center). To walk downtown (15 minutes), leave the station ticket hall near window #8 through the door marked "*Zentrum*" and walk absolutely straight down Rainerstrasse, which leads you under the tracks past Mirabellplatz, changes its name to Dreitaltig-keitsgasse, and takes you to the *Staatsbrucke* (bridge) which deposits you in the old town. For a more dramatic approach, leave the same way but follow the tracks to the river, turn left, and walk the riverside path toward the castle.

Getting Around
Salzburg is served by a fine bus system (info tel. 87 21 45). Single-ride tickets are sold on the bus for 21 AS. Twenty-four-hour passes (sold at TIs and Tobacco shops) cost 30 AS. Salzburg is very bike-friendly and the train station rents good bikes all day until midnight for 50 AS (double if you have no train ticket or pass; no deposit required; go to counter #3 to pay, then pick it up at "left luggage"). I intensified my last visit by having a bike the entire time.

Helpful Hints
The American Express office (Mozartplatz 5, A-5020 Salzburg, open Monday-Friday 9:00-17:30, Saturday 9:00-12:00, tel. 842501) will hold mail for their check- or card-users.

Sights—Salzburg
▲**Salzburg Cathedral** (free, daily 8:00-17:00) claims to be the first Baroque building north of the Alps. Built around 1630, it's modeled after St. Peter's in Rome. Back then, the Bishop of Salzburg was number-two man in the Church hierarchy and Salzburg fancied itself as the "Northern Rome." Check out its 4,000-pipe organ. Sunday Mass (10:00) is famous for its music. For a fee you can tour the excavation site under the church and the Dom Museum in the church.
Residenz—It was Archbishop Wolf Dietrich (not Mozart, or even Julie Andrews) who had the greatest impact on Salzburg. His grandiose vision of Salzburg shaped the city

into the Baroque beauty you'll see today. His palace, the Residenz, next to the cathedral, is impressive—unless you've seen any others. Admission is by tour only (hourly 10:00-15:00, except 13:00; 40 minutes of German only except in July and August; confirm you'll get English before paying the 40 AS).

▲**Carillon**—The bell tower on Mozartplatz chimes throughout the day. The man behind the bells gives fascinating 20-minute tours weekdays at 10:45 and 17:45 but unfortunately only from November through mid-March (in decent weather). You'll actually be up on top among 35 bells as the big barrel turns and the music flies. Buy your 20-AS ticket 10 minutes early. Let the TI know how disappointed you are in the schedule.

▲**Getreidegasse**—Old Salzburg's lively and colorful main drag, famous for its many old wrought-iron signs, still looks much as it did in Mozart's day. "*Schmuck*" means jewelry.

▲**Mozart's Birthplace (Geburtshaus, 1756)**—This best Mozart sight in town, filled with scores, portraits, and old keyboard instruments and violins, is almost a pilgrimage. If you're a fan, you'll have to check it out. It's right in the old town on colorful Getreidegasse #9 (60 AS, daily 9:00-19:00, shorter hours off-season).

▲**Hohensalzburg Fortress**—This castle, one of Europe's mightiest, dominates Salzburg's skyline. The interior is so-so unless you catch a tour (30 AS, confirm that it will be in English as well as German). The basic entry fee (30 AS) gives you only the view and the courtyard. The museum has the noisiest floorboards in Europe. Even so, the prince had a chastity belt. You can see it next to other gruesome torture devices that need no explanation. Upstairs is a mediocre military museum offering a chance to see photos of nice-looking young Nazi officers whose government convinced them that their operation was a just cause. The funicular zips you effortlessly to the castle (32 AS round-trip, every 10 minutes). The castle is open daily 8:00-19:00, until 18:00 in off-season.

▲**Mirabell Gardens and Palace (Schloss)**—The bubbly gardens are always open and free, but to properly enjoy the lavish Mirabell Palace, get a ticket to a *Schlosskonzerte*. Baroque music flying around a Baroque hall is a happy bird

Salzburg

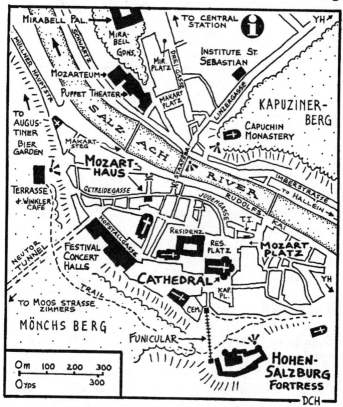

in the right cage. Tickets are around 320 AS (cheaper at the palace and for students) and rarely sold out (tel. 872788).
City Walking Tour—Mediocre two-language 1-hour guided walks of the old town leave from the TI at Mozartplatz (80 AS, 12:15, Monday-Saturday, May-October, tel. 847568).

While walking on your own, be sure to browse through St. Peter's Cemetery, a collection of lovingly tended mini-gardens (at the base of the castle lift). This was where the Trapp family hid out in the *S.O.M.* Tours of the early Christian catacombs leave nearly hourly (tel. 8445780). The nearby open-air market on Universitätsplatz is Salzburg at its liveliest (daily except Sunday).

And for a most enjoyable approach to the castle, consider riding the elevator to the Café Winkler and walking 20 minutes through the woods high above the city to Festung Hohensalzburg (stay on the high paved paths or you'll have a needless climb back up to the castle).

▲▲**Bike Ride to Hallein**—The Salzach River has smooth, flat, and scenic bike paths along each side. On a sunny day, I can think of no more shout-worthy escape from the city. Hallein (with its salt-mine tour, about 12 kilometers away, north or new-town side of river is most scenic, 1 hour each way) is a pleasant destination. Even a quickie ride just from one end of town to the other gives you the best possible views of Salzburg. In the evening, it's a hand-in-hand, flood-lit-spires world.

▲▲*Sound of Music* **Tour**—I took this tour skeptically (as part of my research chores) and liked it. It includes a quick but good general city tour, stops for a luge ride (in season, fair weather, 30 AS extra), hits all the *S.O.M.* spots (including the stately home, gazebo, and the wedding church), and shows you a lovely stretch of the Salzkammergut. The Salzburg Panorama Tours Company charges 300 AS for the 4-hour, English-only tour (from Mirabellplatz daily at 9:30 and 14:00, tel. 874029 for a reservation and a free hotel pickup if you like; travelers with this book who buy their ticket at the Mirabellplatz ticket booth get a 10% discount on this and any other tour they do). This is worthwhile for *S.O.M.* fans without a car or who won't otherwise be going into the Salzkammergut. Warning: Many think rolling through the Austrian country with 30 Americans singing "Do, a Deer" is pretty schmaltzy. There are several similar and very competitive tour companies which offer every conceivable tour from Salzburg. Hotels have their brochures and push them for a healthy commission. The only minibus tours going are Bob's Tours.

▲**Hellbrunn Castle**—The attraction here is a garden full of clever trick fountains and the sadistic joy the tour guide gets from soaking his tourists. The archbishop's 17th-century palace is closed through 1995 (and not worth a look anyway). His Baroque garden, one of the oldest in Europe, is pretty enough, and now features the "I Am 16, Going on 17" gazebo. The burned-out trilingual tour guides sound like every night their wives have to remind them "one language is enough" (daily 9:00-18:00, fewer hours off-season, tel.

82 03 72, 50 AS for the 40-minute tour and admission). The castle is 3 miles south of Salzburg (bus #55 from downtown, twice hourly, 20-minute ride). It's a lot of trouble for a few water tricks.

▲▲**Salzburg Festival**—Each summer from late July to the end of August, Salzburg hosts its famous Salzburger Festspiele, founded in 1920 to employ Vienna musicians in the summer. This fun and festive time is crowded but (except for a few August weekends) there are plenty of beds, and tickets (except for the big shows) are normally available the day of the concert.

Salzburg is busy throughout the year with 1,600 classical performances in its palaces and churches annually (ticket office on Mozartplatz; contact the Austrian National Tourist Office in the U.S.A. for specifics on this year's festival schedule and tickets). I have never planned in advance and have enjoyed great concerts with every visit. While you may find folk evenings twice a week in the summer, Innsbruck is better for these.

Sights—Near Salzburg
▲**Bad Dürnberg Salzbergwerke**—Like its neighbors, this salt-mine tour above the town of Hallein, 8 miles from Salzburg, respects only the German-speakers. You'll get information sheets or headphones but none of the jokes. Still, it's a fun experience—wearing white overalls, sliding down the sleek wooden chutes, and crossing underground from Austria into Germany (daily 9:00-17:00, easy bus and train connections from Salzburg or a great riverside bike ride).
▲**Berchtesgaden**—This Alpine resort just across the German border (20 km from Salzburg) flaunts its attractions very effectively, and you may find yourself in a traffic jam of desperate tourists looking for ways to turn their money into fun. From the station and the TI (tel. 08652/9670), buses go to the idyllic Königsee (19 DM, 2-hour scenic cruises, 4 per hour, stopovers anywhere, tel. 08652/963618) and the salt mines (a 30-minute walk otherwise).

At the salt mines (16 DM, daily 8:30-17:00, winter Monday-Friday, 12:30-15:30, tel. 08652/60020) you put on the traditional miners' outfits, get on funny little trains, and zip deep into the mountain. For 60 minutes you'll cruise subterranean lakes; slide speedily down two long, slick wooden banisters; and learn how they mined salt so long ago. Call for crowd avoidance advice. You can buy a ticket early and browse through the town until your tour time.

Hitler's famous (but overrated) "Eagle's Nest" towered high above Obersalzberg near Berchtesgaden. The site is open to visitors, but little remains of Hitler's Alpine retreat, which he visited only five times. The bus ride up the private road and the lift to the top (a 2,000-foot altitude gain) cost 25 DM from the station, 19 DM from the parking lot. If the weather's cloudy, as it often is in the morning, you'll Nazi a thing.

Berchtesgaden is a train ride from Munich (hrly, one change, 2½ hrs). From Salzburg, ride the scenic and more-direct-than-train bus connection (2/hr, 50 min). Berchtes-gaden caters to long-term German guests. During peak season, it's not worth the headaches for the speedy tourist.

Sleeping in Salzburg
(11 AS = about $1, zip code: 5020, tel. code: 0662)
Finding a room in Salzburg, even during the Music Festival, is usually easy. The tourist offices have pamphlets listing all the pensions, hostels, and private rooms in town. Or, for a couple of dollars, they'll find you an inexpensive bed in a private home in the area of your choice. If you want dorm-style budget alternatives, ask for their list of ten youth hostels and student dorms. Some English is spoken and breakfast is included at all my listings. Most will hold a room with a phone call and more expensive places charge more during the music festival (late July and August).

Sleep code: **S**=Single, **D**=Double/Twin, **T**=Triple, **Q**=Quad, **B**=Bath/Shower and toilet, **CC**=Credit Card (Visa, Mastercard, Amex), **SE**=Speaks English (graded **A** through **F**).

Sleeping on Linzergasse
The first three listings are on lower Linzergasse, directly across the bridge from Mozart-ville and a 15-minute walk from the station. Its bustling crowds of shoppers overwhelm the few shy cars that venture onto it.

Institute St. Sebastian plans to open after major reno-vation in July of 1995 (expected rates: 170-AS dorm beds,

450-AS doubles, breakfast is 35 AS extra, guests with sheets save 25 AS; Linzergasse 41, enter through arch at #37, tel. 871386 or 882606, fax 87138685, reception open 8:00-12:00, 15:00-22:00). This is a friendly, clean, historic convent. Mozart's mom is buried in the courtyard and they usually have rooms available.

Troglodytes love **Hotel zum Jungen Fuchs** (S-220 AS, D-380 AS, T-480 As, 15 AS showers down hall; across from Institute St. Sebastian at Linzergasse 54, tel. 875496). It's wonderfully located in a funky, dumpy old building, very plain but clean, with a tired, elderly management that serves no breakfast and little else.

Hotel Pension Goldene Krone (D-700 AS-750 AS, DB-800 AS-970 AS, TB-1,100 AS-1,200 AS, elevator; Linzergasse 48, tel. 872300) is big, quiet, creaky-traditional but modern, with comforts rare in this price range.

Gasthaus Ganslhof (DB-780 AS, 900 AS during the festival, elevator and lots of ground floor rooms; Vogel-weiderstr. 6, a 10-minute walk up Linzergasse from the old town, tel. 873853, fax 87385323) is clean, central, and comfortable. It's back in the real world, with Motel 6 ambience and a parking lot.

Two plain and decent old places two blocks in front of the train station but a 15-minute walk from the sightseeing action on a slightly sleazy street: **Gasthof Jahn** (D-520 AS-570 AS, spacious DB-640 AS-700 AS, TB-800 AS-900 AS; CC:VM, Elisabethstrasse 31, tel. 871405, fax 875535) is better than the **Pension Adlerhof** (D-490 AS-570 AS, DB-650 AS-720 AS, T-740 AS-790 AS, TB-890 AS-950 AS, public shower is a hike away; Elisabethstrasse 25, tel. 875236, fax 8736636, quirky staff).

Sleeping in or above the Old Town

Gasthaus "Zur Goldenen Ente" (DB-900 AS-980 AS, 100 AS more in August, CC:VMA; Goldgasse 10 in the old center, tel. 845622, fax 8456229), run by the Family Steinwender, is a great splurge if you'd like to sleep in a 600-year-old building above a fine restaurant as central as you can be on a pedestrian street in old Salzburg. Somehow the 15 modern and comfortable doubles fit into this building's medieval-style stone arches and narrow stairs. The breakfast is buffet-big, they have a 70-AS/day deal on the nearby parking lot, and they'll hold a room if you leave your credit-card number. For dinner, try their roast *Ente* (duck). Robert, the cook, also specializes in fish.

Gasthof Hinterbrühl (S-370 AS, D-470 AS, T-540 AS, plus optional 50-AS breakfast; on a village-like square just under the castle at Schanzlgasse 12, tel. 846798) is a smoky, ramshackle old place with spacious rooms, a handy location, and not a tourist in sight.

Naturfreundehaus (D-250 AS, 110 AS per person in 4- to 6-bed dorms, 45-AS breakfast, 70-AS dinner with city view; Mönchsberg 19, 2 minutes from the top of the 25-AS round-trip Mönchsberg elevator, tel. 841729, 01:00 curfew, open May-October) is a local version of a mountaineer's hut. It's a great budget alternative guarded by singing birds and snuggled in the remains of a 15th-century castle wall overlooking Salzburg with magnificent old-town and mountain views. High above the old town, it's the stone house to the left of the glass Café Winkler.

Bed and Breakfasts

These are generally roomy, modern, very comfortable, and come with a good breakfast. Off-season, competition is tough and you can consider it a buyer's market. Most are a bus ride from town, but with the cheap 24-hour pass and the frequent service, this shouldn't keep you away. Unsavory *Zimmer* skimmers lurk at the station. If you have a reservation, ignore them. If you need a place . . . they need a customer.

Brigitte Lenglachner (S-270 AS, bunk bed D-390 AS, D-450 AS, DB-500 AS, T-650 AS, 2 nights minimum; breakfast served in your room; in a chirpy neighborhood a 10-minute walk from the station, cross the pedestrian Pioneer bridge, turn right past park and second left to Scheibenweg 8, tel. 43 80 44) fills her big traditional house with a warm welcome, lots of tourist information, and American tourists.

Moosstrasse, south of Mönchsberg, is lined with *Zimmer*. Those farther out are farmhouses. From the station, catch bus #1 and change to bus #60 immediately after crossing the river. From the old town, ride bus #60. If you're driving from the center, go through the tunnel, straight on Neutorstrasse, and take the fourth left onto Moosstrasse. **Maria Gassner** (SB-300 AS, DB-440 AS, 500 AS, and 600 AS, family deals; 60-AS coin-op laundry; first bus #60 stop after American High School at Moosstrasse 126-B, tel. 824990) rents 10 sparkling clean, comfortable rooms in her modern house. She can often pick you up at the station. **Frau Ballwein** rents seven charming and comfortable rooms in an old farmhouse (S-250 AS, D-400 AS, DBWC-480 AS, Moosstrasse 69A, tel. 824029). Her family operates one of the touristic old horse-buggies. For the cost of a bus ticket, guests can hitch a ride in the buggy downtown as it goes to work at 9:30. **The Ziller Family Farm** rents three huge rooms with kitchenettes in a kid-friendly, horse-filled environment (DB-550 AS, minimum two nights, Moosstrasse 76, tel. 824940). **Gästehaus Blobergerhof** (Hammerauerstrasse 4, Querstrasse zur Moosstrasse, tel. 830227) and **Helga Bankhammer** (D-400 AS minimum two nights, Moosstrasse 77, tel. 830067) are also rural, warm, and reasonable.

Youth Hostels

Salzburg has more than its share of hostels (and tourists). The TI has a complete listing (with directions from the station) and there are nearly always beds available. The most fun, handy, and American is **Gottfried's International Youth Hotel** (4 D-320 AS, 3 Q-140 AS per bed, or 6- to 8-bed dorm-120 AS, sheets not required but rentable-20 AS; 5 blocks from the station towards the center at Paracelsusstr. 9, tel. 87 96 49). This easygoing but impressively run place speaks English first, has cheap meals, lockers, a laundry, tour discounts, no curfew, plays *The Sound of Music* free daily at 13:30, runs a lively bar, and welcomes anyone.

Eating in Salzburg

Salzburg boasts many inexpensive, fun, and atmospheric places to eat. I'm a sucker for the big cellars with their smoky Old World atmosphere, heavy medieval arches, time-darkened paintings, many antlers, and hearty meals to match. These places are famous with visitors but also enjoyed by the locals.

    Gasthaus "Zum Wilder Mann" (enter from Getreidegasse 20 or Griesgasse 17, tel. 841787, food served

11:00-21:00) is the place if the weather's bad and you're in the mood for Hofbräu atmosphere in one small well-antlered room and a hearty cheap meal at a shared table, 2 minutes from Mozart's place. For a quick 100-AS lunch, get the Bauernschmaus, a mountain of dumpling, *kraut*, and peasant's meats.

Stieglkeller (50 yards uphill from the lift to the castle, tel. 84 26 81), a huge, atmospheric institution with several rustic rooms and outdoor garden seating offering a great rooftop view of the old town, is an inexpensive way to get really schnitzeled.

Krimplestätter (Müllner Hauptstrasse 31, 10 minutes north of the old town near the river) employs 500 years of experience serving authentic old-Austrian food in its authentic old-Austrian interior or in its cheery garden. For fine food with a wild finale, eat here and drink at the nearby Augustiner Bräustübl.

Augustiner Bräustübl (Augustinergasse 4, walk through the Mirabellgarten, over the Müllnersteg bridge and ask for "Müllnerbräu," its local nickname; don't be fooled by second-rate gardens serving the same beer nearby—this huge 1,000-seat place is in the huge Augustiner brewery; open daily 15:00-23:00, order carefully, prices can sting; great beer, pick up a 25-AS half-liter or a 50-AS full-liter mug, pay the lady and give Mr. Keg your empty mug). This monk-run brewery is so rustic and crude that I hesitate to show my true colors by recommending it, but I must. On busy nights, it's like a Munich beer-hall with no music but the volume turned up. When its cool you'll enjoy a historic setting with beer-sloshed smoke-stained halls. On balmy evenings you'll eat under trees in a pleasant outdoor beer-garden. Local students mix with tourists eating hearty slabs of *schnitzel* with their fingers or cold meals from the self-serve picnic counter. It'll bring out the barbarian in you. For dessert (after a visit to the *strudel* kiosk), enjoy the incomparable floodlit view of old Salzburg from the nearby pedestrian bridge and then stroll home along the river. Delicious memories.

Stiftskeller St. Peter (next to St. Peter's church at the foot of Mönchsberg, outdoor and indoor seating, daily until midnight, meals 100 AS-200 AS, tel. 8412680) has been in business for over a thousand years. It's classier, with strolling musicians, more central, not too expensive, and your best splurge for traditional Austrian cuisine in medieval sauce. The "Monastery Pot" (hearty soup in a bowl made of dark bread) takes away your munchies. If you start singing "The hills are alive . . ." they'll throw you out.

Café Haydn Stube (1 Mirabellplatz at the entry to the Aicherpassage, Monday-Friday 9:30-20:00), run by the local music school, is cheap and very popular with students. The **Mensa Aicherpassage** (hiding in the basement, Monday-Friday 11:30-14:00) serves even cheaper meals.

Picnics: Classy Salzburg delis serve good, cheap, sit-down lunches on weekdays. Have them make you a sandwich or something hot, toss in a carrot, a piece of fruit, yogurt, and a box of milk and sit at a small table with the local lunch crowd. **Frauenberger** (8:00-14:00, 15:00-18:00, closed Monday and Saturday afternoon and Sunday; it's little hot-dog stand is open until 24:00, across from 16 Linzergasse) is friendly, picnic-ready, cheap and offers indoor or outdoor seating. The University Square, just behind Mozart's house, hosts a bustling produce market daily (except Sunday).

You'll see a mountainous sweet souffle served all over town. The memorable "Salzberger Nockerl" is worth a try (if you have someone to split it with). It's really big enough for four.

Train Connections
Salzburg to: Innsbruck (every 2 hrs, 2 hrs), **Munich** (hrly, 2 hrs), **Vienna** (hrly, 3½ hrs), **Hallstatt** (hrly, 50 min to Attnang Puchheim, 20 minutes wait, 1½ hrs to Hallstatt), **Reutte** (change in Innsbruck, 4 hrs).

Salzkammergut Lake District
Commune with nature in Austria's Lake District. "The hills are alive," and you're surrounded by the loveliness that has turned on everyone from Emperor Franz Josef to Julie Andrews. This is *The Sound of Music* country. Idyllic, majestic, but not rugged, it's a gentle land of lakes, forested mountains, and storybook villages, rich in hiking opportunities and inexpensive lodging. Settle down in the postcard-pretty, fjord-cuddling town of Hallstatt.

Planning Your Time

While there are plenty of lakes, Hallstatt is really the only
one that matters. One night and two hours to browse is all
you need to fall in love with it. To relax or take a hike in the
surroundings, give it two nights and a day. It's a good stop
between Salzburg and Vienna. And a visit here (with a bike
ride along the Danube) balances out your Austrian itinerary.

While the Salzkammergut is well-served by trains and
buses, Eurailers in a hurry can see it from the window of the
half-day *Sound of Music* bus tour (see Salzburg for description).

Hallstatt

Lovable Hallstatt is a tiny town bullied onto a ledge between
a selfish mountain and a swan-ruled lake with a waterfall rip-
ping furiously through its middle. It can be toured on foot in
about 10 minutes. The town is one of Europe's oldest, going
back centuries before Christ. The charm of Hallstatt is the
village and its lakeside setting. Go there to relax, nibble,
wander, and paddle. (In August, tourist crowds trample
much of Hallstatt's charm.)

Tourist Information

The TI (tel. 06134/8208, open daily in summer, often closed
for lunch) can find you a room. Its hotel "guest card" gives
you free parking and sightseeing discounts.

Trains

Hallstatt's train station is a wide spot on the tracks across the
lake. *Stefanie* (a boat) meets you at the station and glides
across the lake into town (20 AS, with each train). The ride
is gorgeous.

Sights—Hallstatt

Prehistory Museum—The humble Prehistory Museum
adjacent to the TI is interesting since little Hallstatt was the
important salt-mining hub of a culture which spread from
France to the Balkans during what archaeologists call the
"Hallstatt Period" (800-400 B.C.). Back then, Celtic tribes
dug for precious salt and Hallstatt was, as its name means,
the "salt place." Your 40-AS Prehistory Museum ticket gets
you into the Heimat (Folk Culture) Museum around the

Salzkammergut and Hallstatt

corner (10:00-18:00 in summer). It's cute but barely worth the trouble. The Janu sport shop across from the TI recently dug into a prehistoric site and now its basement is another small museum.

Hallstatt Church and Cemetery—From near the boat dock, hike up the covered wooden stairway to the church. The church is lovely (500-year-old altars and frescoes) but the cemetery will rot your flesh. Space is so limited in Hallstatt that bones got only 12 peaceful buried years before making way for the freshly dead. The result is a fascinating chapel of bones (10 AS, 10:00-18:00) in the cemetery. Each skull is lovingly named, dated, and decorated, with the men getting ivy and the women roses. They stopped this practice in the 1960s, about the same time the Catholic Church began permitting cremation.

Salt-Mine Tour—If you have yet to do a salt mine, Hallstatt's is as good as any. You'll ride a frighteningly steep funicular high above the town (95 AS, round-trip), take a 10-minute hike, put on old miners' clothes, take an underground train, slide down the banisters, and listen to an English tape-recorded tour while your guide speaks German (130 AS, daily 9:30-16:30, closes early off-season; no children under age 4). The well-publicized ancient Celtic graveyard excavation sites, nearby, are really dead. The scenic 50-minute hike back into town is (with strong knees) a joy.

Hiking and Spelunking—Mountain lovers, hikers, and spelunkers can keep busy for days using Hallstatt as their home base. Get information from the TI on the various caves with their ice formations, the thunderous rivers, mountain lifts, nearby walks, and harder hikes. With a car, consider hiking around nearby Altaussee (flat, 3-hour hike) or along Grundlsee to Tolpitzsee. Regular buses connect Hallstatt with Gosausee for a pleasant walk around that lake. The TI can recommend a great 2-day hike with an overnight in a nearby mountain hut.

Sleeping in Hallstatt
(11 AS = about $1, zip code: A-4830, tel. code: 06134)
Hallstatt's TI can almost always find you a room. July and August can be tight. Early August is worst. A bed in a private home costs about 180 AS with breakfast. It's hard to get a one-night reservation. But if you drop in and they have a spot, they're happy to have you. All prices include breakfast, lots of stairs, and a silent night. "*Zimmer mit Aussicht?*" means "Room with view?" . . . worth asking for.

Gasthof Simony (500 AS-800 AS doubles depending upon the plumbing, view, season, and length of stay; 250 AS for third person, cheaper for families; tel. 8231, SE-B) is my stocking-feet-tidy 500-year-old favorite, right on the square with a lake view, balconies, creaky wood floors, slip-slidey rag rugs, antique furniture, lakefront garden, and a huge breakfast. Call friendly Susan Scheutz for a reservation.

Pension Seethaler (200 AS per person, 180 AS if you stay more than one night, in S, D, T, or Q, no extra for great views; Dr Morton weg 22, tel. 8421, SE-D) is a simple old lodge with 45 beds, perched a little above the lake on the parking-lot side of town.

Pension Sarstein (D-400 AS, DB-500 AS-600 AS; for people with this book, one-night stays are okay; Gosaumühlstr. 83, tel. 8217) has 25 beds in a charming building a few minutes walk along the lake from the center, with a view, run by friendly Frau Fisher. You can swim from her lakeside garden. Her sister, friendly **Frau Zimmermann** (180 AS per person B&B in a double or triple, can be musty; Gosaumühlstr. 69, tel. 8309), runs a small *Zimmer* (as her name implies) in a 500-year-old ramshackle house with low beams, time-polished wood, and fine lake views just down the street. These elderly ladies speak almost no English, but you'll find yourself caught up in their charm and laughing together like old friends.

Helga Lenz (160 AS per person in 2-, 3-, or 4-bed rooms, gives family discounts, welcomes one-nighters; high above the paddleboat dock at Hallberg 17, tel. 8508, SE-B) has a big, sprawling, woodsy house on top of the town with great lake and town views and a neat garden perch. Ideal for those who sleep well in tree houses.

Gasthaus Zauner (DB-1100 AS; Marktplatz 51, tel. 8246, fax 82468) is a business machine offering more normal hotel rooms on the main square, with a restaurant specializing in grilled food. You'll eat better at Gasthaus Weisses Lamm.

The **Gasthaus Mühle Naturfreunde-Herberge** (135 AS per bed with sheets in 2- to 20-bed coed dorms, 35-AS breakfast, cheaper if you BYO hostel sheet, run by Ferdinand; Kirchenweg 36 just below the tunnel car park, tel. 8318) has the best cheap beds in town and is clearly the place to eat well on a budget. Their wonderful pizzas are big enough for two. Closed in November. Restaurant closed on Wednesdays. ("Nature's friends' houses" are found through-out the Alps. Like mountaineers' huts, they're a good, fun, and basic bargain.)

The **youth hostel** (90 AS beds in 2- to 17-bed rooms, extra for sheets and breakfast, Salzbergstrasse 50, just below the salt-mine lift, a 5-minute walk past the tunnel, tel. 8681 or 8279) is clean, without character, and open May through September.

The nearby village of **Obertraun** is a peaceful alternative to Hallstatt in August. You'll find plenty of *Zimmer* and a luxurious youth hostel (135-AS beds with breakfast, tel. 06131/8360).

Train Connections
Hallstatt to: Salzburg (hrly, 1½ hrs to Attnang Puchheim, 20 min wait, 50 min to Salzburg), **Vienna** (hrly, 1½ hrs to Attnang Puchheim, 10 min wait, 2½ hrs to Vienna).

Innsbruck and Hall
Innsbruck is world-famous as a resort for skiers and a haven for hikers. But for traditional small town Tirol, spend your time in Hall, just 5 miles away.

Planning Your Time
When compared to Salzburg and Vienna, Innsbruck is stale strudel. But it's famous, and a quick look is easy and interesting. The nearby town of Hall is as historic with twice the charm and half the tourists. Drivers can use Hall as a convenient overnight stop on the drive from Vienna to Switzerland (having seen Salzburg on the way to Vienna).

Innsbruck
Innsbruck was the Habsburgs' capital of the Tirol. It's medieval center, now a glitzy tourist-filled pedestrian zone, still gives you the feel of a provincial medieval capital. The much-ogled Golden Roof (Goldenes Dachl, 2,657 gilded copper tiles, built by Emperor Maximilian in 1496 as an impressive viewing spot for his medieval spectacles) is the centerpiece. From this square, you'll see the Olympics Museum, the Baroque-style Helblinghaus, and the city tower (climb it for a great view, 20 AS). Nearby are the palace (Hofburg), church (Hofkirche), and Folklife Museum.

Tourist Information
Innsbruck has two TIs, the central office (3 blocks in front of the Golden Roof, daily 8:00-19:00) and the station TI (open until 22:00, tel. 0512/5356).

Innsbruck and Hall

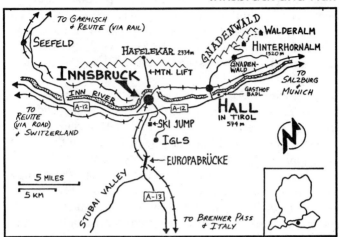

Sights—Innsbruck

Folklife Museum (Tiroler Volkskunst Museum)—
This offers the best look anywhere at traditional Tirolean
lifestyles. Fascinating exhibits range from wedding dresses
and gaily painted cribs and nativity scenes to maternity
clothes and babies' trousers. The upper floors show Tirolean
homes through the ages. (40 AS, open daily in season 9:00-
17:00, closed Sunday afternoon, hard to appreciate without
the English guidebook.)

Olympics Museum—This new museum on the main square
has exciting action videos for winter-sports lovers (22 AS,
daily 9:30-17:30, 32 AS combo tower/Olympics ticket). If
you stand just under the Olympics museum sign and look
down the street, you'll see Innsbruck's Olympic ski jump.

Mountain Lifts and Hiking—A popular mountain-sports
center and home of the 1964 and 1976 Winter Olympics,
Innsbruck is surrounded by 150 mountain lifts, 1,250 miles
of trails, and 250 hikers' huts. If it's sunny, consider riding
the lift right out of the city to the mountaintops above (300
AS, 15% less if ticket purchased at TI). Those who stay
three nights in Innsbruck become members of Club
Innsbruck and can take advantage of free guided hikes,
bike tours, and lots of discounts.

Alpenzoo—This zoo is one of Innsbruck's most popular

attractions (understandable when the competition is the Golden Roof). You can ride the funicular up to the zoo (free if you buy your zoo ticket before boarding) and get a look at all the animals that hide out in the Alps—wildcats, owls, elk, vultures, and more (60 AS, daily 9:00-18:00, special deal at the TI).

Slap-Dancing—For your Tirolean folk fun, Innsbruck hotels offer an entertaining evening of slap-dancing and yodeling nearly every summer night (200 AS includes a drink with the 2-hour show; 21:00; discounted tickets at the TI).

▲▲**Alpine Side Trip by Car to Hinterhornalm**—In Gnadenwald, a village sandwiched between Hall and its Alps, pay a 50-AS toll, pick up a brochure, then corkscrew your way up the mountain. Marveling at the crazy amount of energy put into such a remote road project, you'll finally end up at the rustic Hinterhornalm Berg restaurant (offering three simple 320-AS double rooms without breakfast and a precarious dorm hut or *Lager* with 100-AS beds with cliff-hanger views; tel. 05223/52170, crowded on summer weekends, closed through winter). Hinterhornalm is a hang-gliding springboard. On good days, it's a butterfly nest.

From there it's a level 20-minute walk to the Walder-alm farm, where you can wander around a working dairy farm that shares its meadow with the clouds. The cows ramble along ridgetop lanes surrounded by cut-glass peaks. The lady of the farm serves soup, sandwiches, and drinks (very fresh milk in the afternoon) on rough plank tables. Below you spread the Inn River Valley and, in the distance, Innsbruck.

Side Trip over Brennerpass into Italy?

A short swing into Italy is fast and easy and would give your trip an exciting new twist (45-minute drive, easy border crossing, no problem with car, Austrian schillings accepted in the border region). To get there, take the great Europa Bridge over Brennerpass. It's expensive (about $15), but in 30 minutes you'll be at the border. (Note: traffic can be heavy on summer weekends.) In Italy, drive to the colorful market town of Vipiteno/Sterzing. Just south of town on the east side of the valley, down a small road next to the auto-bahn, is the **Reifenstein Castle**. The lady who lives there gives tours (9:30, 10:30, 14:00, and 15:00, closed Friday) in German, Italian, and a little English. It's a unique and wonderfully preserved medieval castle (4,000L or 30 AS, tel. from Austria 00-39-472/765879).

Train Connections
Innsbruck to: Salzburg (hrly, 2 hrs), **Zurich** (6/day, 3½ hrs), **Venice** (5/day, 5½ hrs), **Bregenz** (6/day, 3 hrs), **Munich** (hrly, 2½ hrs), **Vienna** (hrly, 5 hrs), **Milano** (5/day, 5½ hrs), **Reutte** (every 2 hrs, one change, 2½ hrs, by bus: 4/day, 2½ hrs), **Hall** (2 buses/hr, 30 min), train info tel. 1717.

Hall in Tirol
Hall was a rich salt-mining center when Innsbruck was just a humble bridge (*Brücke*) town on the Inn River. Hall actually has a larger Old Town than does its sprawling neighbor, Innsbruck. Take a "gee, it's great to be alive" walk through this easygoing town. Hall has a colorful morning scene before the daily tour buses arrive, closes down tight for its daily siesta, and sleeps on Sunday. Hall's TI (9:00-12:00, 14:00-18:00, Saturday until 12:00, closed Sunday, tel. 05223/56269) can help you find a room.

Trains
Train travelers will get to Hall via Innsbruck (bus #4, 4/hr, 30 min, 28 AS). Hall is ideally a freeway-handy stopover for drivers. Drivers staying in Hall can side-trip into Innsbruck easily by bus (departs from just over the bridge).

Sights—Hall
Hasegg Castle—This was the town mint. As you walk over the old pedestrian bridge from Gasthof Badl into town, this is the first old building you'll see (you can pick up a town map and a list of sights here).
Salt Museum (Bergbaumuseum)—Back when salt was money, Hall was loaded. Try catching a tour (call first) at this museum, where the town has reconstructed one of its original salt mines, complete with pits, shafts, drills, tools, and the climax of any salt-mine tour—the slippery wooden slide (30 AS, April-October, by tour only; tours go on the

hour except 12:00 and 13:00 from 10:00-17:00; closed
Sunday, tel. 05223/56269).

Walking Tours—The TI organizes town walks in English
which include the salt museum (80 AS including admissions,
10:00 and 14:00, 2 hours).

Swimming—To give your trip a special splash, check out
Hall's magnificent *Freischwimmbad*, a huge outdoor pool with
four diving boards, a giant lap pool, and a kiddies' pool, all
surrounded by a lush garden, a sauna, minigolf, and lounging
locals (35 AS).

Sleeping and Eating in Hall
(11 AS = about $1, tel. code: 05223)

If you'll be arriving late in the day in this popular little town,
call direct to reserve a room. The TI can find you a room
from their list of *Zimmer*, *Pension*, and *Gasthäuser*. *Zimmer*
charge about 200 AS per person but don't accept one-night
stays. Gasthof Badl has maps of Hall and Innsbruck and
information in English. If they're full, they can help you find
another place.

    Gasthof Badl (SB-400 AS, DB-660 AS, TB-930 AS,
QB-1,080 AS, CC:VM, elevator; Innsbruck 4, A-6060, Hall
in Tirol, tel. 05223/56784, fax 567843, SE-A) is a big, comfortable, friendly place run by sunny Frau Steiner and her
daughter, Sonja. It's easy to find, immediately off the Hall in
Tirol freeway exit with an orange-lit "Bed" sign. It's not
cheap, but take it for the convenience, the big breakfast, the
warm welcome, and the fact that they'll hold a room for a
phone call. Freeway noise is no problem. Hall's kitchens
close early but Gasthof Badl's restaurant serves excellent
dinners (from 120 AS) until 22:00.

    For a cheaper room in a private home, **Frieda
Tollinger** (200 AS per person with breakfast; Schopperweg
8, across the river from Badl, tel. 541366 or 41366, SE-F)
rents out three rooms and accepts one-nighters.

Route Tips for Drivers
Into Salzburg from Munich: After crossing the border, stay
on the autobahn, taking the Süd Salzburg exit in the direction of Anif. This road leads you north into town, passing
first the Schloss (and zoo) Hellbrunn and then the TI and a

great park-and-ride service. Get sightseeing information and a 24-hour bus ticket from the TI (daily 9:00-20:00), park your car (free), and catch the shuttle bus (21 AS, every 5 minutes) into town. Mozart never drove in the old town, and neither should you. If you don't believe in P&R, the easiest, cheapest, and most central parking lot is the giant 1,500-car Altstadt lot in the tunnel under the Mönchsberg (150 AS per day). Your hotel may have parking discount passes.

From Salzburg to Hallstatt (50 miles): Get on the Munich-Wein autobahn (blue signs), head for Vienna, exit at Thalgau, and follow signs to Hof, Fuschl and St. Gilgen. The road to Hallstatt leads first past Fuschlsee (mediocre Sommerrodelbahn summer luge ride, 30 AS, open when dry April to mid-October 10:00-17:00, at Fuschl an See), to St. Gilgen (pleasant but touristy), to Bad Ischl (the center of the Salzkammergut with a spa, salt-mine tour, casino, the emperor's villa if you need a Habsburg history fix, and a good tourist office, tel. 06132/23520), and along Hallstattersee to Hallstatt.

Hallstatt is basically traffic-free. Park in the middle of the tunnel at the P-1 sign and waterfall. If this is full, try the lakeside lot (P-2, pleasant 5-minute lakeside walk from town center) just after the tunnel. If you're traveling off-season and staying downtown, you can drive in and park by the boat dock (your hotel "guest card" makes you a temporary resident, giving you permission).

From Hall/Innsbruck to Switzerland: After a morning walk through Hall, you have two choices: a look at Innsbruck or a high-Alp experience. If it's sunny, I'd skip the city and do the Hinterhornalm/Walderalm trip.

For the rainy-day city option, autobahn from Hall to the Innsbruck Ost exit, and follow the signs to Zentrum, then Kongresshaus, and park as close to the old center on the river (Hofgarten) as you can.

Just south of Innsbruck is the Olympic ski jump (from the autobahn take the Innsbruck Süd exit and follow signs to "Bergisel"). Park at the end of the road near the Andreas Hofer Memorial (an Austrian patriot, killed fighting Napoleon) and climb to the empty, grassy stands for a panoramic picnic.

Leaving Innsbruck for Switzerland (from ski jump, go down into town along huge cemetery, thoughtfully placed just beyond the jump landing, and follow blue A12, Garmisch, Arlberg signs), head west on the autobahn (direction: Bregenz). The 8-mile-long Arlberg tunnel saves you 30 minutes but costs 160 AS and lots of scenery. For a joyride and to save a few bucks, skip the tunnel, exiting at St. Anton, and go via Stuben.

After the speedy Arlberg tunnel, you're 30 minutes from Switzerland. Pass Feldkirch (and another long tunnel) and exit the autobahn at Rankweil/Feldkirch Nord, following signs for Altstätten and Meiningen (CH). Crossing the baby Rhine River, you leave Austria.

SWITZERLAND (SCHWEIZ, SUISSE, SVIZZERA)

• 16,000 square miles (half the size of Ireland, or 13 Rhode Islands).
• About 6 million people (400 people per square mile, declining slightly).
• 1 Swiss Franc = about US$.70, 1.4 SF = about $1.

Switzerland is Europe's richest, best-organized, and most mountainous country. Like Boy Scouts, the Swiss count cleanliness, neatness, punctuality, tolerance, independence, thrift, and hard work as virtues, and they love pocket-knives. They appreciate the awesome nature that surrounds them and are proud of their little country's many achievements.

The high average Swiss income, a great social security system, and their strong currency, not to mention the Alps, give them plenty to be thankful for.

Switzerland, 40 percent of which is uninhabitable rocks, lakes, and rugged Alps, has distinct cultural regions and cus-

Switzerland

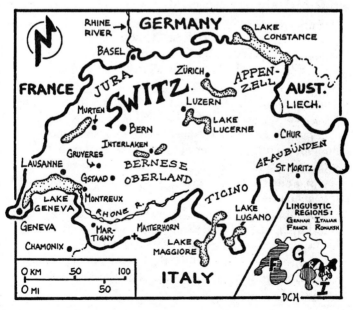

toms. Two-thirds of the people speak German, 20 percent French, 10 percent Italian, and a small group of people in the southeast speak Romansch, a direct descendant of ancient Latin. Within these four language groups, there are many dialects. The sing-songy Swiss German, the spoken dialect, is quite a bit different from High German, which is Switzerland's written German. Most Swiss are multilingual, and English is widely spoken, but an interest in these regional distinctions will win the hearts of locals you meet. As you travel from one valley to the next, notice changes in architecture and customs.

Historically, Switzerland is one of the oldest democracies (yet women didn't get the vote until 1971). Born when three states, or cantons, united in 1291, the Confederation Helvetica as it was called in Roman times (the "CH" decal on cars doesn't stand for chocolate) grew to the 23 of today. The government is decentralized, and cantonal loyalty is very strong.

Fiercely independent, Switzerland loves its neutrality and stayed out of both world wars, but it's far from lax defensively. Every fit man serves in the army and stays in the reserve. Each house has a gun and a bomb shelter. Switzerland bristles with 600,000 rifles in homes and 12,000 heavy guns in place. Swiss vacuum-packed emergency army bread, which lasts two years, is said to also function as a weapon. Airstrips hide inside mountains behind Batmobile doors. With the push of a button, all road, rail, and bridge entries to the country can be destroyed, changing Switzerland into a formidable mountain fortress. Notice the innocent-looking, but explosive, patches checkerboarding the roads at key points like tunnel entrances and mountain summits (and hope no one invades until you get past). Sentiments are changing, and in 1989 Switzerland came close to voting away its entire military. August 1 is the very festive Swiss national holiday.

Switzerland has a low inflation rate and a strong franc. Shops throughout the land thrill tourists with carved, woven, and clanging mountain knickknacks, clocks, watches, and Swiss Army knives (Victorinox is the best brand). To figure out prices roughly in dollars, subtract one-third from the Swiss price (12F = about $8).

Traveling in Switzerland can be expensive. Hotels with double rooms under $50 are rare, but dormitory accommodations are plentiful and reasonable. If your budget is tight, be sure to chase down youth hostels (many with "family rooms") and keep your eyes peeled for *Matratzenlagers* (literally, "mattress dorms"). Groceries are reasonable and hiking is free, but Alpine lifts and souvenirs are pricey.

The Swiss eat when we do and enjoy a straightforward, no-nonsense cuisine. Specialties include delicious fondue, rich chocolates, a melted cheese dish called *raclette*, fresh dairy products (try müesli yogurt), 100 varieties of cheese, and *Fendant*, a good, crisp, local white wine, too expensive to sell well abroad but worth a taste here. The Co-op and Migros grocery stores are the hungry hiker's best budget bet.

You can get anywhere quickly on Switzerland's scenic and efficient trains or its fine road system (the world's most expensive per mile to build). Drivers pay a one-time 30F fee for a permit to use Swiss autobahns. It's easy to slip across the border without buying one, but anyone driving on a Swiss autobahn without this tax sticker is likely to be cop-stopped and fined.

Tourist information offices abound. While Switzerland's booming big cities are cosmopolitan, the traditional culture survives in the Alpine villages. Spend most of your time getting high in the Alps. On Sundays, you're most likely to enjoy traditional sports, music, clothing, and culture.

GIMMELWALD AND THE BERNER OBERLAND

Frolic and hike high above the stress and clouds of the real world. Take a vacation from your busy vacation. Recharge your touristic batteries up here in the Alps where distant avalanches, cowbells, the fluff of a down comforter, and the crunchy footsteps of happy hikers are the dominant sounds. If the weather's good, ride a gondola from the traffic-free village of Gimmelwald to a hearty breakfast at Schilthorn's 10,000-foot revolving Piz Gloria restaurant. Linger among Alpine whitecaps before riding, hiking, or hang gliding down (5,000 feet) to Mürren and home to Gimmelwald.

Your gateway to the wonderfully mountainous Berner Oberland is the grand old resort town of Interlaken. Near Interlaken is Switzerland's greatest open-air folk museum, Ballenberg, where you climb through traditional houses from every corner of this diverse country.

Ah, but the weather's fine and the Alps beckon. Head deep into the heart of the Alps and ride the gondola to the stop just this side of heaven—Gimmelwald.

Planning Your Time

Rather than tackling a checklist of famous Swiss mountains and resorts, choose one area to savor. That area is the Berner Oberland. Interlaken is the administrative headquarters (fine transportation hub, banking, post office, laundry, shopping). Use it for that business and as a springboard for Alpine thrills. With decent weather, explore the two areas (south of Interlaken) which tower above either side of the Lauterbrunnen Valley: Kleine Scheidegg/Jungfrau and the Schilthorn/Mürren. Ideally, homebase three nights in the village of Gimmelwald and spend a day in each area. If on a speedy train trip, you can overnight into and out of Interlaken. For the speediest look, consider a night in Gimmelwald, breakfast at the Schilthorn, an afternoon doing the Mannlichen-to-Wengen hike, and an evening or night train out. Not spending the night is Alpus-interruptus.

Getting Around the Berner Oberland

For over a hundred years this has been the target of nature-worshipping pilgrims. And the Swiss have made the most exciting Alpine perches accessible by lift or train. Part of the fun (and most of the expense) of the area is riding the many lifts. Generally, scenic trains and lifts are not covered on train passes. There are several discount plans for early-birds, families, seniors, groups, and those staying a while. Get a list of discounts and the free fare and time schedule at any station or in Interlaken. Study the "Alpine Lifts in the Jungfrau Region" chart below. Lifts generally go at least twice an hour 7:00-20:00 but you can take advantage of the time schedule to plan efficiently.

Interlaken

When the 19th-century Romantics redefined mountains as something more than cold and troublesome obstacles, Interlaken became the original Alpine resort. Ever since then, tourists have flocked to the Alps "because they're

Interlaken

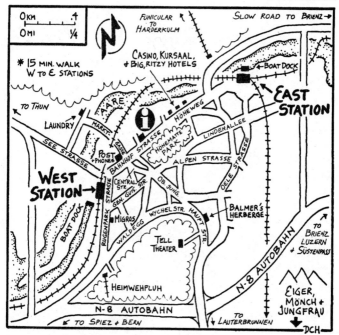

there." Interlaken's glory days are long gone, its elegant old hotels eclipsed by the new, more jet-setty Alpine resorts. Today, its shops are filled with chocolate bars, Swiss Army knives, and sunburned backpackers. Efficient Interlaken is a good administrative and shopping center. Take care of business, give the town a quick look, view the live TV coverage of the Jungfrau and Schilthorn weather in the window of the Schilthornbahn office on the main street (Höheweg), and head for the hills.

Orientation (tel. code: 036)

Tourist Information
The tourist office (on the main street, a 5-minute walk from the West Station, daily 8:00-12:00, 14:00-18:00, less on weekends and off-season; tel. 036/222121) has good information for the whole region and advice on Alpine lift discounts. Pick up a Bern map; while the Jungfrau region map costs 1.50 SF, a perfectly good version of it is in the free Jungfrau region train timetable.

Trains
Interlaken has two train stations. Most major trains stop at the Interlaken-West station. The station's train information desk has some tourist info and an exchange desk with fair rates (daily until 19:00, Sunday until 18:00). An open-late Migros supermarket is across the street. From the Interlaken-East station, private trains (not covered by Eurailpass) take you deep into the mountainous Jungfrau region. Ask at the station about discount passes, special fares, and schedules for the scenic (and non-Eurail) mountain trains (tel. 036/264233). It's a pleasant 15-minute walk between the East and West stations.

Helpful Hints
Telephone: In the center of town, next to the handy post office, you'll find a late-hours long-distance phone booth (daily 7:30-12:00, 13:45-18:30).
Laundry: Helen Schmocker's Wascherei Laundry has a change machine, soap, English instructions, and a pleasant riverside place to hang out (from the post office, follow

Marktgasse over two bridges to Beatenbergstrasse, open daily
7:00-22:00 for self-service, 8 SF to wash and dry 10 pounds;
Monday-Friday 8:00-12:00 and 13:30-18:00 for full service:
drop off 10 pounds and 12 SF in the morning and pick up
clean clothes that afternoon; tel. 221566).

Gimmelwald

Saved from developers by its "avalanche zone" classification,
Gimmelwald is one of the poorest places in Switzerland. Its
economy is stuck in the hay and many of the farmers, unable
to make it in their disadvantaged trade, are subsidized by the
Swiss government. For some travelers, there's little to see in
the village. Others enjoy a fascinating day sitting on a bench
and learning why they say, "If Heaven isn't what it's cracked
up to be, send me back to Gimmelwald."

Take a walk through the town. Notice the traditional
log-cabin architecture and blond-braided children. The
numbers on the buildings are not addresses, but fire insurance numbers. The cute little hut near the station is for stor-
ing and aging cheese, not youth hostelers. Do not confuse
obscure Gimmelwald with touristy and commercialized
Grindelwald just over the Kleine Scheidegg ridge.

Gimmelwald Side of Lauterbrunnen Valley

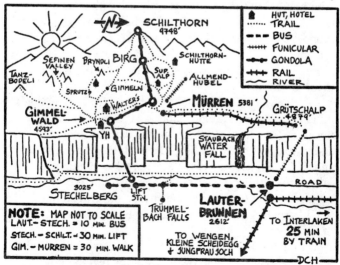

Evening fun in Gimmelwald is found at the youth hostel (lots of young Alp-aholics and a good chance to share information on the surrounding mountains) and up at Walter's Hotel Mittaghorn (see Sleeping, below). Walter's bar is a local farmer's hangout. When they've made their hay, they come here to play. They look like what we'd call "hicks" (former city-slicker Walter still isn't fully accepted by the gang), but they speak some English and can be fun to get to know. Walter knows how many beers they've had according to whether they're talking, singing, fighting, or snoring. For less smoke and some powerful solitude, sit outside (benches just below the rails, 100 yards down the lane from Walter's) and watch the sun tuck the mountaintops into bed as the moon rises over the Jungfrau.

Sights—Alpine Hikes from Gimmelwald

There are days of possible hikes from Gimmelwald. Many are a fun combination of trails, mountain trains, and gondola rides.

▲▲▲**Hike 1: The Schilthorn: Hikes, Lifts, and a 10,000-foot Breakfast**—If the weather's good, have breakfast atop the Schilthorn, in the slowly revolving, mountain-capping restaurant (of James Bond movie fame). The early-bird special gondola tickets (rides before 9:00) take you from Gimmelwald to the Schilthorn and back with a great continental breakfast on top for 55 SF—cheaper than the normal round-trip without breakfast. (Buy tickets from Walter or at the gondola station.) Bear with the slow service, and ask for more hot drinks if necessary. If you're not revolving, ask them to turn it on.

The Gimmelwald–Schilthorn hike is free, if you don't mind a 5,000-foot altitude gain. You can ride up and hike down, or for a less scary hike, go halfway down by cable car and walk down from the Birg station. Lifts go twice an hour, and the ride (including two transfers) takes 30 minutes. Watch the altitude meter in the gondola. Buy the round-trip excursion early-bird fare (cheaper than the Gimmelwald-Schilthorn-Birg ticket) and decide at Birg if you want to hike or ride down.

Linger on top. Piz Gloria has been newly renovated. There's a souvenir shop, the rocks of the region on the

restaurant wall, telescopes, a "touristorama" film room showing explosive highlights from the James Bond thriller that
featured the Schilthorn, and a multi-screen slide show. (It's
free and self-serve. Push the button for slides or, after a long
pause for the projector to rewind, push for 007.)

Watch hang gliders set up, psych up, and take off, flying 30 minutes with the birds to distant Interlaken. Walk
along the ridge out back to the "No High Heels" signpost.
This is a great place for a photo of the "mountain-climber
you." For another cheap thrill, ask the gondola attendant to
crank down the window, stick your head out, and pretend
you're hang gliding, ideally, over the bump going down from
Gimmelwald. (For an expensive thrill, you can bungee-jump
from the Stechelberg-Mürren service gondola.)

Think twice before hiking down from the Schilthorn
(weather can change, have good shoes). Hiking down from
Birg is easier but still very steep and gravelly. Just below Birg
is the Schilthorn-Hutte. Drop in for soup, cocoa, or a coffee
schnapps. You can spend the night in the hut's loft (40
mattresses, open July-September, tel. 551167 or 552512).
Youth hostelers scream down the ice fields on plastic-bag
sleds from the Schilthorn. (English-speaking doctor in
Mürren.)

The most interesting trail from Birg (or Mürren) to
Gimmelwald is the high one via Suppenalp, Schiltalp,
Gimmeln, and the Sprütz waterfall. Mürren has plenty of
shops, bakeries, banks, a TI, a modern sports complex for
rainy days, and accommodations (see Sleeping, below). Ask
at the Schilthorn station in Mürren for a gondola souvenir
pin or sticker.

▲▲▲**Hike 2: The Männlichen-Kleine Scheidegg Hike—**
This is my favorite easy Alpine hike, entertaining you all the
way with glorious Jungfrau, Eiger, and Mönch views. (That's
the Young Maiden being protected from the Ogre by the
Monk.)

If the weather's good, descend from Gimmelwald bright
and early. Catch the post bus to the Lauterbrunnen train station (or drive, parking at the large multi-storied pay lot
behind the station). Buy a ticket to Männlichen and catch the
train. Ride past great valley views to Wengen, where you'll
walk across town (buy a picnic, but don't waste time here if

Alpine Lifts in the Berner Oberland

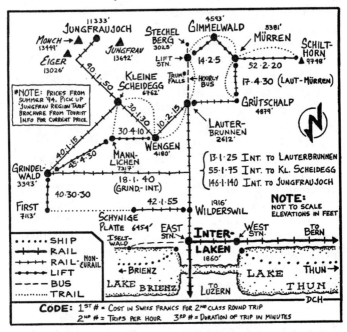

train or hike downhill (30 gorgeous minutes to Wengeralp, 90 more steep minutes from there into the town of Wengen). If the weather turns bad, or you run out of steam, catch the train early at the little Wengeralp station along the way. After Wengeralp, the trail to Wengen is steep and, while not dangerous, requires a good set of knees. Wengen is a fine shopping town. (For accommodations, see Sleeping, below.) The boring final descent from Wengen to Lauterbrunnen is knee-killer steep, so catch the train. Trails may be snow-bound into early summer. Ask about conditions at lift sta-tions. If the Männlichen lift is closed, take the train straight from Lauterbrunnen to Kleine Scheidegg. Many take the risk of slipping and enjoy the Kleine Scheidegg to Wengeralp hike even with a little snow.

▲▲**Hike 3: Schynige Platte to First**—The best day I've had hiking in the Berner Oberland is the demanding 6-hour ridge walk high above Lake Brienz on one side and all that Jungfrau beauty on the other. Start at Wilderswil (just above Interlaken) where you catch the little train up to Schynige

Alpine Lifts in the Berner Oberland

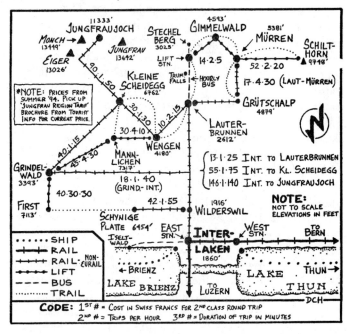

MONCH → ▲ 13449'
JUNGFRAUJOCH 11333'
EIGER ▲ 13026'
▲ JUNGFRAU 13642'
STECHELBERG 3025'
GIMMELWALD 4593'
MÜRREN 5381'
SCHILT-HORN ▲ 9748'

LIFT STN. → 14·2·5
52·2·20
17·4·30 (LAUT–MÜRREN)

KLEINE SCHEIDEGG 6762'
40·1·50
30·1·30
TRÜM FALLS
← HOURLY BUS

#NOTE: PRICES FROM SUMMER '94. PICK UP 'JUNGFRAU REGION TARIF' BROCHURE FROM TOURIST INFO FOR CURRENT PRICE.

GRÜTSCHALP 4879'
10·2·15
LAUTER-BRUNNEN 2612'

30·4·10 X
WENGEN 4180'
40·1·15
45·4·30
MÄNN-LICHEN 7317'

{ 13·1·25 INT. TO LAUTERBRUNNEN
{ 55·1·75 INT. TO KL. SCHEIDEGG
{ 146·1·140 INT. TO JUNGFRAUJOCH

GRINDEL-WALD 3393'
18·1·40 (GRIND–INT.)
40·30·30

FIRST 7113'
42·1·55
WILDERSWIL 1916'

NOTE: NOT TO SCALE ELEVATIONS IN FEET

SCHYNIGE PLATTE 6454'
ISELT-WALD
EAST STN.
INTER-LAKEN 1860'
WEST STN.
TO BERN

•••••• SHIP
┼─┼─┼ RAIL
┼•┼•┼ RAIL NON-EURAIL
•─•─• LIFT
─ ─ ─ BUS
•••••• TRAIL

← BRIENZ
LAKE BRIENZ
TO LUZERN
LAKE THUN
THUN →
DCH

CODE: 1ST # = COST IN SWISS FRANCS FOR 2ND CLASS ROUND TRIP
2ND # = TRIPS PER HOUR   3RD # = DURATION OF TRIP IN MINUTES

train or hike downhill (30 gorgeous minutes to Wengeralp, 90 more steep minutes from there into the town of Wengen). If the weather turns bad, or you run out of steam, catch the train early at the little Wengeralp station along the way. After Wengeralp, the trail to Wengen is steep and, while not dangerous, requires a good set of knees. Wengen is a fine shopping town. (For accommodations, see Sleeping, below.) The boring final descent from Wengen to Lauterbrunnen is knee-killer steep, so catch the train. Trails may be snow-bound into early summer. Ask about conditions at lift stations. If the Männlichen lift is closed, take the train straight from Lauterbrunnen to Kleine Scheidegg. Many take the risk of slipping and enjoy the Kleine Scheidegg to Wengeralp hike even with a little snow.

▲▲**Hike 3: Schynige Platte to First**—The best day I've had hiking in the Berner Oberland is the demanding 6-hour ridge walk high above Lake Brienz on one side and all that Jungfrau beauty on the other. Start at Wilderswil (just above Interlaken) where you catch the little train up to Schynige

Platte (2,000 meters). Walk through the Alpine flower display garden and into the wild Alpine yonder. The high point is Faulhorn (2,680 meters, with its famous mountain-top hotel). Hike to a chairlift called First (2,168 meters), where you descend to Grindelwald and catch a train back to your starting point, Wilderswil (or, if you have a regional train pass or no car but endless money, return to Gimmelwald via Lauterbrunnen from Grindelwald over Kleine Scheidegg).

▲**Other Hikes near Gimmelwald**—For a not-too-tough 3-hour walk (there's a scary 20-minute stretch that comes with ropes) with great Jungfrau views and some mountain farm action, ride the funicular from Mürren to Allmendhübel (1,934 meters), and walk to Marchegg, Saustal, and Grütschalp (a drop of about 500 meters), where you catch the panorama train back to Mürren. An easier version is the lower "Bergweg" from Allmenhübel to Grütschalp via Winteregg. For an easy family stoll with grand views, walk from Mürren just above the train tracks to either Winteregg (40 min, restaurant, playground, train station) or Grütschalp (60 min, train station) and catch the panorama train back to Mürren. An easy, go-as-far-as-you-like trail from Gimmelwald is up the Sefinen Valley. Or, you can wind from Gimmelwald down to Stechelberg (1 hour).

You can get specifics at the Mürren TI. The TI, Hotel Belmont, and Hotel Mittaghorn each have a "Hiking Possibilities: Schilthorn—Panoramaland" flier that describes 12 recommended hikes. For a more extensive rundown on the area (hikes, flora, fauna, culture, travel tips) get Don Chmura's fine 5-SF Gimmelwald guidebook (available at Hotel Mittaghorn).

Rainy Day Options

If clouds roll in, don't despair. They can roll out just as quickly and there are some good bad-weather options. There are easy trails and pleasant walks along the floor of the Lauterbrunnen Valley. If all the waterfalls have you intrigued, sneak a behind-the-scenes look at the valley's most powerful one, Trümmelbach Falls (8 SF, on the Lauterbrunnen-Stechelberg road, daily April-October 9:00-18:00). You'll ride an elevator up through the mountain and climb through several caves to see the melt from the Eiger, Mönch, and Jungfrau grinding like God's bandsaw through the mountain at the rate of up to 20,000 liters a second (nearly double the beer consumption at Oktoberfest). The upper area, "chutes 6 to 10," are the best, so if your legs ache you can skip the lower ones and ride the lift down. Lauterbrunnen's Heimatmuseum (3 SF, mid-June through September, Tuesday, Thursday, Saturday, and Sunday 14:00-17:30, just over the bridge) shows off the local folk culture.

Mürren's slick Sports Center (pool open only mid-June through October) offers a world of indoor activities (7 SF for use of the swimming pool and whirlpool).

Boat Trips from Interlaken—From Interlaken there are regular boat trips on Lake Thun and Lake Brienz. The super-cute and quiet village of Iseltwald is just a bus or boat ride from Interlaken. On Lake Thun, both Spiez and Thun are visit-worthy towns.

▲▲**Ballenberg**—Near Interlaken, the Ballenberg Open-Air Museum is a rich collection of traditional and historic farmhouses from every region of the country. Each house is carefully furnished, and many feature traditional crafts-people at work. The sprawling 50-acre park, laid out roughly as a huge Swiss map, is a natural preserve providing a won-derful setting for this culture-on-a-lazy-Susan look at Switzerland.

The Thurgau house (#621) has an interesting wattle-and-daub (half-timbered construction) display and house #331 has a fun bread museum. Use the 2-SF map/guide. The more expensive picture book is a better souvenir than guide. Open daily April-October 10:00 to 17:00; 12-SF entry, half-price after 16:00 (houses close at 17:00, park stays open later); craft demonstration schedules are listed just inside the entry; tel. 036/511123. There's a reasonable outdoor cafete-ria inside the west entrance, and fresh-baked bread, sausage, and mountain cheese, or other cooked goodies are on sale in several houses. Picnic tables and grills with free firewood are scattered throughout the park. The little wooden village of Brienzwiller (near the east entrance) is a museum in itself with a lovely little church. Trains go regularly from Inter-laken to Brienzwiller, an easy walk from the museum.

Sleeping in the Alps
(1.4 SF = about $1, tel. code: 036)

To inhale the Alps and really hold it in, sleep high in Gimmelwald.

Sleep code: **S**=Single, **D**=Double/Twin, **T**=Triple, **Q**=Quad, **B**=Bath/Shower, **WC**=Toilet, **CC**=Credit Card (Visa, Mastercard, Amex), **SE**=Speaks English (graded **A** through **F**).

Sleeping and Eating in Gimmelwald
(4,500 feet, zip code: 3826)

Poor, happily stuck in the past, avalanche-zone Gimmelwald has a happy youth hostel, a cranky pension, and a creaky hotel. The only bad news is that the lift costs 7 SF each way.

The **Mountain Hostel** (9 SF per bed in 2- to 15-bed rooms, 2 SF for sheets, closed mid-December through February; 50 yards from the lift station, tel. 551704, SE-B) is goat-simple, as clean as its guests, cheap, and very friendly. Its 45 beds are often taken in July and August, so call ahead to Lena, the elderly woman who runs the place. The hostel has low ceilings, a self-serve kitchen (pack in groceries, 20- and 50-cent coins for the stove), coed washrooms, and enough hot water for ten (1 SF, 5 minutes) hot showers a day (or you can drop by the Mürren Sports Center with a towel and 3 SF).

This relaxed hostel is struggling to survive. Please read the signs, respect its rules, and leave it cleaner than you found it. Treat it and Lena with loving care. Without Lena, there's no hostel in Gimmelwald. The place, because of the spirit of its rugged but sensitive visitors and the help of Marc (a local Englishman), almost runs itself. It's one of those rare places where a family atmosphere spontaneously combusts and spaghetti becomes communal as it softens.

The **Pension Gimmelwald** (20-SF dorm beds on its top floor without breakfast, D-90 SF, DB-110 SF, two-night minimum, open mid-June through October, tel. 551730), next door, serves meals.

Hotel Mittaghorn, the treasure of Gimmelwald, is run by Walter Mittler, a perfect Swiss gentleman (D-60 SF, T-85 SF, Q-105 SF, loft beds-25 SF, all with breakfast, family discounts; CH-3826 Gimmelwald/Bern, tel. 551658; SE-A;

reserve by telephone only and then you must reconfirm by telephone the day before your arrival, at this time you can order dinner, a deal at 15 SF if Walter's cooking; don't show up without a reservation; closed for a week in early May and mid-November through March).

Hotel Mittaghorn is a classic, creaky, Alpine-style place with memorable beds, ancient down comforters (short and fat, wear socks and drape the blanket over your feet), and a million-dollar view of the Jungfrau Alps. The hotel has two rooms with private showers and one shower for everyone else (1 SF for 5 minutes). Walter is careful not to get too hectic or big and enjoys sensitive Back Door travelers. He runs the hotel with the help of Don von Gimmelwald (actually Don Chmura, "von" Winnipeg), keeping it simple but with class. This is a good place to receive mail from home (mail barrel in entry hall).

To some, Hotel Mittaghorn is a fire just waiting to happen, with a kitchen that would never pass code, lumpy beds, teeny towels, and nowhere near enough plumbing, run by an eccentric grouch. These people enjoy Interlaken, Wengen, or Mürren, and that's where they should sleep. Be warned, you may meet more of my readers than you hoped for, but it's a fun crowd, an extended family.

Gimmelwald feeds its goats better than its people. The hostel has a decent members' kitchen but serves no food. There are no groceries in town. The wise and frugal buy food from the Co-ops in Mürren or Lauterbrunnen and pack it in. Walter, at Hotel Mittaghorn, is Gimmelwald's best cook (not saying much, but he is good). His salad is best eaten one leaf at a time with your fingers. There's no menu, and dinner's served at 19:30 sharp. When Walter's in the mood, his place is the best bar in town: good cheap beer, strong *kaffee fertigs* (coffee with schnapps), and Heidi cocoa (cocoa *mit schnapps*) or Virgin Heidis.

Meals (including hamburgers I'll never forget) are also served at Pension Gimmmelwald next to the hostel. For a rare bit of ruggedness and the best budget food in the center of Mürren, eat at the Stägerstübli. Brian's sandwich bar at the Hotel Belmont across from the Mürren train station is ideal for those who blew their budget on Alpine lifts.

Sleeping in Mürren (5,500 feet, zip code: 3825)

Mürren is as pleasant as an Alpine resort can be. It's traffic-free, filled with bakeries, cafés, souvenirs, old-timers with walking sticks, GE employees enjoying incentive trips, and Japanese making movies of each other with a Fujichrome backdrop. Its chalets are prefab-rustic. Sitting on a ledge 2,000 feet above the Lauterbrunnen valley, surrounded by a fortissimo chorus of mountains, it has all the comforts of home and then some, with Alp-high prices. Mürren's Tourist Office can find you a room, give hiking advice, and change money (in the Sporthaus, mountain bikes for rent, open daily 9:00-12:00, 13:00-18:30, less off-season, tel. 551616).

Hotel Belmont (D-100 SF, DB-130 SF, with breakfast, discounts for rooms without views, CC:VM; across from the train station, tel. 553535, fax 553531, SE-A) offers Mürren's best budget rooms. Andreas and Anne Marie Goetschi, former travelers with a great "back door" travel perspective, make this a friendly home away from home in Mürren. Their restaurant is economical and the attached "Brian's sandwich bar" is a fun hangout. **Hotel Alpenblick** (tel. 551327, fax 551391, closed off-season), next door, and **Hotel Alpina** (tel. 551361) also have affordable rooms.

Chalet Fontana (35 SF-45 SF per person in doubles or triples with breakfast and kitchenette, tel. 552686; across the street from the Stägerstübli in the town center, mid-June through September), run by Denise Fussel, is well-worn and basic but a rare budget option in Mürren. Off-season you can rent a room here cheaper through the Ed Abegglen shop next door (tel. 551245).

Sleeping in Wengen (4,200 feet)

Wengen is a fancy Mürren on the other side of the valley. It's traffic-free and an easy lift ride above Lauterbrunnen. Wengen is halfway up to Kleine Scheidegg and Männlichen. It has more tennis courts than budget beds. **Hotel Berner-hof** (D-80 SF, DB-120 SF with breakfast, more during peak times and for one night, tel. 552721 or 553358) has dorm beds (20 SF, no sheets). The **Chalet Bergheim**, open June through mid-October, has reasonable doubles, and six 20-SF dorm beds (plus 6 SF for sheets and

11 SF for breakfast, tel. 552755). The **Chalet Schweizerheim Garni** (D-100 SF, tel. 551581, summer only) is the cheapest hotel in Wengen.

Sleeping in Kleine Scheidegg (6,762 feet)
For 30-SF dorm beds with breakfast high in the mountains, you can sleep at Kleine Scheidegg's **Bahnhof Buffet** (tel. 551151) or at **Restaurant Grindelwaldblick** (12-bed dorm rooms, no sheets, tel. 533043, open June-October).

Sleeping below Gimmelwald, near the Stechelberg Lift (2,800 feet)
The local **Naturfreundehaus Alpenhof** (60 coed beds, 4-8 per room, 16 SF per bed, 7-SF breakfast, 13-SF dinner, no sheets; Stechelberg, tel. 551202; closed November; near Stechelberg bus stop) is a rugged Alpine lodge for local hikers at the far end of Lauterbrunnen Valley. The neighboring **Hotel Stechelberg** (D-78 SF, DB-98 SF and 118 SF including breakfast, tel. 552921, SE-B) has 13 clean and quiet rooms. **Klara von Allmen** (D-50 SF, minimum two nights; just over the river from the Stechelberg post office at big "*Zimmer*" sign, Pfang, 3824 Stechelberg, tel. 552554, SE-F) rents out three rooms in a quiet, scenic, and folky setting.

Sleeping in Lauterbrunnen (2,600 feet)
Masenlager Stocki (12 SF a night with sheets in an easy-going little 30-bed coed dorm with a kitchen; tel. 551754; across the river, take the first left; closed November through mid-December) is a great value. Two campgrounds just south of town work very hard to provide 15- to 25-SF beds. They each have dorms, 2-, 4-, and 6-bed bungalows, no sheets, kitchen facilities, and big English-speaking tour groups. **Camping Jungfrau** (tel. 552010), romantically situated just beyond the stones hurled by Staubbach Falls, is huge and well organized, with a Heidi Shop and clocks showing the time in Sydney and Vancouver. It also has fancier cabins and trailers for the classier camper. **Schützenbach Campground** (tel. 551268), on the left just past Lauterbrunnen toward Stechelberg, is simpler.

Sleeping in Interlaken
(1.4 SF = about $1, tel. code: 036)

I'd head for Gimmelwald. Interlaken is not the Alps. But if you must stay, here are two good choices: **Hotel Lotschberg** (DBWC-100 SF-180 SF, CC:VMA, 2-minute walk from the West Station, look for the wall painting, at General Guesan Strasse 31, 3800 Interlaken, tel. 036/222545), with easy parking and a sun terrace, is run by English-speaking Susie and Fritz. And backpackers enjoy **Balmer's Herberge** (17-SF dorm beds, 28 SF per person in simple doubles, and 12 SF in overflow on-the-floor accommodations, all with breakfast; Haupstrasse 23, in Matten, a 15-minute walk from either Interlaken station, tel. 221961). This Interlaken institution is run by a creative tornado of entrepreneurial energy, Eric Balmer. With movies, ping-pong, laundromat, a secondhand English book-swapping library, rafting excursions, plenty of tips on budget eating and hiking, and a friendly, hardworking, mostly American staff, this little Nebraska is home for those who miss their fraternity (but not their parents).

Train Connections

Interlaken to: Bern (hrly, 60 min), **Spiez** (2/hr, 15 min), **Brienz** (hrly, 20 min). While there are a few long trains from Interlaken, you'll generally connect from Bern where trains go to **Frankfurt** (4½ hrs), **Munich** (4/day, 5½ hrs), **Lausanne** (hrly, 70 min), **Paris** (4/day, 4½ hrs), and **Zurich** (hrly, 75 min).

Interlaken and Gimmelwald: Take the train from the Interlaken-East station to Lauterbrunnen, then cross the street to catch the funicular to Mürren. You'll ride up to Grütschalp where a special scenic train (*panorama fahrt* in German) rolls you along the cliff into Mürren. From there, either walk an easy, paved 30 minutes downhill to Gimmelwald or walk 10 minutes across Mürren to catch the gondola (7 SF and a 5-minute steep uphill backtrack) to Gimmelwald. A good bad-weather option (or vice versa) is to ride the post bus from Lauterbrunnen (leaves at 5 minutes past the hour) to Stechelberg and the base of the Schilthornbahn (a big, gray gondola station, tel. 036/231444 or 552141).

By car, it's a 30-minute drive from Interlaken to Stechelberg. The parking lot at the gondola station is safe and free. Gimmelwald is the first stop above Stechelberg on the Schilthorn gondola (7 SF, 2 trips/hr at :25 and :55; get off at first stop, walk into the village, hard right at PTT, signs direct you up the path on a steep 300-yard climb to the chalet marked simply "Hotel"). This is my home in Switzerland, Walter's Hotel Mittaghorn. Note that for a week in early May and from mid-November through early December, the Schilthornbahn is closed for servicing.

APPENZELL

Welcome to cowbell country. In moo-mellow and storybook-friendly Appenzell, you'll find the warm, intimate side of the land of staggering icy Alps. Savor Appenzell's cozy small-town ambience.

Appenzell is Switzerland's most traditional region—and the butt of much local humor because of it. This is Landsgemeinde country, where entire villages would meet in town squares to vote (featured on most postcard racks). Until 1991, the women of Appenzell couldn't vote on local issues.

A gentle beauty blankets the region overlooked by the 8,200-foot peak, Säntis. As you travel, you'll enjoy an ever-changing parade of finely carved chalets, traditional villages, and cows moaning "milk me." While farmers' daughters make hay in bikinis, old ladies walk the steep roads with scythes, looking as if they just pushed the grim reaper down the hill. When locals are asked about their cheese, they clench their fists as they answer, "It's the best."

If you're here in early September there's a good chance you'll get in on—or at least have your road blocked by—the ceremonial procession of flower-bedecked cows and whistling herders in traditional, formal outfits. The festive march down from the high pastures is a spontaneous move by the herding families, and when they finally do burst into town (a slow-motion Swiss Pamplona), the people become children again, dropping everything and running into the streets.

The center of the Appenzell region is Appenzell town. The nearby village of Ebenalp, snuggled into a cliff, is my top choice for a home base.

Planning Your Time

The area's charms are subtle and its public transportation a little disappointing. For many on a fast trip with no car, the area is not worth the trouble. But by car it's a joy. And anyone hoping to get a broad feel for Switzerland has to stop here. Ideally, it's an interesting way for drivers to connect Tirol and Bavaria with the Berner Oberland (Jungfrau region): drive in from Tirol in time to get up the lift and hike down to Ebenalp; descend the next morning and spend the day sampling the small town charms of Appenzell; and get to the Interlaken area that night.

Transportation Connections

Those with a car have the region by the tail. Those without will need a little more time and patience. The hourly train connects Appenzell with **Wasserauen** (15 min) and **Herisau** (30 min) from where the bigger train goes hourly to **St. Gallen** (20 min) and **Luzern** (2 hrs). Regional buses connect all towns several times a day.

Sights—Appenzell

Appenzell Town—This is the most "typical" town around, where the kids play "barn," not "house," while mom and dad watch yodeling on TV. The tourist information office (9:00-12:00, 14:00-17:00, Saturday 9:00-12:00, tel. 071/874111) is on the main street, Hauptgasse, next to the City Hall. Ask about an Appenzeller folk evening (most nights, July-September, often free, dinner usually optional). The little folk museum next to the TI is good. The Appenzeller *bier* is famous, good, and about the only thing cheap in the region. For accommodations, see Sleeping, below.

Appenzell Region

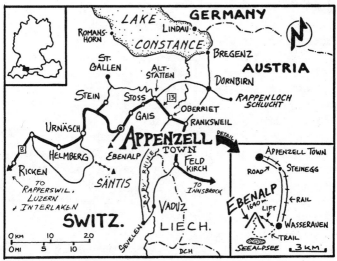

Ebenalp—This cliff-hanger of a town is a thin-air alternative to Appenzell town. Ride the lift from Wasserauen, 5 miles south of Appenzell town, to Ebenalp (5,000 feet). On the way up, you'll get a sneak preview of Ebenalp's cave church and guest house, and from the top, a sweeping view of the entire region all the way to Lake Constance (Bodensee).

From the top of the lift, take a 12-minute hike downhill through a prehistoric cave, past a hermit's home (now a tiny museum, always open) and the 400-year-old Wildkirchi cave church (hermit monks lived there from 1658-1853), to a 150-year-old guesthouse built precariously into the cliffside. Originally used by pilgrims who climbed here to have the hermit pray for them, Berggasthaus Ascher now welcomes tourists. See Sleeping, below.

From Ebenalp's sunny cliff perch, you can almost hear the cows munching on the far side of the valley. Only the parasailers, like neon jellyfish, tag your world 20th-century. In the distance, nestled below Säntis Peak, is the Seealpsee (lake). The interesting 90-minute hike down to the lake is steep but a joy.

The Ebenalp lift runs twice an hour until 19:00 in July and August, 18:00 in June and September, otherwise the last lift is at 17:00 (19 SF round-trip, 15 SF one-way, pick up the free one-page hiking map, tel. 071/881212).

▲▲**Stein**—In the town of Stein, the Appenzell Showcase Cheese Dairy (*Schaukäserei*) is open daily 8:00-19:00 (cheese-making normally 9:00-11:00 and 13:00-15:00). It's fast, free, and well explained in the free English brochure (with cheese recipes). The lady at the cheese counter loves to cut it so you can sample it. They also have yogurt and cheap boxes of cold iced tea for sale. Stein's TI and a great folk (*Volkskunde*) moo-seum are next door. This is the ultimate cow-culture museum with old-fashioned cheese-making demonstrations, peasant houses, fascinating and complex embroidering machinery, lots of cow art, and folk craft demonstrations daily in the summer (7 SF, 10:00-17:00, closed for lunch and on Monday morning, may open a little early if you ask nicely; borrow English booklet; tel. 071/591159.)

▲**Urnäsch**—This appealing one-street town has my

nomination for Europe's cutest museum. The Appenzeller Museum (on the town square, 4 SF, open daily in summer 13:30-17:00, less in spring and fall, closed in winter; good English description brochure; will open for groups of five or more if you call the director at 581487 or 582322) brings this region's folk-customs to life. Warm and homey, it's a happy little honeycomb of Appenzeller culture. The Gasthaus Ochsen, three doors down from the museum, is a fine traditional hotel (D-80 SF, tel. 071/581117) with good food, low ceilings, and wonderful atmosphere. Peek into its old restaurant.

Sleeping in Appenzell
(1.5 SF = about $1, zip code: 9050, tel. code: 071)

Sleeping in the town of Appenzell
The town is small but quite touristy. Hotels are expensive; the *Zimmer* are a 10-minute walk from the center.

Sleep code: **S**=Single, **D**=Double/Twin, **T**=Triple, **Q**=Quad, **B**=Bath/Shower, **WC**=Toilet, **CC**=Credit Card (**V**isa, **M**astercard, **A**mex), **SE**=Speaks English (graded **A** through **F**).

The **Gasthaus Hof** offers by far the best cheap beds in town in its modern Matratzenlager (20 SF per bed in 6- to 8-bed rooms with breakfast, sheets 6 SF more; centrally located just off the Landsgemeindeplatz, tel. 872210, Herr Dörig). Outside of peak times, you'll be sleeping alone in a warehouse of bunkbeds. Gasthaus Hof serves good 20-SF *Rösti*, the area's cheesy potato specialty.

Hotel Adler (D-100 SF, DB-140 SF, CC:VMA, elevator; a block from the TI, just over the bridge, tel. 871389, fax 871365; SE-A), above a delicious café in a fine location, offers three kinds of rooms: modern, newly refurbished traditional Appenzeller, or old and basic. **Hotel Taube** is also good (D-100 SF, DB-120 SF, CC:VMA; between the station and the main street, Hirschengasse 8, tel. 871149). The only inexpensive hotel in town, **Pension Union** (D-70 SF, DB-80 SF; between the station and the main street, tel. 871420, SE-F) is a peaceful, grandfatherly old place.

Haus Lydia (D-75 SF; Eggerstandenstrasse 53, CH 9050 Appenzell, east of the center over the bridge and past the Mercedes-Esso station, tel. 874233) is an Appenzell-style home filled with tourist information and a woodsy folk atmosphere, on the edge of town with a garden and a powerful mountain view. This wonderful six-room *Zimmer* is run by Frau Mock-Inauen.

Johann Ebneter speaks English and runs a friendly and modern *Zimmer* in the same area (D-80 SF; Mooshalden-strasse 14, tel. 873487).

Sleeping in Ebenalp

There's no real reason to sleep in Appenzell town. The Ebenalp lift in Wasserauen is a few minutes' drive or train ride south. For a memorable experience, stay in the **Berggasthaus Ascher** (13 SF for a dorm bed, blankets but no sheets required or provided, 10 SF for breakfast, good dinners; run by Claudia and Bennie Knechtle-Wyss and their five little children; 9057 Weissbad, 12 minutes by steep trail below top of lift, tel. 071/881142; open daily May-October). Their 150-year-old house has only rainwater and no shower. While it's often festive and can sleep 40 people (literally four hikers to three mattresses), if you come outside a weekend you'll normally get a small woody dorm to yourself. The hut is actually built onto the cliffside; its back wall is the rock. From the toilet you can study this alpine architecture. Sip your coffee on the deck, behind drips from the gnarly over-hang a hundred yards above. The goats have their cliff hut adjacent. The guestbook goes back to 1941 and the piano, in the comfortable dining/living room, was brought in by heli-copter. For a great 45-minute pre-dinner check-out-the-goats hike, take the high trail towards the lake; circle clock-wise back up the peak to the lift and down the way you originally came.

Less atmospheric and more normal is the **Berg Gasthaus Ebenalp**, just above the lift (23-SF dorm bed with breakfast, D-74 SF; family Sutter; tel. 071/881194). From Wasserauen at the base of the lift, you can walk 30 minutes uphill to **Berggasthaus Seealpsee**, situated on an idyllic alpine lake by the same name (D-76 SF, loft dorm beds-10 SF plus 10 SF for breakfast; Dörig family; 9057 Weissbad, tel. 071/881140).

Route Tips for Drivers

Hall to Appenzell (130 miles): From the Austria/
Switzerland border town of Feldkirch, it's an easy scenic
drive through Altstätten and Gais to Appenzell. At the Swiss
border you must buy an annual road-use permit for 300 AS
or 30 SF if you want to use the Swiss autobahns (you do). It's
easy to slip across the border without buying one. But anyone driving on a Swiss autobahn without this tax sticker is
likely to be cop-stopped and fined.

From picturesque Altstätten, you'll wind up a steep
mountain pass and your world becomes H.O.-gauge. The
Stoss railroad station, straddling the summit of a mountain
pass, has glorious views. Park here, cross to the chapel and
walk through the meadow, past munching cows, to the monument that celebrates a local Appenzeller victory over
Habsburg Austria. From this spectacular spot, you can see
the Rhine Valley, Liechtenstein, and the Austrian Alps.

Side Trip through Liechtenstein?—If you must see the
tiny and touristy country of Liechtenstein, take this 30-
minute detour: from Feldkirch south on E77, drive through
Schaan to Vaduz, the capital. Park near the City Hall, post
office, and tourist office. Passports can be stamped (for a
small fee) in the tourist office. Stamp collectors make a bee-
line for the post office across the street while the prince
looks down on his 4-by-12-mile country from his castle, a
20-minute hike above Vaduz (it's closed but offers a fine
view; catch the trail from Café Berg). Liechtenstein's banks
(open until 16:30) sell Swiss francs at uniform and good
rates. To leave, cross the Rhine at Rotenboden, immediately
get on the autobahn heading north from Sevelen to the
Oberriet exit, and check another country off your list.

Appenzell to Interlaken/Gimmelwald (120 miles): It's
a 3-hour drive from Appenzell to Ballenberg and another
hour from there to the Gimmelwald lift. Head west out of
Appenzell town on the Urnäsch road, taking the first right
(after about 2 miles, easy to miss, sign to Herisau/Wattwil)
to Stein. In Stein, Schaukäserei signs direct you to a big,
modern building. From there, wind scenically south to
Urnäsch and down the small road (signs to Hemberg) to
Wattwil. Somewhere along the Urnäsch-Hemberg road, stop
to ask an old local if this is the way to Wattwil (or San

Jose)—just to hear the local dialect and to see the healthy outdoor twinkle in his or her eyes up close. Drive through Ricken, into the town of Rapperswil, following green signs to Zurich over the long lake bridge, and southward following blue signs to Einsiedeln and Gotthard. You'll go through the town of Schwyz, the historic core of Switzerland that gave its name to the country.

From Brunnen, one of the busiest, most expensive to build, and most impressive roads in Switzerland wings you along the Urnersee. It's dangerously scenic, so stop at the parking place after the first tunnel (on right, opposite Stoos turn-off) where you can enjoy the view and a rare Turkish toilet. Follow signs to Gotthard through Flüelen, then autobahn for Luzern, vanishing into a long tunnel that should make you feel a little better about your 30-SF autobahn sticker. Exit at the Stans-Nord exit (signs to Interlaken). Go along the Alpnachersee south toward Sarnen. Continue past Sarnensee to Brienzwiller before Brienz. A sign at Brienzwiller will direct you to the Ballenberg Freilicht (Swiss Open-Air) Museum/Ballenberg Ost. You can park here, but I prefer the west entrance, a few minutes down the road near Brienz.

From Brienzwiller, take the new autobahn to Interlaken along the south side of Lake Brienz. Cruise through the old resort town down Interlaken's main street from the Ost Bahnhof, past the cow field with a great Eiger-Jungfrau view on your left and grand old hotels, the TI, post office, and banks on your right, to the West Bahnhof at the opposite end of town. Park there. Gimmelwald is a 30-minute drive and a 5-minute gondola ride away.

WEST SWITZERLAND

Enjoy urban Switzerland at its best in the charming, compact capital of Bern. Ramble the ramparts of Murten, Switzerland's best-preserved medieval town, and resurrect the ruins of an ancient Roman capital in nearby Avenches. The Swiss countryside offers up chocolates, Gruyères cheese, a folk museum, and summer skiing. On Lake Geneva, the Swiss Riviera, explore the romantic Château Chillon and stylishly syncopated Montreux.

South of Murten, the predominant language is French, *s'il vous plaît*, and as you'll see, that means more than language. For West Switzerland, Murten—Morat, if you're speaking French—is the ideal homebase.

Planning Your Time

Nothing in the region merits a lot of time on a quick trip. Bern, Lake Geneva, and Murten are each worth half a day. Bern is easily seen en route to Murten. I'd establish a homebase in Murten from which to explore the southwest in a day by car. Without a car you might use a better transportation hub such as Bern or Montreux.

For a day by car from Murten: 8:45, depart; 10:00, tour Chateau Chillon; 11:30, quick visit or drive through Montreux, Vevey, and the Corniche de Laveau; 14:00, cheese-making demo in Gruyeres or Moleson; 15:30, Gruerien folk museum in Bulle; 18:00, Roman ruins in Avenches; 19:00, home in Murten for salad by the sea.

Bern

Stately but human, classy but fun, the Swiss capital gives you the most (maybe even the only) enjoyable look at urban Switzerland. User-friendly Bern is packed into a peninsula bounded by the Aare River.

Tourist Information

Start your visit at the tourist office inside the train station (daily 9:00-20:30, until 18:30 in winter, tel. 031/3116611). Pick up a map of Bern (and any other Swiss cities you'll be visiting), a list of city sights, and information on the

Parliament tour, the clock, or whatever you're interested in, and confirm your plans.

Getting Around

Bern is easy. From the train station, it's all downhill through the heart of town to the bear pits and Rose Garden (a 15-minute stroll), the catch trolley #12 back up to the station (buy the cheapest, yellow-button ticket from the machine at the stop).

Sights—Bern

▲▲**The Old Town**—Window-shopping and people-watching through the lovely arcaded streets and busy market squares are Bern's top attractions. This is my favorite shopping town: prices are so high there's no danger of buying. Great browsing. (Shops open 8:00-18:30, Saturday 8:00-16:00, Thursday until 21:00, closed Sunday and Monday until 14:00.)

Bern

Map of Bern showing: Train Stn., Main Post, Kunst Museum (Klee), Kornhaus-Bridge, Kornhaus-Keller, Rose Garden, Unterfor Bridge, To Autobahn N-1 Zurich/Basel, To Autobahn Exit Neufeld, Spitalgasse, Marktgasse, Bärenplatz, Kramgasse, Ger-Gasse, Junk-Gasse, Nydegg, Münster, Clock Tower, Laupenstrasse, To Autobahn N-12 Fribourg, Bundesgasse, Funicular, Hostel, Alp. Post Mus., Bundeshaus (Parliament Bldg.), Aarebad River Baths, Kirchenfeld Bridge, Bern. Hist. Museum, Natur. Hist. Museum, Aare River, Muristrasse, Bear Pits, To Autobahn N-6 Luzern/Interlaken, To Autobahn N-12 Fribourg, Eiger Strasse, Kirchenfeld Strasse, Thunstrasse. Scale: 0 KM to .5, 0 Mi to ¼. —DCH—

Clock Tower (Zytglogge-turm)—The clock performs at 4 minutes before each hour. Apparently this slowest-moving 5-minute non-event in Europe was considered entertaining in 1530. To pass the time during the performance, read the TI's brochure explaining what's so interesting about the fancy old clock. Enthusiasts can tour the medieval mechanics daily at 16:30 (May-October, tickets 5 SF at the TI or on the spot).

Cathedral—The 1421 Swiss late-Gothic *Münster*, or cathedral, is worth a look (10:00-17:00, Sunday 11:00-17:00, closed Monday, shorter hours off-season). Climb the spiral staircase 100 yards above the town for the view, exercise, and a chance to meet a live church watchman. Peter Probst and his wife, Sigi, live way up there, watching over the church, answering questions, and charging tourists for the view.

Parliament (Bundeshaus)—You can tour Switzerland's imposing Parliament building (free 45-minute tours most days at 9:00, 10:00, 11:00, 14:00, 15:00, and 16:00, tel. 031/322 8522 to confirm; closed about March, June, September, and December; minimum group size: five people). Don't miss the view from the Bundeshaus terrace. You may see some national legislators, but you wouldn't know it—everything looks very casual for a national capital.

Einstein's House—Einstein did much of his most important thinking while living in this house on the old town's main drag. It was just another house to me, but I guess everything's relative (2 SF, Kramgasse 49, 10:00-17:00, Saturday until 16:00, closed Sunday, Monday, December, and January).

▲Bear Pits and Rose Garden—The symbol of Bern is the bear, and some lively ones frolic their days away (8:00-18:00) to the delight of locals and tourists alike in the big, barren, concrete pits (or *Graben*) just over the river. Up the paved pathway is the Rosengarten—worth the walk for the great city view. The Rosengarten restaurant's 16-SF lunch special comes with a great view (tel. 031/331 32 06).

▲▲The Berner Swim—For something to write home about, join the local merchants, legislators, publishers, students, and carp in a lunchtime float down the Aare River. The Bernese, proud of their very clean river and their basic ruddiness, have a tradition—sort of a wet, urban *paseo*. On hot summer days, they hike upstream 5 to 30 minutes and float playfully or sleepily back down to the excellent (and free) riverside baths and pools (*Aarebad*) just below the Parliament building. If the river is a bit much, you're welcome to enjoy just the Aarebad. If the river is not enough, a popular daytrip is to raft all the way from Thun to Bern.

▲▲**Museum of Fine Arts (Kunstmuseum)**—While it features 1,000 years of local art and some Impressionism, the real hit is its fabulous collection of Paul Klee's playful and colorful paintings. If you don't know Klee, I'd love to introduce you. (6 SF, 10:00-17:00, Tuesday until 21:00, closed Monday, 4 blocks from the station, #12 Holdergasse).

Other Bern Museums—Across the bridge from the Parliament building on Helvetiaplatz are several museums (Alpine, Berner History, Postal) that sound more interesting than they are. Nearly all are open 10:00-17:00 and closed on Monday.

Sleeping in Bern
(1.5 SF = about $1, tel. code: 031)
These are in the old town about a 10-minute walk from the station.

Sleep code: **S**=Single, **D**=Double/Twin, **T**=Triple, **Q**=Quad, **B**=Bath/Shower, **WC**=Toilet, **CC**=Credit Card (**V**isa, **M**astercard, **A**mex), **SE**=Speaks English (graded **A** through **F**).

Hotel Hospiz sur Heimat (S-62 SF, SB-85 SF, D-92 SF, DB-120 SF, T-123 SF, TB-147 SF, Q-164 SF, CC: VMA, elevator; Gerechtigkeitsgasse 50, on the main street near the bridge and bears, tram #12 from the station, tel. 311 04 36, fax 312 3386) is Bern's best budget hotel value.

Hotel Goldener Schlüssel (S-60 SF, SB-82 SF, D-96 SF, DB-120 SF, CC:VM, elevator, Rathausgasse 72, CH-3011 Bern, tel. 311 0216, fax 311 5688) is a basic, comfortable, crank-'em-out old hotel in the center.

Bern's big, newly renovated, sterile, well-run **IYHF hostel** (15-SF beds, nonmembers 21 SF, breakfast 5 SF; down the stairs from the Parliament building, by the river, at Weihergasse 4, 3005 Bern, tel. 311 6316 or 226316) has 8- to 26-bed rooms and provides an all-day lounge, laundry machines, and cheap meals (office open 7:00-9:30 and 15:00-24:00).

West Switzerland

Train Connections

Bern to: Frankfurt (4½ hrs), **Munich** (4/day, 5½ hrs), **Lausanne** (hrly, 70 min), **Paris** (4/day, 4½ hrs), and **Zurich** (hrly, 75 min), **Murten** (hrly, 30 min), **Fribourg** (2/hr, 30 min), **Interlaken** (2/hr, 60 min).

Murten

The finest medieval ramparts in Switzerland surround the 4,600 people of Murten (or Morat, in French). We're on the lingua-cusp of Switzerland: 25 percent of Murten speaks French; a few miles to the south and west nearly everyone does. Murten is a mini-Bern with three parallel streets, the middle one nicely arcaded with breezy outdoor cafés and elegant shops (closed Mondays). Its castle is romantically set, overlooking the tiny Murtensee and the rolling vineyards of gentle Mount Vully in the distance. Try some Vully wine. Murten is touristic but seems to be enjoyed mostly by its own people. Nearby Avenches, with its Roman ruins, glows at sunset.

Tourist Information

The TI (tel. 037/715112, open April-October about 9:00-12:00, 14:30-18:00, closed Saturday afternoon and Sunday) tries to be helpful, but there's not much to say. Ask about their free town walks (10:30 in the summer). Hourly trains connect Murten with Fribourg (30 min), where major trains leave frequently for Bern and Lake Geneva.

Sights—Murten

Rampart Ramble—The only required sightseeing is to do the rampart ramble (free, always open, easy stairway access on east side of town). **Town Museum**—The town history museum in an old mill (closed Monday) is not quite worth a look. **Lakeside Fun**—You can rent a bike just outside the wall or at the train station for a lakeside ride. The lake-front offers a popular but pricey restaurant (Les Bain), a lavish swimming pool, and 1-hour lake cruises (free with train passes, departing daily in summer at 15:40).

Avenches—Avenches, 4 miles south of Murten, was Aventicum, the Roman capital of the Confederation Helvetica. Back then its population was 50,000. Today it could barely fill the well-worn ruins of its 15,000-seat Roman amphitheater. You can tour the Roman museum but the best experience is some quiet time at sunset at the evocative Roman theater in the fields, a short walk out of town (always open). Avenches, with a pleasant, small-French-town feel, is a quieter place to stay than Murten. See Sleeping, below. (TI tel. 037/751159).

Sleeping and Eating in Murten and Avenches
(1.5 SF = about $1, tel. code: 037)

Sleeping in Murten

Hotel Ringmauer (that's German for "ramparts," S-55 SF, D-100 SF, CC:VM; 2 Deutsche Kirchgasse, near the wall on the side farthest from the lake, tel. 711101) is Murten's only good accommodations deal, and this place is great. Run by Frau Kramer (SE-A), the Ringmauer is friendly, very characteristic, a block from the town center, clean as a croissant, and has showers and toilets within a naked dash of each room. It's my nominee for the "best modern hallway art in an old hotel" and the "best bathroom hardware" awards. It's a bowl-of-apples and homemade-marmalade kind of place with a good restaurant (try the tasty 10-SF *Rösti*; restaurant closed on Saturday).

Hotel Murtenhof (DB-120 SF-200 SF, CC:VMA, SE-A; next to the castle on Rathausgasse, tel. 715656, fax 715059), a full-fledged hotel, is a worthwhile splurge with all the comforts and a lake view.

I eat on **Hotel Murtenhof's terrace** every night for their salad bar (summer only): 7 SF for a small plate, 14 SF for the big one; the small one—carefully stacked—is plenty, comes with wonderful bread and a sunset over the lake). The small plate is meant as a side dish (no bread) but you can usually just come in, stack up the salad, eat it, and get away with a 7-SF meal. The romantic terrace is a good place to try the Vully wine—just point to the vineyards across the lake. (Handy toddlers' play area next to restaurant.) For a cheap hot meal, the Migros and Co-op supermarkets (just outside three of the town gates) have cafeterias.

Sleeping in Avenches

The Avenches **IYHF hostel** (21 SF for bed, sheets, and breakfast, more for nonmembers; Rue du Lavoir 5, 3 blocks from the center at the medieval *lavoir*, or laundry), the only hostel in the area, is a beauty. It's run by the Dhyaf family, with 4- to 8-bed rooms, a homey TV room, ping-pong, a big backyard, and a very quiet setting near the Roman theater (7:00-9:00 and 17:00-22:00, tel. 037/752666, fax 752717).

Hotel de L'Union (D-80 SF, DB-100 SF, TB-150 SF; rue Centrale 23, tel. 037/751384) is a simple old place, mostly a restaurant with a few two- and three-bed rooms upstairs, shower down the hall, right on the central square of Avenches, 2 blocks from the Roman amphitheater. It's nothing special except for its price and location.

Swiss Countryside

The Swiss countryside is sprinkled with tasty chocolates, summer skiing, smelly cheese, and sleepy cows. If you're traveling between Murten, Montreux, and Interlaken, take in a few of the countryside's sights, tastes, and smells.

Getting Around

By public transportation, you'll find plenty of cross-country trolleys and buses using Fribourg and Bulle as hubs. For example: **Bulle-Gruyères** (15 min, 7/day), **Fribourg-Bulle** (45 min, hrly), **Avenches-Fribourg** (30 min, 7/day), **Murten-Fribourg** (30 min, hrly).

Sights—Swiss Countryside

▲**Caillers Chocolate Factory**—The town of Broc is chock full of mourning chocoholics. The last great Swiss chocolate factory tour is now dead . . . for hygienic reasons. While you can no longer drool in front of a molten river of your favorite chocolate, you can see a 40-minute movie and stuff yourself with free melt-in-your-hands samples at the Caillers Chocolate factory, the smell of which dominates the town (free, May-October, Monday afternoon through Friday, closed July, reservation required, tel. 029/65 151, follow signs to Nestlé and Broc Fabrique). Broc town is just the sleepy, sweet-smelling home of the chocolate-makers. It has a small, very typical hotel, the Auberge des Montagnards (D-60 SF, great Gruyères view, elegant dining room, tel. 029/61526).

▲▲**Musée Gruèrien**—Somehow the unassuming little town of Bulle built a refreshing, cheery folk museum that manages to teach you all about life in these parts and leave you feeling very good. It's small and easy (10:00-12:00, 14:00-17:00, closed Sunday morning and Monday, 4 SF plus 1 SF for the excellent English guide, tel. 029/27260). When it's over, the guide reminds you, "The Golden Book of Visitors awaits your signature and comments. Don't you think this museum deserves another visit? Thank you!"

▲**Gruyères**—This ultra-touristy town, famous for its cheese, fills its fortified little hilltop like a bouquet. Its ramparts are a park, and the ancient buildings serve the tourist crowds. The castle is mediocre, and you don't need to stay long, but make a short stop for the setting. Minimize your walk by driving up to the second parking lot. Hotels in Gruyères are expensive.

▲▲**Gruyères Fromagerie**—There are two very different cheese-making exhibits to choose from. Five miles above Gruyères, a dark and smoky 17th-century farmhouse in

Moleson gives a fun look at the old and smelly craft (mid-May through mid-October 9:30-18:30, tel. 029/62434). Closer, slicker, and very modern, the cheese-production center at the foot of Gruyères town (follow Fromagerie signs) opens its doors to tourists with a good continuous English audiovisual presentation (free, daily 8:00-18:30). Cheese is made at each place (usually 10:00-11:00 and 14:00-15:00). The cute cheese shop in the modern center has lunches and picnic stuff (closed from 12:00-13:30).

▲**Glacier des Diablerets**—For a grand Alpine trip to the tip of a 10,000-foot peak, take the three-part lift from Reusch or Col du Pillon. A quick trip takes about 90 minutes and costs 40 SF. You can stay for lunch. From the top, on a clear day, you can see the Matterhorn and even a bit of Mont Blanc, Europe's highest mountain. This is a good chance to do or watch some summer skiing. Normally expensive and a major headache, it isn't bad here. A lift ticket and rental skis, poles, boots, and a heavy coat cost about 65 SF. The slopes close at 14:00. The base of the lift is a 2-hour drive from Murten or Gimmelwald.

▲▲**Taveyanne**—This enchanting and remote hamlet is a huddle of log cabins used by cowherds in the summer. These days the hamlet's old bar is a restaurant serving a tiny community of vacation-goers and hikers. Taveyanne is 2 miles off the main road between Col de la Croix and Villars. A small sign points down a tiny road to a jumble of huts and snoozing cows stranded at 5,000 feet. The inn is **Refuge de Taveyanne** (1882 Gryon), where the Seibenthal family serves hearty meals in a prize-winning rustic setting—no electricity, low ceilings, huge charred fireplace. This is French Switzerland, but these people speak some English. For a back-on-the-farm experience, consider sleeping in their primitive loft. It's never full (5 mattresses, access by a ladder outside, 9 SF, urinate with the cows, open May-October, closed Tuesdays except in July and August, tel. 025/681947). A fine opportunity to really know bell prize-winning cows.

▲**Simmental**—The most scenic drive or train ride from Interlaken to Lake Geneva is through the Simmen Valley (*tal* means valley). Famous in the United States for its great milk-cows, it's known locally for its fine medieval churches (the most in the Berner Oberland) and for the American farmers who come to see the cows. The Erlenbach Church (park at the market square) is worth a look. An English brochure explains that, as in most local churches, the beautiful paintings decorating the interior survived, ironically, because they were whitewashed over by Baroque people.

Lake Geneva (Lac Leman)

This is the Swiss Riviera. Separating France and Switzerland, surrounded by Alps, and lined with a collage of castles, museums, spas, resort towns, and vineyards, Lake Geneva's crowds are understandable. This area is so beautiful that Charlie Chaplin and Idi Amin both chose it as their second home.

Getting Around Lake Geneva

Buses connect towns along Lake Geneva every 15 minutes. Boats carry visitors comfortably to all sights of importance. The 15-SF ride from **Lausanne to Chillon** takes 2 hours with stops in **Vevey** and **Montreux** (6 trips daily in each direction, Eurailers sail free, tel. 021/6170666). The 10-minute Montreux-Château Chillon cruise is fun even for those with a car.

Sights—Lake Geneva

Montreux—This expensive resort has a famous jazz festival each July (TI tel. 021/9631212). The casino is an entertainment center with a wimpy gaming room and the Bar du Festival, which plays great videos of the latest jazz festival. A beer here makes for an enjoyable evening. **Vevey**—Near Montreux, Vevey is a smaller and more comfortable resort town. **Corniche de Lavaux**—The Swiss Wine Road winds ruggedly through picturesque towns and the stingy vineyards that produce most of Switzerland's tasty but expensive wine, *Fendant*. Hikers can take the boat to Cully and explore on foot from there. A car tour is quick and frightening (from Montreux, go west along the lake through Vevey, following blue signs to Lausanne along the waterfront, taking the Moudon/Chexbres exit). Explore some of the smaller roads. **Lausanne**—This is the most interesting city on the lake. You can park near its impressive cathedral and walk through the colorful old town. The Collection de l'Art Brut (11

Avenue des Bergieres, 10:00-12:00, 14:00-18:00, closed
Saturday and Sunday morning and Monday, follow signs to
Palais de Beaulieu) is a fascinating and thought-provoking
collection of art by those who have been labeled criminal or
crazy by society.

Geneva—It bores me. This big city is sterile, cosmopolitan,
expensive, and full of executives, diplomats, and tourists
looking for profits, peace, and cheap rooms.

▲▲▲**Château Chillon**—Wonderfully preserved, this 13th-
century castle, set wistfully at the edge of Lake Geneva, is a
joy. Follow the free English map-brochure from one fascinating room to the next (or call to find out when an English
group is scheduled)—tingly views, dank prison, battle-
scarred weapons, interesting furniture, and even 700-
year-old toilets. The long climb to the top of the keep (#25
in the brochure) isn't worth the time or sweat. Curl up on
a window sill to enjoy the lake (daily 9:00-18:30, less off-
season, 6 SF, 2 SF extra to join a tour, private tours for
30 SF, easy parking, tel. 021/963 3912).

Sleeping near Montreux
and Château Chillon
(1.5 SF = about $1, tel. code: 021)

If you want to sleep on the lake, Montreux is expensive. But
the town of Villeneuve, 3 miles east, has the same palmy
lakeside setting without the crowds or glitz. Its main drag
runs parallel to the shore, 1 block in. It's a short walk from
the waterfront promenade to the château and Montreux.

Le Romantica (D-70 SF, DB-80 SF; Grand-Rue 34,
1844 Villeneuve, tel. 021/960 1540, SE-F) is a rare value
with a frumpy, very French atmosphere. Even the stools are
overstuffed. **Hotel du Soleil** (DB-120 SF; Grand-Rue 20,
tel. 021/960 4206) is renovated with all the comforts, an
expensive but likable place. The depressing **Hotel de l'Aigle**
(D-76 SF; Grand-Rue 48, tel. 021/960 1004, SE-F) has only
location and price going for it.

Haut Lac youth hostel (dorm bed, sheets, and break-
fast-21 SF, D-63 SF, non-members pay 7 SF extra, closed
9:00-17:00, cheap meals served; Passage de l'Auberge 8, 1820
Territet town, tel. 021/963 4934, train noise is a problem),
at the edge of Montreux, is on the lake, a 10-minute stroll

north of the château and a long stroll from the fun of
Montreux.

Train Connections

Lausanne to: Basel (2/hr, 2½ hrs), **Bern** (hrly, 70 min),
Milan (hrly, 3½ hrs), **Geneva** (3/hr, 50 min), **Montreux**
(2/hr, 20 min).

Route Tips for Drivers

Interlaken to Bern to Murten (50 miles): From Lauterbrunnen, drive toward Interlaken and catch the autobahn
(direction Spiez, Thun, Bern). After Spiez, the autobahn will
take you right to Bern. Circle the city on the autobahn, taking the fourth Bern exit, Neufeld Bern, into the center. Signs
to Zentrum will take you to the Bahnhof. Turn right just
before the station into the Bahnhof Parkplatz (2-hour meter
parking outside, all-day lot inside, 2 SF per hour). You're just
an escalator ride away from a great tourist information center
and Switzerland's compact, user-friendly capital. From the
station, drive out of Bern following blue Lausanne signs, then
green signs to Neuchatel and Murten. Notice the big gray
Jacob Suchard Tobler chocolate factory overlooking the autobahn at the Bern-Brunnen autobahn exit. This is the home
of Toblerone, recently purchased by Philip Morris and no
longer giving tours. In about 20 minutes you'll be in Murten.

    Parking within Murten's walls is medieval. If you have a
dashboard clock (free at TIs and banks) you can try the blue
spots near the Ringmauer Hotel, but it's best to settle for
the large free lots just outside either gate and walk in. It's a
tiny town.

Murten to Lake Geneva (50 miles): The autobahn corridor from Bern to Lausanne/Lake Geneva makes everything
very speedy. Murten and Avenches are about 10 minutes
from the autobahn. Broc, Bulle, and Gruyères are within
sight of each other and the autobahn. It takes about an hour
to drive from Murten to Montreux. The autobahn (direction:
Simplon) takes you high above Montreux (pull off at the
great view-point rest stop) and Château Chillon. Take the
first exit east of the castle (Villeneuve). Signs will direct you
along the lake back to the castle (easy parking). Continue
along into Montreux.

APPENDIX

Public Transportation

The chart below lists the major train segments you may use, with average duration of journey, approximate 1995 cost in U.S. dollars for a one-way second-class ticket (for first class, just add 50% and spit out your gum), and about how many trips are made per day. Any journey of six or more hours can be done overnight.

Train Almanac for Germany, Austria, and Switzerland
Approximate 1995 Cost

From–To	Length of Trip	in $, one-way, 2nd class	Trips/ Day
Frankfurt–Würzburg	1 hr. 20 min.	24	20
Frankfurt–Berlin	8 hrs.	74	7
Frankfurt–Munich (train)	4 hrs.	62	17
Frankfurt–Munich (bus tour)	11 hrs	60	1
Frankfurt–Köln	2 hrs. 10 min.	34	20
Frankfurt–Amsterdam	5 hrs. 30 min.	66	11
Würzburg–Rothenburg, via Steinach	1 hr.	9	20
Rothenburg–Munich (bus)	5 hrs.	34	1
Rothenburg–Füssen	6 hrs.	39	1
Füssen–Reutte in Tirol (bus)	45 min.	3	11
Reutte–Munich, via Garmisch	3 hrs.	24	8
Munich–Füssen	1 hr.	18	12
Munich–Salzburg	2 hrs.	24	15
Munich–Vienna	5 hrs. 30 min.	60	7
Munich–Venice	9 hrs.	57	2
Vienna–Venice	10 hrs.	63	5
Salzburg–Vienna	3 hrs. 20 min.	36	16
Vienna–Mauthausen	2 hrs.	18	20
Vienna–Innsbruck	5 hrs. 30 min.	66	8

Train Almanac for Germany, Austria, and Switzerland, continued

From–To	Length of Trip	in $, one-way, 2nd class	Trips/ Day
Vienna–Zürich	9 hrs. 30 min.	99	5
Vienna–Budapest	3 hrs. 30 min.	29	4
Vienna–Prague	6 hrs.	38	4
Innsbruck–Zürich	4 hrs.	46	7
Zürich–Munich	4 hrs. 30 min.	55	5
Zürich–Paris	6 hrs. 30 min.	77	5
Zürich–Luzern	50 min.	15	20
Luzern–Interlaken	2 hrs.	15	20
Interlaken Ost– Gimmelwald	1 hr. 30 min.	8	20
Interlaken–Montreux	3 hrs.	33	16
Interlaken–Bern	1 hr.	15	20
Montreux–Lausanne	20 min.	6	30
Lausanne–Murten	1 hr.	14	12
Murten–Bern	1 hr.	14	12
Bern–Freiburg (Germany)	3 hrs.	33	4
Freiburg–Baden-Baden	1 hr. 20 min.	14	3
Baden-Baden–Koblenz	2 hrs. 30 min.	38	20
Koblenz–Cochem	40 min.	8	17
Cochem–Trier	45 min.	9	17
Koblenz–Mainz, train	50 min.	14	40
Koblenz–Mainz, boat	6 hrs.	34	5
Koblenz–Bonn	30 min.	8	40
Bonn–Köln	30 min.	6	40
Koblenz–Frankfurt	1 hr. 30 min.	18	20
Frankfurt–Frankfurt Airport	15 min.	3	50
Berlin–Munich	10 hrs.	9	3
Berlin–Vienna	12 hrs.	75	1
Berlin–Amsterdam	10 hrs.	93	5
Berlin–Copenhagen	10 hrs.	58	2

Train Lines: Germany, Austria, and Switzerland

Telephoning
International Access Codes (use when calling from . . .)
Austria–00
Germany–00
Switzerland–00
U.S.A.–011

Country Codes (use when calling to . . .)

Austria–43	Great Britain–44
Belgium–32	Italy–39
Canada–1	Netherlands–31
France–33	Switzerland–41
Germany–49	U.S.A.–1

Cost of Public Transportation in Germany

FIRST CLASS CONSECUTIVE DAY EURAILPASSES

15-day	$498
21-day	648
1-month	798
2-months	1098
3-months	1398

FIRST CLASS EURAIL FLEXIPASSES

Any 5 days in 2 months	$348
Any 10 days in 2 months	560
Any 15 days in 2 months	740

Germany:
Point-to-point 2nd class rail fares in $US.

GERMAN RAILPASSES

	1st cl	1st twin	2nd cl	2nd twin	Junior
5 days in a month	$260	$208	$178	$142	$138
10 days in a month	410	328	286	228	188
15 days in a month	530	424	386	276	238

1994 prices. The discounted "twin" pass is for the traveling companion of anyone who buys a regular pass in the same class. "Twins" must travel together at all times. Junior passes are for anyone under 26. The German railpass covers all the Eurail bonuses in Germany (boats on the Rhine and Mosel, Romantic Road bus tour, and so on). These passes are available in Germany, but since the 15% VAT (value-added tax) is added on, they are more expensive over there than in the USA.

GERMAN RAIL 'N DRIVE PASSES

4 days of rail and 2 days of Hertz car rental in a month. 1994 prices are listed below. Add up to 4 extra 1st class rail days for around $40/day, or around $30/day 2nd class. Prices (except for extra car days) are per person for two traveling together.

	1st cl	2nd cl	extra car day
A: Ford Fiesta-type car	$238	$178	$48
B: Ford Escort-type car	258	198	62
C: Ford Sierra-type car	268	208	70

Cost of Public Transportation
in Switzerland and Austria

SWISS PASSES AND SWISS FLEXIPASSES

	1st cl	2nd cl
8 days	$266	$186
15 days	312	214
1 month	430	296
Any 3 days in 15	222	148

1994 prices. A 4-day Swiss Pass is sold in Switzerland for 200 SF, or about $142, 2nd class.
These passes cover all the trains, boats and buses with 25% off on the high mountain rides.

SWISS RAIL 'N DRIVE PASSES

Any 3 days rail and 3 days Avis car out of 15 days:

	1st cl	2nd cl	extra car day
A-Economy	$289	$215	$49
B-Small	335	259	75
C-Medium	359	285	89
D-Small automatic	349	269	79

1994 prices listed are per person with two traveling together. Solo travelers pay about $100
more. This covers the same extras as the Swiss Pass.

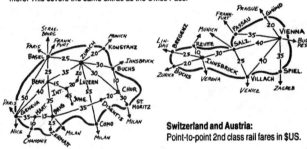

Switzerland and Austria:
Point-to-point 2nd class rail fares in $US.

AUSTRIAN RABBIT FLEXIPASSES

	1st cl	2nd cl
Any 4 days out of 10 days	$153	$103
Same flexipass for juniors under 26	95	64

1994 prices. Children under 7 travel free. Bonuses include 50% off on Danube ships and on
Lake Constance. These passes are available in the USA or at train stations in countries outside
of Austria. Prices are about the same in Germany (236 DM first class, 158 DM second class)
but require you to get off the train at the border to exchange your voucher for the actual ticket.

U.S.A Direct Toll-Free Access Numbers
(for calling home from Europe)

Your credit card will be billed about $2.50 plus the cheaper USA-to-Europe long-distance rate.

	ATT	MCI	SPRINT
Austria	022-903-011	022-903-012	022-903-014
Germany	0130-0010	0130-0012	0130-0013
Switzerland	155-00-11	155-02-22	155-97-77

Climate Chart

The first line indicates average daily low in Germany, Austria, and Switzerland. The second line indicates average daily high. The third line indicates days per month of no rain.

	J	F	M	A	M	J	J	A	S	O	N	D
Germany Frankfurt	29°	31°	35°	41°	48°	53°	56°	55°	51°	43°	36°	31°
	37°	42°	49°	58°	67°	72°	75°	74°	67°	56°	45°	39°
	22	19	22	21	22	21	21	21	21	22	21	20
Austria Vienna	26°	28°	34°	41°	50°	56°	59°	58°	52°	44°	36°	30°
	34°	38°	47°	57°	66°	71°	75°	73°	66°	55°	44°	37°
	23	21	24	21	22	21	22	21	23	23	22	22
Switzerland Frankfurt	29°	30°	35°	41°	48°	55°	58°	57°	52°	44°	37°	31°
	39°	43°	51°	58°	66°	73°	77°	76°	69°	58°	47°	40°
	20	19	21	19	19	19	22	21	20	20	19	21

Metric Conversions (approximate)

1 inch = 25 millimeters
1 foot = 0.3 meter
36-24-36 = 90-60-90
1 yard = 0.9 meter
1 mile = 1.6 kilometers
1 square yard = 0.8 square meter
1 acre = 0.4 hectare

Basic German Survival Phrases

English	German	Pronunciation
Hello (good day).	Guten Tag.	GOO-ten tahg
Do you speak English?	Sprechen Sie Englisch?	SHPREH-khen zee ENG-lish
Yes. / No.	Ja. / Nein.	yah / nīn
I don't understand.	Ich verstehe nicht.	ikh fehr-SHTAY-heh nikht
I'm sorry.	Entschuldigung.	ent-SHOOL-dee-goong
Please.	Bitte.	BIT-teh
Thank you.	Danke.	DAHNG-keh
Goodbye.	Auf Wiedersehen.	owf VEE-der-zay-hen
Where is...?	Wo ist...?	voh ist
...a hotel	...ein Hotel	īn hoh-TEHL
...a youth hostel	...eine Jugend-herberge	Ī-neh YOO-gend-hehr-behr-geh
...a restaurant	...ein Restaurant	īn res-tow-RAHNT
...a grocery store	...ein Lebensmittelgeschäft	īn LAY-bens-mit-tel-geh-SHEHFT
...the train station	...der Bahnhof	dehr BAHN-hohf
...the tourist information office	...das Touristen-Informationsbüro	dahs too-RIS-ten-in-for-maht-see-OHNS-bew-roh
...the toilet	...die Toilette	dee toh-LEH-teh
men / women	Herren / Damen	HEHR-ren / DAH-men
How much does it cost?	Wieviel kostet das?	vee-FEEL KOS-tet dahs
Cheaper.	Billiger.	BIL-lig-er
Included?	Eingeschlossen?	ĪN-geh-shlos-sen
I would like...	Ich hätte gern...	ikh HEH-teh gehrn
Just a little. / More.	Nur ein bißchen. / Mehr.	noor īn BIS-yen / mehr
A ticket.	Ein Karte.	īn KAR-teh
A room.	Ein Zimmer.	īn TSIM-mer
The bill.	Die Rechnung.	dee REHKH-noong
one	eins	īns
two	zwei	tsvī
three	drei	drī
four	vier	feer
five	fünf	fewnf
six	sechs	zex
seven	sieben	ZEE-ben
eight	acht	ahkht
nine	neun	noyn
ten	zehn	tsayn
hundred	hundert	HOON-dert
thousand	tausend	TOW-zend

For another 112 pages of user-friendly German, check out *Rick Steves' German Phrase Book*. See JMP catalog to follow for ordering information.

INDEX

RICK STEVES'

FREE TRAVEL NEWSLETTER/CATALOG

My Europe Through the Back Door travel company will help you travel better *because* you're on a budget — not in spite of it. Call us at (206) 771-8303, and we'll send you our *free newsletter/catalog* packed full of info on budget travel, railpasses, guidebooks, videos, travel bags and tours:

EUROPEAN RAILPASSES

We sell the full range of European railpasses, and with every Eurailpass we give you these important extras — *free:* my hour-long "How to get the most out of your railpass" video; your choice of one of my ten "Best of..." regional guidebooks and phrasebooks; and our sage advice on your 1-page itinerary. Call us for a free copy of our 64-page *1995 Back Door Guide to European Railpasses.*

BACK DOOR TOURS

We offer a variety of European tours for those who want to travel in the Back Door style, but without the transportation and hotel hassles. If a tour with a small group, modest Back Door accomodations, lots of physical exercise, and no tips or hidden charges sounds like your idea of fun, call us for details.

CONVERTIBLE BACK DOOR BAG $75

At 9"x21"x13" our specially designed, sturdy bag is maximum carry-on-the-plane size (fits under the seat) and your key to footloose and fancy-free travel. Made of rugged water resistant cordura nylon, it converts easily from a smart looking suitcase to a handy rucksack. It has padded hide-away shoulder straps, top and side handles, and a detachable shoulder strap (for use as a suitcase). Lockable perimeter zippers allow easy access to the roomy 2,500 cubic inch central compartment. Two large outside compartments are perfect for frequently used items. We'll even toss in a nylon stuff bag. More than 40,000 Back Door travelers have used these bags around the world. I live out of one for three months at a time. Available in black, grey, navy blue and teal green.

MONEYBELT $8

Absolutely required for European travel, our sturdy nylon, ultra-light, under-the-pants pouch is just big enough to carry your essentials (passport, airline tickets, travelers checks, gummi bears, and so on) comfortably. I won't travel without one, and neither should you. Comes in neutral beige, with a nylon zipper. One size fits all.

All items are field tested by Rick Steves and completely guaranteed.
Prices are good through 1995 (maybe longer), and include shipping (allow 2 to 3 weeks).
WA residents add 8.2% tax. Sorry, no credit cards or phone orders. Send checks in US $ to:

Europe Through the Back Door   ❖   120 Fourth Avenue North
PO Box 2009, Edmonds, WA 98020   ❖   Phone: (206)771-8303

Other Books from John Muir Publications

Travel Books by Rick Steves

Asia Through the Back Door, 4th ed., 400 pp. $16.95

Europe 101: History, Art, and Culture for the Traveler, 4th ed., 372 pp. $15.95

Mona Winks: Self-Guided Tours of Europe's Top Museums, 2nd ed., 456 pp. $16.95

Rick Steves' Best of the Baltics and Russia, 1995 ed. 144 pp. $9.95

Rick Steves' Best of Europe, 1995 ed., 544 pp. $16.95

Rick Steves' Best of France, Belgium, and the Netherlands, 1995 ed., 240 pp. $12.95

Rick Steves' Best of Germany, Austria, and Switzerland, 1995 ed., 240 pp. $12.95

Rick Steves' Best of Great Britain, 1995 ed., 192 pp. $11.95

Rick Steves' Best of Italy, 1995 ed., 208 pp. $11.95

Rick Steves' Best of Scandinavia, 1995 ed., 192 pp. $11.95

Rick Steves' Best of Spain and Portugal, 1995 ed., 192 pp. $11.95

Rick Steves' Europe Through the Back Door, 13th ed., 480 pp. $17.95

Rick Steves' French Phrase Book, 2nd ed., 112 pp. $4.95

Rick Steves' German Phrase Book, 2nd ed., 112 pp. $4.95

Rick Steves' Italian Phrase Book, 2nd ed., 112 pp. $4.95

Rick Steves' Spanish and Portuguese Phrase Book, 2nd ed., 288 pp. $5.95

Rick Steves' French/German/Italian Phrase Book, 288 pp. $6.95

A Natural Destination Series

Belize: A Natural Destination, 2nd ed., 304 pp. $16.95

Costa Rica: A Natural Destination, 3rd ed., 400 pp. $17.95

Guatemala: A Natural Destination, 336 pp. $16.95

Undiscovered Islands Series

Undiscovered Islands of the Caribbean, 3rd ed., 264 pp. $14.95

Undiscovered Islands of the Mediterranean, 2nd ed., 256 pp. $13.95

Undiscovered Islands of the U.S. and Canadian West Coast, 288 pp. $12.95

For Birding Enthusiasts

The Birder's Guide to Bed and Breakfasts: U.S. and Canada, 288 pp. $15.95

The Visitor's Guide to the Birds of the Central National Parks: U.S. and Canada, 400 pp. $15.95

The Visitor's Guide to the Birds of the Eastern National Parks: U.S. and Canada, 400 pp. $15.95

The Visitor's Guide to the Birds of the Rocky Mountain National Parks: U.S. and Canada, 432 pp. $15.95

Unique Travel Series

Each is 112 pages and $10.95 paperback.

Unique Arizona
Unique California
Unique Colorado
Unique Florida
Unique New England
Unique New Mexico
Unique Texas
Unique Washington

2 to 22 Days Itinerary Planners

2 to 22 Days in the American Southwest, 1995 ed., 192 pp. $11.95

2 to 22 Days in Asia, 192 pp. $10.95

2 to 22 Days in Australia, 192 pp. $10.95

2 to 22 Days in California, 1995 ed., 192 pp. $11.95

2 to 22 Days in Eastern Canada, 1995 ed., 240 pp $11.95

2 to 22 Days in Florida, 1995 ed., 192 pp. $11.95

2 to 22 Days Around the Great Lakes, 1995 ed., 192 pp. $11.95

2 to 22 Days in Hawaii, 1995 ed., 192 pp. $11.95

2 to 22 Days in New England, 1995 ed., 192 pp. $11.95

2 to 22 Days in New Zealand, 192 pp. $10.95

2 to 22 Days in the Pacific Northwest, 1995 ed., 192 pp. $11.95

2 to 22 Days in the Rockies, 1995 ed., 192 pp. $11.95

2 to 22 Days in Texas, 1995 ed., 192 pp. $11.95

2 to 22 Days in Thailand, 192 pp. $10.95

22 Days Around the World, 264 pp. $13.95

Other Terrific Travel Titles

The 100 Best Small Art Towns in America, 224 pp. $12.95

Elderhostels: The Students' Choice, 2nd ed., 304 pp. $15.95

Environmental Vacations: Volunteer Projects to Save the Planet, 2nd ed., 248 pp. $16.95

A Foreign Visitor's Guide to America, 224 pp. $12.95

Great Cities of Eastern Europe, 256 pp. $16.95

Indian America: A Traveler's Companion, 3rd ed., 432 pp. $18.95

Interior Furnishings Southwest, 256 pp. $19.95

Opera! The Guide to Western Europe's Great Houses, 296 pp. $18.95

Paintbrushes and Pistols:

How the Taos Artists Sold the West, 288 pp. $17.95

The People's Guide to Mexico, 9th ed., 608 pp. $18.95

Ranch Vacations: The Complete Guide to Guest and Resort, Fly-Fishing, and Cross-Country Skiing Ranches, 3rd ed., 512 pp. $19.95

The Shopper's Guide to Art and Crafts in the Hawaiian Islands, 272 pp. $13.95

The Shopper's Guide to Mexico, 224 pp. $9.95

Understanding Europeans, 272 pp. $14.95

A Viewer's Guide to Art: A Glossary of Gods, People, and Creatures, 144 pp. $10.95

Watch It Made in the U.S.A.: A Visitor's Guide to the Companies that Make Your Favorite Products, 272 pp. $16.95

Parenting Titles

Being a Father: Family, Work, and Self, 176 pp. $12.95

Preconception: A Woman's Guide to Preparing for Pregnancy and Parenthood, 232 pp. $14.95

Schooling at Home: Parents, Kids, and Learning, 264 pp., $14.95

Teens: A Fresh Look, 240 pp. $14.95

Automotive Titles

The Greaseless Guide to Car Care Confidence, 224 pp. $14.95

How to Keep Your Datsun/Nissan Alive, 544 pp. $21.95

How to Keep Your Subaru Alive, 480 pp. $21.95

How to Keep Your Toyota Pickup Alive, 392 pp. $21.95

How to Keep Your VW Alive, 25th Anniversary ed., 464 pp. spiral bound $25

TITLES FOR YOUNG READERS AGES 8 AND UP

American Origins Series
Each is 48 pages and $12.95 hardcover.
Tracing Our English Roots
Tracing Our French Roots
Tracing Our German Roots
Tracing Our Irish Roots
Tracing Our Italian Roots
Tracing Our Japanese Roots
Tracing Our Jewish Roots
Tracing Our Polish Roots

Bizarre & Beautiful Series
Each is 48 pages, $9.95 paperback, and $14.95 hardcover.
Bizarre & Beautiful Ears
Bizarre & Beautiful Eyes
Bizarre & Beautiful Feelers
Bizarre & Beautiful Noses
Bizarre & Beautiful Tongues

Environmental Titles
Habitats: Where the Wild Things Live, 48 pp. $9.95
The Indian Way: Learning to Communicate with Mother Earth, 114 pp. $9.95
Rads, Ergs, and Cheeseburgers: The Kids' Guide to Energy and the Environment, 108 pp. $13.95
The Kids' Environment Book: What's Awry and Why, 192 pp. $13.95

Extremely Weird Series
Each is 48 pages, $9.95 paperback, and $14.95 hardcover.
Extremely Weird Bats
Extremely Weird Birds
Extremely Weird Endangered Species
Extremely Weird Fishes
Extremely Weird Frogs
Extremely Weird Insects
Extremely Weird Mammals
Extremely Weird Micro Monsters
Extremely Weird Primates
Extremely Weird Reptiles
Extremely Weird Sea Creatures
Extremely Weird Snakes
Extremely Weird Spiders

Kidding Around Travel Series
All are 64 pages and $9.95 paperback, except for *Kidding Around Spain* and *Kidding Around the National Parks of the Southwest*, which are 108 pages and $12.95 paperback.
Kidding Around Atlanta
Kidding Around Boston, 2nd ed.
Kidding Around Chicago, 2nd ed.
Kidding Around the Hawaiian Islands
Kidding Around London
Kidding Around Los Angeles
Kidding Around the National Parks of the Southwest
Kidding Around New York City, 2nd ed.
Kidding Around Paris
Kidding Around Philadelphia
Kidding Around San Diego
Kidding Around San Francisco
Kidding Around Santa Fe
Kidding Around Seattle
Kidding Around Spain
Kidding Around Washington, D.C., 2nd ed.

Kids Explore Series
Written by kids for kids, all are $9.95 paperback.
Kids Explore America's African American Heritage, 128 pp.
Kids Explore the Gifts of Children with Special Needs, 128 pp.
Kids Explore America's Hispanic Heritage, 112 pp.
Kids Explore America's Japanese American Heritage, 144 pp.

Masters of Motion Series
Each is 48 pages and $9.95 paperback.
How to Drive an Indy Race Car
How to Fly a 747
How to Fly the Space Shuttle

Rainbow Warrior Artists Series
Each is 48 pages and $14.95 hardcover.
Native Artists of Africa
Native Artists of Europe
Native Artists of North America

Rough and Ready Series
Each is 48 pages and $12.95 hardcover.
Rough and Ready Cowboys
Rough and Ready Homesteaders
Rough and Ready Loggers
Rough and Ready Outlaws and Lawmen
Rough and Ready Prospectors
Rough and Ready Railroaders

X-ray Vision Series
Each is 48 pages and $9.95 paperback.
Looking Inside the Brain
Looking Inside Cartoon Animation
Looking Inside Caves and Caverns
Looking Inside Sports Aerodynamics
Looking Inside Sunken Treasures
Looking Inside Telescopes and the Night Sky

Ordering Information
Please check your local bookstore for our books, or call **1-800-888-7504** to order direct. All orders are shipped via UPS; see chart below to calculate your shipping charge for U.S. destinations. **No post office boxes please; we must have a street address to ensure delivery**. If the book you request is not available, we will hold your check until we can ship it. Foreign orders will be shipped surface rate unless otherwise requested; please enclose $3 for the first item and $1 for each additional item.

For U.S. Orders

Totaling	Add
Up to $15.00	$4.25
$15.01 to $45.00	$5.25
$45.01 to $75.00	$6.25
$75.01 or more	$7.25

Methods of Payment
Check, money order, American Express, MasterCard, or Visa. We cannot be responsible for cash sent through the mail. For credit card orders, include your card number, expiration date, and your signature, or call **1-800-888-7504**. American Express card orders can only be shipped to billing address of cardholder. Sorry, no C.O.D.'s. Residents of sunny New Mexico, add 6.25% tax to total.

Address all orders and inquiries to:

John Muir Publications
P.O. Box 613
Santa Fe, NM 87504
(505) 982-4078
(800) 888-7504